First Person Glimpses into Premortality

# Trailing Clouds of

# Glory

Harold A. Widdison, Ph.D.

First Person Glimpses into Premortality

# Trailing Clouds of

Harold A. Widdison, Ph.D.

BONNEVILLE BOOKS TM

ISBN 13: 978-0-88290-772-7

Published by Horizon Publishers, an imprint of Cedar Fort, Inc.
2373 W. 700 S., Springville, UT 84663
Distributed by Cedar Fort, Inc. www.cedarfort.com

Library of Congress control number: 2004110435

Cover design by Brian Halley
Cover design © 2012 by Lyle Mortimer
Typeset by Janice Bernice

Printed in the United States of America

10  9  8  7  6  5  4  3  2  1

# Preface

When I was a young boy, on warm Montana nights I would lay on my back, hands behind my head, staring into the black star studded skies. My eyes would wander from the Big Dipper, to the Milky Way, to the North Star. On some evening the skies would be filled with the wavering curtains of green, yellow, and red—the aurora borealis. On occasion the brilliant light of a shooting star would flash across the sky disappearing behind the surrounding Rocky Mountains. What stories that shooting star could tell about the vast regions of space it had come from. I felt that I, too, had come to earth from somewhere far out in the vast regions of space like this shooting star. But if my origin was not of earth, where did I come from? What was it like there? Why did I leave that sphere? Would I ever return? And, if so, how would I return?

It was not until many years later that I found some answers to these questions. As a medical sociologist seeking information about the causes of physical and emotional disabilities, I met people who could answer these questions firsthand. Some had vivid memories from when they were young children of where they had come from and how they arrived on earth. Others had long forgotten memories triggered through some traumatic event. These individuals remembered living in a place far from earth and very different from earth, a place of brilliant light, peace and serenity, a place of total acceptance and love, a place they knew they had to leave in order to move forward and progress. From these individuals I learned that we did not evolve out of some primal ooze but had our origins at a place other than earth. We are definitely not here on earth by some cosmic accident.

The individuals who shared their memories and experiences did so with the desire that I and others could realize that all mankind has divine origins and that our lives are important. From them I learned that there is a strong bond between those who are currently on earth, those who are still to come to earth, and those who have already been to earth.

Reflecting back on those brilliant flashes of light I saw coming from the heavens when I was a boy, I cannot help but wonder if some of them just might be light reflected by heavenly travelers coming to earth.

Note: For the reader's information, where a reference is given, the material was taken from a published source. All other quotes come from individuals interviewed by the author.

# Acknowledgments

This book would have been impossible without the help of many individuals most of whom felt the need to share their experiences and memories. For some, sharing was only done after serious and prayerful contemplation. Their accounts are deeply personal and usually held sacred to them. Many felt that they needed to share their experience to help others deal the loss of a loved one so they would know that death is not the end of existence or of relationships. Some wanted those questioning the meaning of life, especially their own life, to know they are loved unconditionally by God and have divine origins. Others were instructed by angelic beings to share their experience so that mankind would know that God is real. To all of these individuals, I express my heartfelt gratitude for their confidence and trust.

I would also like to acknowledge each and every one of these individuals by name but as many did not want themselves identified, mostly to protect the confidentiality of their families, I honored their request here and in the body of the book. Nevertheless, I want to acknowledge that this book would not have been possible without their help.

I would like to thank all those who read the manuscript providing many helpful suggestions as to content and style. Specifically, Bill Burke, Debbie Dyson, Kathy Fowkes, Arvin Gibson, Elaine Holmes, Craig Lundahl, Tom Nibley, Barbara Rommer, Stan Swarts, Shirley Testi, and RaNelle Wallace. I especially give thanks to Sarah Hinze. Through her interest in the pre-birth experience she was able to refer me to a number of individuals that I interviewed for this book. But especially, I wish to thank my wife, Marie, who spent many hours patiently reading and re-reading the manuscript. From the editing of the very early tape recordings to the final manuscript, her fine editorial touches are here.

# Contents

Preface

Acknowledgments

Chapter 1      Our Original Home      11

Chapter 2      The Appearance of the Heavenly Home  27

Chapter 3      Life in the Heavenly Home      43

Chapter 4      Preparations for Earth Life      69

Chapter 5      The Mission Begins      83

Chapter 6      Leaving Home      109

Chapter 7      The Journey to Earth      125

Chapter 8      Arriving On Earth      137

Chapter 9      Children's Memories of
Their Heavenly Home      155

Chapter 10      Unique Qualities Brought to Earth      169

Chapter 11      Why Adversity?      189

Chapter 12      Why Disabilities and Handicaps?      209

Chapter 13      Comfort From Home      229

Chapter 14      Protection From Home      261

Chapter 15      Assurances That a Child Is On the Way  287

Chapter 16    Parental Visits With
              Their Unborn Children              305

Chapter 17    Playful Visits from Home           323

Chapter 18    Adoption                           337

Chapter 19    Abortion                           353

Chapter 20    Returning Home                     377

Chapter 21    Mission Completed:
              Our Final Reward                   389

              Epilogue                           413

              Sources Cited                      417

# Chapter One
## Our Original Home

Margaret Fairbourn had lived through two world wars, the Great Depression, many moves necessitated by the ill health of her first husband, the deaths of both her husbands in automobile accidents, and the deaths of six of her seven siblings. She started experiencing many health problems in her mid-70s, including leukemia. At first Margaret was devastated when the doctor told her she had cancer. In her mind, leukemia meant a lingering and extremely painful death. Of death itself she had no fear but she did fear what she would have to go through before she died.

Not long before she died, Margaret told her doctors that she had lived a long full life and was now ready to go home. Her use of the term "home" puzzled them because she was living at home with her daughter's family. Seeing their confusion, she told them, "This is my earthly home. I want to go to my real home, my home in heaven. I want to see my parents, my brothers and sister, and especially my husband. I miss them and I want to go home. So don't hook me up to any machines or use heroic measures to keep me here."

As she grew closer to death, Margaret requested that her daughter buy her brand new clothing to be buried in. She said, "I want to look my best when I return home." She conveyed absolutely no fear of death. To the contrary, she looked forward to her trip "home." When she finally died after an eight-year battle with the leukemia, her face radiated peace. She was home at last.

Margaret is my mother (the author).

Cambria Henderson was not dying, but she had an experience where her mind was opened and memories of her pre-mortal home were recalled.

"I was standing on a balcony, taking in one last sentimental view of what had been my home ever since I could remember," wrote Cambria. "My long white robe gently rippled in the breeze and the gold railing on my balcony shone brilliantly in the light. The fairway below, the river beyond, and the sky above me was as beautiful and as vibrantly alive as they had ever been. The city in the distance was a pearlescent hue, pulsating with energy and light."

Another individual who actually visited his heavenly home was Larry Tooley, an electrician who was critically injured in an industrial accident. His injuries were so serious that all medical signs indicated he was dead. While in this state his spirit left his body and entered another realm where he experienced an extensive review of his life. Then he was pleasantly surprised to meet an old friend, also named Larry, who had died years earlier. This other Larry served as his escort. The following is Larry's reported experience.

Larry Tooley said to the other Larry, "I've never felt like this before. It feels as if all my senses have increased a hundred fold."

Larry smiled at me. "That's how I felt, too, when I first crossed over."

I felt I was again in possession of superior knowledge and intelligence that had been withheld from me since I had first gone to earth.

"Yes," said Larry as if reading my thoughts. "Since you've crossed over, the veil has been taken from your mind. You'll soon regain all your powers and knowledge. It only takes a little time and the right words to jog your memory."

"It seems I've already had my memory jogged," I half-said to myself as I thought about the life I'd just been through.

"Ah, yes," he said. "That was just a recall of your earth life. I'm talking about a recall of your former knowledge and powers."

"What powers are you talking about?" I asked.

"I'll try and explain as we go along," he said.

I looked around me. Everything was beginning to look familiar. "I feel like I've returned home," I said.

"You have," he assured me.[1]

Larry Tooley discovered that death of the body does not mean death of the self. Even when all his bodily functions ceased, he continued to exist. Not only did he maintain consciousness, but his awareness and his knowledge expanded to a higher level—a level which he recognized he had known before he was born. As he passed through this heavenly realm, his memories flooded back and he recognized where he was—he was back home.

Claudia Epstein lost all desire to go on living when her twenty-four-year-old sister, Ruth, and her husband, Daniel Moore, were killed in an airplane crash in September of 1988. Claudia was at the airport watching them take off when their commuter plane began to falter and then nose dived onto the runway. Totally shattered, Claudia went into a depression and, at times, seriously thought of ending her life.

One night, as she sat reading near the fireplace, she could no longer hold back her grief and slipped into a deep depression. She reached for a bottle of rum and the sleeping pills a doctor had prescribed to help calm her restless nights.

"I had begun to contemplate how easy it would be to wash down the bottle of sleeping pills with the rum and just drift away into oblivion, when I unmistakably felt a physical presence behind me. I turned to see Ruth and Dan standing behind me in the center of the room. I saw them as solidly as I had ever seen them. They were smiling and holding hands. For the first time in months, I smiled also.

"Please, please do not continue to grieve so for us, dear one," Ruth said in her familiar soft, lilting voice. "Dan and I are happier than ever. Our love is even stronger here than it was on earth."

Dan put his arm around Ruth and added, "It is so beautiful here, Claudia, and so filled with love. Don't grieve for us. We are truly in a better place."

Claudia could not hold back her tears. "Why did you have to leave me? It just isn't fair."

"You consider such a concept as 'fair' from a human point of view, Sis," Ruth replied. "Although it is difficult to understand, all things are part of God's larger plan. And this is our true home. We were only strangers in a strange land on Earth."[2]

Claudia discovered that she and we are only strangers in a strange land, that our true home is in a land far from this earthly home where love, unconditional acceptance, and peace prevail. This very brief visit let Claudia know that she had not lost Ruth and Dan and that they are still together. Before this experience ended Ruth told Claudia, "One day, when it is your time, you will join us here and the three of us will be together again. Until that day, dear, be happy and live a life of joy and fulfillment."

Rebecca had an experience during which her physician declared her to be clinically dead. However, much to the surprise of her physician, she revived. She reported that during the time she was thought to be dead, she was met by her deceased brother who served as her escort.

As they walked through the beautiful streets of a heavenly city she asked, "Frank, where are we?"

"Home, little sister." he answered tenderly.

Are these unusual uses of the term *home*? Not according to seasoned hospice and terminal care workers. For example, Maggie Callanan,[3] who has served as a hospice nurse for many years providing daily assistance to dying people, reports that the most frequent comments of those close to death were about going home. They would say things such as "I'm ready to go home now" or "I'm going home soon."

This book explores what many individuals learned about their original home through near-death experiences, death bed visions, or after death communications. When many credible individuals report having similar experiences, a careful examination of their accounts can help us to understand the significance of what they experienced, as well as provide keys to understanding ourselves— our origins, our nature, and our destiny. In conducting the research for this book many individuals were interviewed and numerous books and journals were reviewed to see what they revealed about the following:

- Is earth our only home?
- Did we reside in a heavenly home before birth?
- Do we return to a heavenly home at death?
- What is our purpose while on earth?
- How does knowledge of a heavenly home change the meaning of life and death?

It is with a sense of exploration that we proceed, for our quest provides keys to understanding ourselves—our origins, our nature, our destiny, and our universe. To understand the types of situations and experiences being examined and evaluated, it is important to identify the four basic types of data collected and analyzed.

## Types of Information Collected

### Near-Death Experiences (NDEs)

The witness experiences clinical death but is resuscitated. While the physical body is lifeless, the witness experiences continued and/or expanded consciousness. The witness may see persons and places not of this earth, yet which are familiar to the experiencer from a time before birth. Research has exploded in this area since the 1975 publication of philosopher/psychiatrist Raymond Moody's groundbreaking book on NDEs, *Life After Life*.[4]

### Pre-Birth Memories (PBM) and Pre-Birth Experiences (PBS)

The witness, through dreams, visions, hearing, sensing a presence, etc., recalls aspects of life in heaven before birth, or has contact with spirits there. Some NDErs have seen souls or spirits on the other side waiting to be born. This category was formalized by researcher/experiencer Sarah Hinze in her pioneering books, *Life Before Life* (1993)[5] and Coming from the Light (1997)[6] Other major authors in this area include Elizabeth M. Carman and Neil J. Carman's 1999 book, *Cosmic Cradle*,[7] and Elisabeth Hallett's books, *Soul Trek* and *Stories of the Unborn Soul*.[8]

### Nearing Death Awareness (NDA) and Deathbed Visions (DBVs)

The dying witnesses, in moments, days, or weeks prior to death begins speaking of going home and the need to pack for a journey. They often report the appearance of beings (often deceased loved ones) who have come to take them *home* and excitedly report glimpses of a fantastically beautiful place they will soon enter. Maggie Callanan and Patricia Kelly provide numerous examples of nearing death awareness in their 1992 book, *Final Gifts*.[9] Two early researchers, Karlis Osis and Erlendur Haraldsson reported the observations of nurses and physicians in both India and the United States of what their patients said and did just before and as they died in their 1977 book, *At the Hour of Death*.[10]

### After Death Communications (ADCs)

The witness, through dreams, visions, hearing, sensing a presence, etc., receives communication from a deceased person or persons. These communications provide not only comfort and reassurance to the bereaved but often information about where the deceased is and what he or she is doing. A large collection of ADC accounts is found in *Hello From Heaven* (1995) by researchers/experiencers Bill & Judy Guggenheim.[11] Louis E. LaGrand has also compiled a large number of such experiences in his two books, *After Death Communications* (1997) and *Messages and Miracles* (1999).[12,13]

*The Eternal Journey* (1997) by Craig Lundahl and Harold Widdison was one of the first works to comprehensively combine data from all of the four areas listed above. [14]

Utilizing information gleaned from individuals who have had one or more of the above types of experiences, I will look at what it reveals about who we are and our true origins.

### Adults' Reports of a Heavenly Home

Frances Gomez was catapulted from her speeding motorcycle over a bridge railing into the river below. Desperately gasping for air, she sank into the river's murky depths. Suddenly all pain ceased as her spirit silently slipped from her body but not into oblivion.

"My floating body was pulled back by a voice saying, 'Come on, Frances, let's go!'. . .I started going down some kind of tunnel . . .at tremendous speed. . .There was no feeling of loss, or sadness about leaving my husband and daughters. There was only an aura of serenity that kept increasing, and a knowledge that everything was connected somehow. I was going home to the world where I had once existed as a magnificent, spiritual being of light." [15]

One can only begin to imagine the trauma of free-falling from a racing motorcycle into deadly waters. Yet when the breath of life ran out, Frances did not lose consciousness. Rather, her consciousness changed.

1. When her spirit left her body she could still think and feel, but was freed from physical pain.

2. Fear was replaced by serenity because she was restored to her "interconnectedness with all things in the universe."

3. She recognized she was returning to her former home, a heavenly home where she had existed as "a magnificent spiritual being of light."

How extraordinary! Is it possible that we all are "magnificent spiritual beings of light?"

During childhood, Angie Fenimore suffered incredible abuse. Her body healed but for years the scars on her soul ran so deep she could not escape depression, anxiety, and feelings of betrayal. With marriage and two young sons, Angie did find bright moments but despite her best efforts she could not permanently lift herself above the relentless whirlpool of hopelessness. So damaged was her self-esteem that she eventually lost the will to live.

There were suicide attempts, fearful and half-hearted at first. Then came the day when she was determined to end her emotional pain and do it right by downing a large quantity of drugs with alcohol and then slitting her wrists. Drugs ingested, oozing wrists wrapped in towels to protect the couch, Angie laid back to await death. Soon the room was spinning, fading in and out.

Angie's spirit exited her body and initially entered a dark, frightening realm. She prayed desperately for help and was at last delivered into the presence of a powerful Being of Light.

"I was captivated by his beauty. Yet as much as God filled me with wonder and awe, I was certain that I was not meeting Him for the first time. There was a tremendous familiarity about Him. While

I was not remembering (all the) details of a life before my mortal birth, I was reacquainting myself with the life that I shared with the Father, a spirit life that seemed to extend to the beginning of the universe."[16]

Angie's spirit did not return directly to her heavenly home, perhaps because of the negative way she chose to die. But through her pleading prayer she was eventually rescued from darkness by a Being who she remembered as her God and Father, with whom she had associated before coming to earth. Of great importance is the effect the memories of her former self and her former life had on her when she returned to earth. She now knew she had existed since "the beginning of the universe" and had a father in heaven who loved her. The abuse she experienced on earth nearly destroyed her. But the discovery of her true self changed her completely. Angie found happiness and a true sense of purpose to her life and an awareness she was a beloved daughter of God.

In the next case a woman felt her spirit trying to leave her body. With all her strength she fought against dying. In spite of her efforts her spirit left her body and floated up above the earth. An angelic escort appeared. Mary told him she did not want to accompany him but that did no good and she was taken away from earth toward an unusual light. Upon reaching this light, her sentiments underwent a dramatic change.

"The light radiated an extreme feeling of love. I could tell I had been there before and (I) was so happy to be going home. The closer I came, the happier I was and the more I anticipated being home . . . (The feeling) was similar to a feeling of arriving home in your driveway or city, when you have been gone for a long, long time, and you can't wait to run into the house and see your family and loved ones

. . . I felt my heart would burst with joy and happiness."[17]

Before Mary understood her destination, she fought dying. Even the appearance of an angelic escort did not relieve her fears. It wasn't until she met the Being of Light and felt his loving reassurance that all resistance melted away. It was then that she recognized she knew him and the place where they were. She was back home.

During a major operation, Gary died. His spirit passed from his body and he was met by an angelic being. Together, they traveled through a tunnel. Gary instinctively recognized that it was through this same tunnel he had come to earth many years before. There was no doubt about it!

Gary pondered, "Maybe this is the way all beings pass between the worlds."[18]

Gary's sense of "recognizing" a place he'd been before is typical of many individuals who have traveled to this realm. From his experience and many others, it appears that escorts or guides accompany each of us during all or part of the "journey between worlds."

During a complete cardiac arrest, Gloria McCracken's vital signs shut down, but not her consciousness.

"I left my body and zoomed straight up into a clear, vast sky—dark, but feeling as though dawn was imminent. I felt the most wonderful peace and love envelop me.

*Welcome home,* I heard in my mind.

My thinking was racing. *Will I be rejected since I have not led a blameless life?* and *How could I ever have forgotten about this very familiar existence?*

Then I heard, "Good job, you tried really hard and never gave up."[19]

"Welcome home" is a beautiful greeting here on earth but how much more beautiful it be must to hear these words at the doorstep of our eternal home, especially knowing that we are welcome even if we have not been perfect during our earthly lives. And how astounded we will be that we could have forgotten such a special, loving place.

The next account is about an NDA (Nearing Death Awareness) and is an experience many older people battling terminal illnesses or suffering the debilitating effects of age report having.

An elderly gentleman was sitting in a favorite chair enjoying the view from his porch when he experienced this remarkable vision.

"The sky suddenly opened up. It seemed to peel back like a canvas prop and there was heaven revealed to me. When I got up and turned around I saw my body sitting in the chair and there was a blue bruise over my right eye that hadn't been there before. I turned around again and looked up at where the sky opened up and it was so, so beautiful. There was light pouring out of the opening and it was living light. It came towards me and when it touched me I felt a warmth and peace and a complete awareness of all my memories and recollections of what I experienced during my entire life. I found myself floating up toward the light and it was as if I was returning home to a place I had left many years before . . . my real home.

I floated up through the hole in the sky and I recognized everything. It was as though I had never left."[20]

My real home! Though he had thought for the many years he had lived on earth that earth was his real home, this experience clearly revealed to him that earth was only a temporary residence.

The gracious individuals who have shared the experiences related in this book invariably say they have not just discovered, but have rediscovered things they knew long before earth life. These memories are normally blocked by a veil of forgetfulness.

But when this veil is parted, albeit briefly, certain truths about our previous existence are remembered:

1. We existed long before earth birth, possibly to "the beginning of the universe."
2. We have a creator/father with whom we lived in a heavenly home before birth.
3. We are "magnificent beings of light" with power to choose light or darkness through our earthly tests.
4. We can earn the right of returning to our heavenly home as more mature spiritual beings by trying hard to fulfill our earth missions.

Perhaps these were among the truths that stirred the poet Wordsworth's soul when he wrote:

> . . . *Our birth is but a sleep and a forgetting;*
> *The soul that rises with us, our life's Star,*
> *Hath had elsewhere its setting,*
> *And cometh from afar:*
> *Not in entire forgetfulness,*
> *And not in utter nakedness,*
> *But trailing clouds of glory do we come*
> *From God, who is our home:*
> *Heaven lies about us in our infancy!*[21]

## Children's Reports of a Heavenly Home

Wordsworth's concluding phrase, "Heaven lies about us in our infancy!" raises an interesting question. Is it possible that children recall their heavenly home? After all, they were there more recently than adults. "Absolutely!" according to internationally renowned physician, Dr. Elisabeth Kubler-Ross. The pioneering researcher in her classic book, *On Death and Dying,*[22] was a key figure in launching the hospice movement that has done so much to help people die with dignity. Dr. Kubler-Ross reported:

"It is true that I am best known for my research on the death process, but I believe every bit as much that we lived before birth as I do that we live after death. I have interviewed thousands of children during my career. Many children before the age of five or six, while their memories are still pure—before they begin school and become earthbound or tainted by worldly stuff—can tell you things about our heavenly home, about the journey to earth, about guardian angels, about choosing their parents, about entering their mother's womb, about their birth and so forth. After a couple of years in public school, memories of heaven are mostly forgotten, or these children are too embarrassed to recount them because they are now 'sophisticated.' They have become earthbound."

We all become earthbound when we forget who we really are—magnificent eternal beings with a divine heritage from a heavenly home, here temporarily on earth. We need not look far, often no further than within, to see how our happiness, our potential, our self-esteem suffers when we forget our eternal heritage, that we are all children of the Light, and that thee light is God. Such was the case of Angie whom we met earlier. Children's experiences can be most helpful here.

Dr. Melvin Morse, the pediatrician who wrote *Closer to the Light*,[23] purposely chose only young subjects for his research on near-death. He observed that children are more likely to give pure descriptions and explanations because they have had little exposure to the belief systems of the world and are, therefore, less likely to embellish or distort their accounts.

What follows are a few brief examples of children's memories and experiences of "home."

While driving to the grocery store, eighteen-month-old Jonathan said to his mother, "Mommy, I really miss my Father."

His mother responded, "Your daddy will be home before we get back from the store."

In a matter of fact way Jonathan clarified, "No, not my Daddy. I mean my Father in Heaven. I used to sit and talk with him and I really miss him."

Jonathan's comment truly surprised his mother as she didn't believe such things and certainty hadn't taught them to her son.

Another young mother recounted an experience she had with her four-year-old daughter, Sachi.

Soon after her brother was born, little Sachi began to ask her parents to leave her alone with the new baby. They worried that like most four-year-olds, she might feel jealous and want to hit or shake him, so they said no. But she showed no signs of jealousy. She treated the baby with kindness and her pleas to be left alone with him became urgent. They decided to allow it.

Elated, she went into the baby's room and shut the door, but it opened a crack—enough for her curious parents to peek in and listen. They saw little Sachi walk quietly up to her baby brother, put her face close to his and say quietly, "Baby, tell me what God feels like. I'm starting to forget."[24]

Sachi realized that her recollections of her former home and her relationship with God were fading and she logically assumed that as her brother had just come from heaven, he would have a clear recollection of their heavenly home and their Heavenly Father and he could share them with her.

Suzy was chatting with her three-year-old son, Devin, when he suddenly said,

"Mommy, let's go home."

"Where's home?" I asked.

"Far far away," said Devin. Pointing upward, he went on: "Up in the sky. This the dirt place. Our home up there."[25]

Jonathan's feelings of homesickness, Devin's memories of the location of his real home, and the little girl's desires to talk to her newborn brother reflect that they still retain memories of their original home and are not products of cultural conditioning. The age and innocence of these young children who have so recently come from their heavenly home are potent evidence of its existence.

To return to Larry Tooley, part of whose NDE experience was related earlier, he found himself in an indescribably beautiful city of light. The feelings he felt while there were like no others he had ever felt before. He could feel the utter divinity of the city. As he stood there trying to comprehend all that was occurring around him, he began to remember his premortal life.

"More memories came flooding back as I recalled an earlier time. It was a time when we were all part of God's celestial world. It was a time in which we all participated in the preparations for our mortal existence on the earth. Most of us remained true and faithful to Father, thus earning the right to come to the earth and take a body. We had gained the right then to leave our celestial home so that we might be tried and tested on earth."[26]

Larry's memories of his and our original home provide a bridge between this and subsequent chapters. What is intriguing in his account is his observation that we had gained the right to come to earth. We were not forced to come to earth, we earned the right to come. And what were we to do on earth? These questions and what the right to come to earth entails for each of us will be explored in subsequent chapters.

## Summary Thoughts

It is a generally held belief in most cultures and throughout history that we are more than an accident of evolution, that we did not evolve out of some primal ooze but came from God "trailing clouds of glory" as is so poignantly described by the poet Wordsworth. We are all, in reality, children of God with the divine spark of God in us. We are but temporary sojourners on earth and, contingent on how we function on earth, will also have the right to eventually return to that Being who gave us life and to our real home.

## Chapter Two
## The Appearance of the Heavenly Home

What does our premortal home look like? What do its inhabitants do? Some of the answers to these questions will be addressed in this chapter by examining accounts of individuals who have been permitted brief glimpses into the heavenly realm and some few individuals who actually visited it.

### Why We Do Not Remember Our Heavenly Home

Several individuals discovered why they couldn't remember anything about a heavenly home. One such individual was David Goines who was thirteen at the time of his experience. He was hit by a cement truck while riding his bicycle to school. The next thing he knew, he was sitting on a marble bench admiring the beautiful scenery around him. Next to him on the bench sat an old gentleman who spoke to him.

"'Well, you've had a rough day,' the old gentleman said, as if he knew all about it.

"With a tired sigh I said, 'I sure have!' No further explanation seemed necessary as we both sat there. Then, I remembered just how much trouble I was really in.

"Hoping he would have an answer I could stand to hear, I asked, 'Am I dead?'

"He smiled to reassure me and said, 'No, you are not dead. Your body is in a lot of trouble, but it is being well taken care of and you do not need to worry.'

"I demanded of him, 'How am I here, in this place, when I know that my body is back there in the hospital?'

"And, 'Where is this place? How do I see this place and you, if I'm not with my body? How can I be in two places at once?'

I began to feel very upset.

"He replied, 'I am here on behalf of your Heavenly Father's love for you and to remind you of where you came.' My first thought was, the hospital? He smiled and said, 'No. I mean your Father's house.'

"It was at that moment that I realized that I knew everything that he was saying was true and that I had known this long before I was born. I remembered that before I was a physical being I was a spiritual being, and it all made perfect sense. I was mildly puzzled that I could have ever forgotten such things when he reminded me that to experience a physical life it was necessary, at least for a while, to forget a little of our prior knowledge so that we might more fully experience physical things—be physically challenged, make choices of free agency, and yes, even make mistakes so that we could learn from them in ways that only a physical life could impart. If we retained all of our prior knowledge, we might not bother to experience the physical life for its fulfillment; we might decide to skip the pain and thus miss the pleasure.

"I also remembered the promise I had made to my Heavenly Father upon accepting the opportunity, challenges and responsibility of a physical life to make the most of this opportunity for myself and for Him and to return to His house with the knowledge and experience gained. This is why we need to forget our prior existence when we take a physical body. Because in order for us to appreciate, benefit, and learn all we can from our physical life, we have to re-discover what we knew before but now in physical ways.

"Likewise, through this physical life we must also discover how to return to our Heavenly Father. By the good that we do to each other in earth life, by the ways we improve our minds, and by the ways that we learn to cope with a physical body and physical life, by these things we earn our right of safe passage back to our Father's House. In so doing, we likewise magnify and glorify (honor) our Father. It is our Father's love that sends us on the journey and it is our love for Him that will allow us to go back *home* to His loving arms again."[1]

Our memories of heaven are blocked, requiring that we learn to live by faith while on earth. But in quiet moments or on specific occasions, we may sense that our true self exceeds the bounds of the present.

## What Our Heavenly Home Is Like
### Cities

Many individuals during their near-death experiences reported seeing radiant cities of light. Cecil L. Hamilton was seven years old when he drowned trying to save his brother. Cecil was later revived, but his brother did not. While Cecil was on the bottom of the river struggling to live, the following happened.

"A peaceful feeling came over me. I felt my spirit come out of my body and I went into a black void. That was a little frightening.

"A long way off there was a pinprick of light. I moved toward it, slowly at first, then faster and faster as if I were on top of a train accelerating. Then I stopped and stepped fully into the light. I noticed everything—sky, buildings, grass—emitted its own light. And everything was much more colorful than what we see here. A river meandered around. On the other side was a city, and a road running through it to another city, and another city, and another and another.

"Right in front of me but across the river were three men. They projected themselves to me. They didn't walk or fly—they projected over. I didn't recognize them, yet I knew one was Lynn Bibb. (He died a matter of weeks before I was born.) I knew these three men were looking out for me, like a welcoming committee to escort me over to the first city.

"The first city was like first grade. People stayed there until they were ready to go to the next city—your eternal progression, from city to city."[2]

Cecil not only saw a number of cities but learned that their residents were being prepared in one city to move to the next. Although not stated directly, the impression was that continued progression would ultimately lead to the presence of God. While every city of light is impressive and inspiring, evidently the light emanating from the various cities is not of uniform intensity. This fact was also testified to by Lorenzo Dow Young.

Lorenzo died and met a heavenly messenger—his guide.

"The guide said, 'Now let us go!'

"Space seemed annihilated. Apparently we went up, and almost instantly were in another world. It was of such magnitude that I formed no conception of its size. It was filled with innumerable hosts of beings, who seemed as naturally human as those among whom I had lived. With some I had been acquainted in the world I had just left. My guide informed me that those I saw had not yet arrived at their final abiding place.

"Again my guide said, 'Now let us go.'

"In a moment we were at the gates of a beautiful city. A porter opened it and we passed in. The city was grand and beautiful beyond anything that I can describe. It was clothed in the purest of light, brilliant but not glaring or unpleasant.

"The people, men and women, in their employments and surroundings seemed contented and happy. I knew those I met without being told who they were.

"My guide would not permit me to pause much . . . but rather hurried me on through this place to another still higher but connected with it. It was still more beautiful and glorious than anything I had before seen. To me its extent and magnificence were incomprehensible."[3]

Lorenzo's guide took him to three heavenly sites. In the first, beings returning from earth waited to be assigned their place in heaven. The second site was a beautiful city of light and the third, another city of light even more grand than the first. Lorenzo pleaded with his guide to stay but was told he was only permitted to visit these "heavenly cities," but could only stay briefly because he had not yet filled his mission in mortality.

While not many individuals who have had near-death experiences reported seeing multiple cities of light, the single city they did see or visit was extremely impressive and awe-inspiring. Invariably, they commented on the light. It was more than illuminating. It permeated their very being and they could actually feel it. They reported that light is not reflected from some source outside the city, like a sun, but emanates from every aspect of the city itself. There is no need for a sun because everything in the city produces light that radiates a sense of peace, acceptance, and understanding, and which is all-pervasive.

Linda Allen reported that she was shown a big city:

"It had golden colors and there was what looked like a big explosion coming up from the city. There were colors that we do not have on earth. These colors were so brilliant and intense that they would hurt our eyes if we looked at them on earth. But not there. It was a glorious glowing city of buildings and streets. The streets had bricks. They were like golden bricks. The buildings, and I know that this sounds really strange, were smart. They were intelligent. They were buildings of knowledge."[4]

During his near-death experience, Larry Tooley was met by an escort who accompanied him as they moved toward a brilliant light.

"As we approached the light I was told, 'We can go no farther. Just ahead lies the bounds of our travel.'

"The hillside ahead continued its ascent, ending at the base of a mountain. Cliffs rose steeply, disappearing into a hazy mist. Very high mountains protruded through the mist as fleecy clouds slowly drifted across their craggy peaks. Regal splendor crowned this celestial scene.

"At the base of the mountains lay a glorious city. Tall spires and pinnacles rose in exalted splendor, challenging the clouds above for dominance.

"Light radiated, undulating from the pearlized buildings. A thousand different shades of color filled the spectrum. I struggled to comprehend the sheer immensity of the city that lay below me. At first I failed to see the delicate details of the domed spires until I studied the scene in more detail.

"Each spire's dome was capped in pure gold. Pinnacles the color of platinum rose among the spires.

"My emotions overcame me as I sank to my knees in the tall grass at my feet. Through each arched doorway and window shimmered a faint blue light."[5]

### Buildings

Larry Tooley saw magnificent buildings but, from a distance. Faith, however, was able to visit a heavenly city and enter a building.

"It is magnificent, so magnificent that words do not exist that can adequately describe what I witnessed but I will try. I was taken to this awe-inspiring building. There were steps leading up to massive doors. On either side of the doors were great fluted columns with ornate capstones. As I entered the two gigantic doors I found myself in a large foyer leading to a grand room, round in shape, with stairs ascending up on the far side. In the center of the round room was a round translucent crystalline table with a gorgeous bowl filled with fruit and flowers. It had a central column supporting it and three small legs radiating out from its base. The ends of the legs had what looked to me like the feet of some animal. Hanging over the table was a glorious chandelier that radiated light.

"The floor of the room appeared to be made out of white marble. Leading into the room were three doors, one directly across from me, one to my left and one to my right. The stairway across from me wound up to a marble balcony.

"On the walls were what appeared to me to be pictures of beloved leaders who had lived on earth. The doorways had arches as did the windows. Around the windows hung gorgeous tapestries and curtains. The combination of colors, textures, and materials gave the appearance of serenity, peacefulness, and beauty."

Rebecca saw multiple buildings during her heavenly visit and commented on their beauty and grandeur.

"As we walked my eyes drank in the splendor of my environment. The houses, as we approached and passed them, seemed wondrously beautiful to me. They were built of the finest marble, encircled by broad verandas, the roofs or domes supported by massive or delicate pillars or columns; and winding steps led down to pearl and golden walks. The style of the architecture was unlike anything I had ever seen, and the flowers and vines that grew luxuriantly everywhere surpassed in beauty even those of my brightest dreams.

"Turning to the left, my escort led me through the beautiful marble columns that everywhere seemed substituted for doorways into a large oblong room. The entire walls and floor of the room were still of that exquisite light gray marble, polished to the greatest luster; and over walls and floors were strewn exquisite long-stemmed roses of every variety and color from the deepest crimson to the most delicate shades of pink and yellow."

Roy Mills, whose extensive near-death experience will be

reported on later, told about seeing a great hill with an enormous glowing building on top of it. The dazzling building seemed to him to be as big as a small city with two enormous luminous front doors.[6]

Sarah saw a building that appeared to be made of white alabaster marble with a pinkish hue, more beautiful than anything she had ever seen on earth. As she concentrated she realized that she could see through the walls and watch activity going on inside. One room that caught her attention was a large study room or library which had rows of huge ancient books and beautiful carved desks, yet simplistic in decor. People moved about freely and happily. She saw another room where women were preparing food. She also saw a man sitting in what looked like a module, working at a type of machine—like a computer, placing colored crystals with pointed ends in spaces.

### Vegetation

In addition to the building on the top of a hill mentioned above, Roy Mills said he also saw breathtakingly beautiful gardens and rolling green hills as far as his eyes could see. The colors were magnificent, beyond anything he had ever seen on earth.

Becky recalled walking through gently rolling hills covered with green grass and flowers.

"This exquisitely beautiful scene appeared to stretch before me forever. Everything had spirit about it. I could sense not only life in the grass and flowers, but they also radiated a knowing—a communication that conveyed love, peace, and joy all blended together. And the colors! Even the colors radiated life, knowledge, friendliness, and good will. They were beautiful beyond earth description—brilliant, yet at the same time soft, gentle, twinkling; luxurious pastels that seemed to send their beauty right into my soul."

Frances was very impressed with the flowers she saw.

"There were so many flowers and trees. They were alive. The flowers were so bright; they had colors I had never seen before. The blue ones seemed to be polarized light. Yellows felt as if the sun was inside them. Their brightness was as intense as looking at the sun in this world, except that there, it didn't hurt my eyes. They were incredibly beautiful and they were made of light."

Arlene described the beautiful garden she found herself in.

"The grass was such a lovely shade of green and the stems of flowers grew up out of the grass. I did not recognize any of the flowers but they were exceptionally beautiful, colorful, and delicate. They were so beautiful that when I returned to earth I set out on a quest to learn as much about flowers as I could and searched in every botany book I could find. But the flowers I saw were not of this world. Their petals are very sheer but brilliant in their colors. They seem to have the loveliest parts of many different flowers I have seen on earth combined. There are no words to describe the beauty of the flowers I saw."

During her experience, Holly Draper saw herself preparing to come to earth. In one scene, she was playing with other children by a fountain located just in front of a great building. There was a bench surrounding the fountain where she remembers trailing her hand in the water marveling at its color and composition. On the side of the fountain away from the great building, was an open area with grass, trees, flowers with butterflies flitting about them, and birds. It was a warm peaceful place with a delicate fragrance. The flowers were in sculptured gardens highlighted by majestic trees in full bloom. There was a wide variety of trees each of which fitted in and complemented the scene. Faith did not actually see birds but she could hear their songs which added to the sense of peace and serenity.

### Inhabitants

While the beauty and grandeur of the heavenly realm greatly impressed all those who were privileged to see it, it was the inhabitants who excited them the most. As discussed in greater detail in later chapters, many recognized beings they had known on earth. These beings emanated light and were perfect in shape and form regardless of what they had last looked like on earth. The beings were usually there to escort them and inform them that they had to return to earth.

Some people reported the presence of angelic beings who emanated light of a greater quality and intensity than those who had once lived on earth. These beings also radiated a sense of acceptance and unconditional love that was impossible for the experiencers to describe.

But there is one being who stands out from all the others. The light radiating from him exudes not only love and acceptance, but an overwhelming aura of power, strength, and authority. The light radiating from this being is so intense and beautiful that those who have seen it are absolutely sure that they were in the presence of the Supreme Being. Many intuitively recognized him when they came into his presence as memories came flooding back of who he is and the relationship they had had with him before coming to earth. Some were told by a voice resonating with authority that they were in the presence of God, but most knew this fact without such a pronouncement. In other places in this book you will read accounts of people who met this being and how being in his presence transformed them.

### The Being of Light

Many children in sharing their near-death experience, report seeing a Being of Light and use masculine terms to describe who they saw. This being often takes them into his arms where they get a close up view of him. They comment on the love emanating from his face, the piercing quality of his eyes, and the color of his eyes and hair. One woman, who had lost the ability to pray because her religious tradition taught that God was an essence much like a gas that had no shape or form, was greatly surprised and delighted to discover that he does have a visible body and that she is his daughter. She learned that she and the spirits of all humankind were created by him and in his image.

Many children have had the experience of meeting the inhabitants of heaven. Melvin Morse in his fascinating book, *Closer to the Light,*[7] believes that the reason why many more children than adults meet the Being of Light is because of their purity and innocence. Their experiences, a few of which are described below, are very touching and informative.

Kevin, a rambunctious three-year-old, was observed by his mother Linda standing pensively by the big picture window in the living room. He stood very still for a long time—which was amazing for a tiny active boy. He just stood there staring through the window and not moving. When Kevin finally walked away from the spot, she asked him what he had been doing. Very matter of factly he replied, "I was talking with God."[8]

Small children's experiences differ somewhat from their adult counterparts. For many their memories of home are still sharp and they remember who God is and their relationship with him. For example, a four-year-old boy named Rocky was leaning against the screen on his bedroom window when it gave way, and he fell two stories landing on his head. He was rushed to the hospital where his attending physicians gave him no chance to survive. But he did.

When he was released from the hospital two weeks later, he was partially paralyzed and spoke very hesitantly, one word at a time. Before the words came, he would point and gesture to indicate what he wanted. Often he would catch his mother Berta's eye and he would point up. Thinking that he was attempting to communicate about his fall, his mother would say, "Yes Rocky, you fell out the window."

He would shake his head, indicating that this was not what he meant. One day when his words were coming a bit easier, he told his mother, "Me, Heaven."

Startled, she looked at him and said, "What?"

He repeated, "Me, Heaven" at the same time pointing upward, then at himself. She asked him if he had gone to heaven and he nodded his head.

After a number of months his powers of communications improved significantly and he was able to tell his mother what he had experienced.

"When I fell out of the window I was hurt really bad. They took me to the hospital where the doctors were working on me. I floated up near the ceiling and I could see them doing something on the side of my head where I got hurt. That's when Jesus came and took my hand and took me to heaven. I saw people there and they had families and they live in homes like here."

He added that Heavenly Father had also visited him.[9]

Not all children who report seeing a Being of Light identify him as God. Numerous children report that the being they met was Jesus . These reports come not only from those reared in families from the Christian tradition. Children from non-religious homes, Jewish homes, and other non-Christian traditions have reported to their astonished parents that they met Jesus. One young mother reported an experience she had with her four-year-old daughter.

"My daughter Ruth liked to sleep with me and on occasion I would let her. This particular morning she woke me up hugging and shaking me. She was very excited and when she shook me into some sense of consciousness, she told me, 'Mom, Mom, Jesus told me I'm going to heaven! I've been there and it's beautiful: gold and silver streets, and Jesus and God are there!' She was extremely excited, so excited that I had a hard time following what she was saying.

"My daughter was not an excitable child. Normally she was a calm, contemplative child, intelligent, verbally-skilled, and precise in her speech. To find her so excited that she was stammering, searching for the right words, was very unusual. She had never been this excited before, even at Christmas or the circus. Never!

"I tried to calm her, but she continued chattering. When they first handed her to me as a newborn, I was elated, but my elation was tempered by a feeling that she would not be with me long. I had almost forgotten that feeling until now. Her talk about dying, which is something she never did before, brought back this uneasy feeling.

"I tried to settle her down by holding her on my lap. I told her, 'If you went to heaven, I'd miss you,' squeezing her tightly, with my eyes clenched tightly, 'but I'm glad that you had such a happy dream.' Losing her was something I did not even want to think about.

"She pulled away, looked up at me and emphatically stated, 'It was not a dream, it was real! But you don't have to worry Mom, 'cause Jesus said that I could take care of you and you won't have to worry about anything.'

"I am not a very religious individual, and when Ruth suddenly started talking about Jesus, heaven, and her going there, it was completely out of character. To my knowledge, Ruth hadn't heard of the golden streets of heaven, yet she was excitedly describing them to me now.

"She continued talking a steady stream about how wonderful heaven was. I again told her that I was glad she had had such a lovely dream. She stopped me, insisting 'Mommy, it was not a dream but was really, really real.' She lay there in my arms for a while chattering and said that I shouldn't worry or feel sad 'cause

Jesus would take care of me. She finally sat up, climbed out of our bed and ran off to play.

"It was just too much to think about. I lay there contemplating what she had just said, Jesus, heaven, her leaving me, it was just too much to even think about. So I got up and fixed breakfast. The rest of the day was normal, except between 3:00 and 3:30 that afternoon, Ruth was murdered.

"Through all the pain and anguish I felt at her death, I also felt a sense of calm. When things got really bad I would remember her words, 'Jesus said that I could take care of you.' And she has."[10]

In the next case, a young five-year-old girl had been raised in a violent and abusive home by parents who considered themselves to be atheists.

One day during a violent argument, her father grabbed his gun, shot and killed his wife, and then himself.

Neighbors heard the shots and came into the house. Horrified, they took the little girl out and called the police. In spite of all she had seen, she did not seem to be severely trauma-tized. Some suspected that she would eventually experience some type of post traumatic stress disorder. She was placed in a foster home with a number of other children pending a final placement. The couple she was placed with were deeply religious and tried to help their young charges to understand Christian principles. One day they were giving a lesson on Christ. The woman held up a large picture of Jesus and asked her young students if anyone knew who this was. The little girl who had just been placed in their home raised her hand. The woman, being a bit surprised knowing the type of home she came from, asked, "You know who he is?"

The little girl said, "Yes, He is the one who held me when my daddy shot my mommy and himself. He said that he loved me and that I would be OK."

No one can predict the long-term effect that this experience will have on this little girl, but she knows she is not alone, that Christ loves her and will be there when she needs Him.

Researchers in the United States are just now beginning to receive NDE accounts concerning children raised in China and other non-Christian societies. One account involves a four-year-old Chinese boy, Go Hing, who was pronounced dead after a drowning accident. He was washed and dressed for burial when he unexpectedly sat up. Needless to say this greatly surprised and startled all those present.

When he sat up, he told his mother of a man who held out his hand and pulled him from the water. His mother asked him if he knew the man's name, assuming it was the headmaster of the school where the accident occurred. "Don't you know?" responded the boy. "It's Jesus."

This family had fled from mainland China and had never had contact with Christians. His mother had never even heard of Jesus.[11]

After her son's statement that it was Jesus who saved him, his mother sought out books that referenced Jesus to find out who he was.

## Summary Thoughts

From the foregoing accounts and many others, it is apparent that our premortal home is a place of indescribable beauty. In general appearance it reminds observers of cities on earth but without pollution or disorder. The vegetation reflects a pleasing order and seems designed to add to the overall beauty and grandeur of the scene. The cities emanate light as does everything in them, including their inhabitants. Some individuals were shown more than one city with the different cities evidently having differing functions and emanating different intensities of light. These cities of light are awe- inspiring and impossible to describe. To a significant degree the appearance of our earthly home seems to be patterned after our celestial home. Perhaps our attempts to beautify our earthly homes are an unconscious desire to recreate our heavenly home on earth.

As to the inhabitants of heaven, they are equally impressive. Not only do they emanate light but they exude an aura of unconditional love. While everyone there emanates light, there is one Being who emanates light like no other and leaves such an impression on observers that their lives are forever changed. Who is this Being of Light? Children and adults alike report that it is God or Jesus, and many refer to him as their Father in Heaven.

## Chapter Three
## Life in the Heavenly Home

There is no way of knowing all that goes on in our premortal/postmortal home, but some conclusions may be drawn from the accounts of many individuals who have had brief visits to the heavenly realm. The first and perhaps most important observation is that heaven is organized, purposeful. Furthermore, observers sensed a definite aura of urgency associated with this activity.

Joe stated that the great city he saw was, ". . . a place of intense light, a place of intense activity, more like a bustling city than a lonely country scene."

A second man said, "Everyone was busy doing something. They were continually occupied with errands and seemed to be very happy."

A girl named Ella Jensen. said, "I saw no evidence of idleness whatever. Everyone, even the small children, seemed actively involved in some pursuit."[1]

George Ritchie, as he was being escorted by angelic beings during his experience, noted:

"Everyone seemed caught up in some all-engrossing activity. Not many words were exchanged among them. And yet I sensed no unfriendliness between these beings, rather a sense of total concentration.

"Whatever else these people might be, they appeared utterly and supremely self-forgetful, absorbed in some vast purpose beyond themselves."[2]

According to Lorenzo Young—"The people in the City were very busy but organized. But in spite of the intense level of activity, everything was in harmony and there was no disorder."[3]

During his brief visits to the world of spirits, Jedediah reported the following:

"I have been into the spirit world two nights in succession and, of all the dreads that ever came across me, the worst was to have to again return to my body, though I had to do it. But O, the order and government that were there. When in the spirit world, I saw the order of righteous men and women; beheld them organized in their several grades, and there appeared to be no obstruction to my vision; I could see every man and woman in their grade and order. I looked to see whether there was any disorder there, but there was none, neither darkness, disorder or confusion. All were organized and in perfect harmony.[4]

Angie Fenimore said that she could actually *feel* the intensity felt by the spirits she saw rushing to do the work of God. She was told that the time when the Savior would return to the earth was near, and everyone in Heaven was aware of this fact and was working toward that end.[5]

A man had died of a cancer that had severely disfigured him. But when his wife Abigail saw him during her near-death experience he was no longer disfigured or ill-looking, but appeared to be in perfect health. She was excited to see him and wanted to speak with him, but he said that he could not stop and visit. When she inquired what he was doing he said, "I can't stop; there are so many things to get done." He did not look frazzled or over-burdened, only very preoccupied with some very important task.

Before she was sent back to her physical body she saw him one more time. This time he was with others in a building listening intently to someone. He glanced over and saw her. It was obvious he knew what she wanted as he signaled her that he could not chat with her because there was something very important for him to hear. As soon as the speaker had finished everyone, including her husband, hurried out of the building and went in many directions as if they had an important task to fulfill. All the people this woman saw were radiant, full of life, vitality, and happiness, yet their actions and countenances revealed a deep sense of urgency.

Katie was an eight-year-old girl who hit her head on the side of a public swimming pool and drowned. After she was resuscitated, she hesitantly shared with her parents what had happened. She said that a pretty, glowing woman had taken her by the hand to a beautiful place. While she was looking around, her grandfather who had died several years earlier came up to her. He said, "What are you doing here? It is not your time. I need to speak to you but I can't right now." Looking at her escort he said, "As soon as I can, I will be back." He glanced down at Katie and repeated, "It's not your time, but I will speak with you later." He then rushed off.[6]

This grandfather seemed surprised to see his granddaughter in the spirit world but his pressing responsibilities would not permit him to stop and chat with her.

## Types of Activities

### Teaching/Learning

Premortality is evidently a place where an individual grows, develops and learns until he or she is ready for earth life. Apparently this preparation is directed by angelic beings and senior (more advanced) spirits as evidenced by the following account.

Roy Mills reports how he was prepared to come to earth:

"Before I came to earth I was taken to a place where I received instruction as to what I must do while on earth. The place where I received my instruction was what I called the Angel School. The Angel School has many rooms for instruction and as we progressed, we were taken from one room to the next. In these rooms we were taught about things we would need to know while on earth. When the angels in one room finished teaching I would be taken to a new room, each room focused on specific topics.

"In Angel School we were each assigned tutors who watched over and helped prepare us for earth. In my case I was assigned two young male angels. They were helpful, dedicated and fun-loving. I discovered that we all have specific names in Heaven and they told me theirs, but after I left home I could not remember them. They took me to one room where I met three other spirits being prepared for earth life. I was told to get to know these three spirits as they were going to be my best friends on earth."[7]

What is instructive here is the fact that not only are those about to go to earth being prepared, but those doing the instruction have unique personalities and identities. In Roy's case they were males with fun-loving personalities.

Cherie Logan discovered that her unborn son's tutor was a brother he was yet to have.

One night while Cherie was praying, she was visited by her unborn son, Ryan. She was impressed by his excitement and exuberance. He was trying to be calm and dignified but could not conceal a thrilling energy. He told her that he had just completed his training and that Nathan (his brother just older than he) had been his tutor until he, Nathan, had had to leave for earth. Ryan had been very concerned that he would not be able to complete the training he needed to have prior to coming to earth but his instruction and preparation had been taken over by another angelic being. With his instruction completed, Ryan was now ready to come. [8]

It is very apparent to those who have been permitted a glimpse into the premortal existence that great emphasis is placed on preparing spirits for earthlife and untold numbers are evidently involved in this enterprise. In Chapters Four, Five, Six, and Seven, the significance of earthly missions, the preparations for going to earth, and the actual departure for earth are discussed in detail.

### Escorting Spirits to Earth

Coming to earth is not a solitary experience. Discussed in detail in Chapter Six, angelic escorts are assigned to each spirit to assure that the spirit will traverse unscathed what is apparently a dark region occupied by malevolent beings.

### Watching Over Those On Earth

When beings are escorted to earth, they are given assurances that if they will seek help and guidance from home, they will receive it. In Chapters Twelve, Thirteen, and Fourteen, numerous accounts are presented and discussed that document the fact that guardian angels watch over those on earth, that comfort is given when needed, and that help is only a prayer away when trials and adversity seem overwhelming. However, this help is evidently dependent on whether what is requested is in harmony with heavenly objectives and will not interfere with the earthly missions of others.

### Escorting Spirits Home

Dr. Kubler-Ross reports that there are two major concerns that haunt parents who have had children murdered or die by mischance (such as getting lost and dying of exposure). Their first concern is the amount of pain the child may have had to suffer and the second is that no one was with the child when he or she died. Dr. Kubler-Ross has worked with thousands of dying people, including children, and has discovered that at the moment of death, pain is not a significant problem and that no one, especially a child, is alone when he or she steps through the door we call death.

Hospice workers have reported that as their patients draw close to death they often begin to chat with unseen relatives, friends, or angelic beings who seem to be assembling to escort them home. Their faces literally light up and many become very animated. They often say phrases such as, "I'm coming! I'm coming!" or, "Oh, how beautiful!" Often they will reach up toward something or someone before they die. Evidently we neither come into this world alone nor leave it alone.

### Keeping Records

It would seem that detailed records are kept in heaven as attested to in the following accounts.

Janette Whetten saw her daughter who had been stillborn standing by a large group of people. In her hands she held what appeared to be a clipboard on which she seemed to be keeping track of those going to and coming from earth.

During his near-death experience George Ritchie[9] saw many people in a large room working on strange-looking machines recording information and Harriet also saw a large room filled with individuals rapidly documenting what she was told were records of her family.

### Working

George Ritchie, during his visit to the heavenly city, discovered that it was compartmentalized into places each with a specific purpose. For example, he observed a place where music was being created and refined, a second place where the great books and writings of the universe were stored, and a third place where laboratories were filled with beings focusing on the problems facing those on earth.[10]

### Serving On Councils

It was not unusual for individuals during their near-death experiences to be told that it was not their time to die or that they had not yet completed their missions on earth and so couldn't stay. But in some cases, individuals who died didn't want to stay and petitioned to be allowed to return to earth.

One young father appeared before a council in heaven and pleaded to be able to go back to help his wife raise their young family. While his petition was being heard he was told to wait outside the room. He was later informed that his petition had been granted. Evidently decisions are not made on the spur of the moment possibly because they have implications for those already on earth, for those yet to be born, or for those who have returned to heaven. Nor are they made in all cases by a single "judge" but by groups of individuals in councils. Such was the case of Kathleen, who found herself in front of a group of people she discovered were her progenitors and who were making a judgment as to whether she should continue her life on earth. (See Chapter Four for details.)

### Relationships

There is no way of determining how long we were in our heavenly home before we came to earth but from various accounts it was probably a very long time. During this time, many of us formed relationships that would extend beyond heaven to earth. Plans were made to become a member of a specific family, or to marry. Following are examples of both.

Sometimes the problems and stresses associated with everyday living can be virtually overwhelming so that having additional children seems out of the question. It might therefore take divine intervention to help put things into an eternal perspective.

Ben was a young man who had three very active, very energetic sons. He and his wife had been in the midst of a financial crisis and were just starting to see daylight when his wife discovered she was pregnant. Ben was devastated. The expenses associated with a new baby would destroy them! As his wife's pregnancy progressed, Ben became increasingly despondent and depressed. One day, as he was lying in bed feeling totally overwhelmed, he began thinking how their problems would be eliminated if only his wife would miscarry. In the midst of these dark feelings he glanced up and saw a stern-looking young man standing in front of him. He pointed his finger at Ben and said, "You promised!" then disappeared. Ben was shocked by this stern rebuke. But then he began to remember—he remembered that he had made a promise to that young man just as he had said. Ben had made a commitment to him while still in the premortal world to become his father. At that point Ben realized that although this promise would not be easy to fulfill, he must fulfill it.

What a wake up call! Here was a young man looking straight into Ben's eyes and stating that Ben had promised to provide him a home on earth. It was not an idle promise but one that this young man was counting on.

Apparently this is not a unique situation. Bonnie was also confronted by the spirit of the baby she was carrying. It was 1975 and Bonnie was in her sixth month of pregnancy and hospitalized for the treatment of a major blood clot. To attack the blood clot, her doctors were injecting increasingly larger amounts of a blood thinner but without success. One day she woke up feeling very woozy and lethargic. Then suddenly everything changed.

"All the strange feelings and pain disappeared. Much to my delight, I discovered that I was no longer in my body but up in a corner of the room looking down at a body lying in the bed which I recognized as mine. As I sat up there looking down at that body, I became increasingly disgusted with it. I did not like how it looked nor all the restrictions that came with it. There was no way that I would return to that body if I had any say in the matter.

"As I sat up there, an aide came into the room with my lunch. She put the tray on my bedside table and left without saying a word. I can remember thinking that I should go down and eat the food, but didn't. About thirty minutes later she came back and removed the tray, without looking at me, saying a word, or even looking to see what I had eaten. As I watched her leave I heard someone say to me, not in words but telepathically, "Are you ready to go?"

"Without any hesitation I said, 'Yes.'

"The next instant I found that I had been transported into a dazzling light. The environment in which I found myself seemed to be one more of knowledge than place. I was delighted to discover that any question I had was immediately answered and that the depth and breadth of the answer was total and comprehensive. For example, if I thought about a shirt, I learned the specific plant the fabric was made of, the seed from which it grew, the genetic strain that made up seed and on and on. I would also know how the dye was created and how it was printed on the cloth, including every detail of how the printing machine was made and how it worked. I knew everything there was to know about the shirt. It was an amazing experience.

"At this time I had two little boys and one of the things shown me were all the hardships they would experience without me. I also understood what constitutes tragedy and adversity and the fact that they are always accompanied with opportunities for spiritual growth. I could see the ways that my sons' lives would be affected by my death. But I also clearly understood that whatever came into their lives, be it good or bad, would ultimately be for their good. I also realized that in the light with me was my father, who had died four months earlier, other family members, and a wondrous Being of Light.

"The Being of Light told me that I needed to go back to my body to complete the work I had yet to do on earth. His desire was supported by my father and all the others with him. But the atmosphere there was so wonderful, warm, peaceful, and loving that I was determined to stay and told him so. I knew that I didn't have to do anything I didn't want to do. He would not force me to go back.

"As part of my experience I had both a life review and a life preview. I saw in detail all the tragedies, adversity and hardships and blessings I had experienced and the role they had played in my life. But I also saw all those I would yet experience in my life and I knew with absolute certainty that I was not strong enough to endure them. I was then reminded by the Being of Light that I was carrying a baby to whom I had specific obligations, but even that did not overcome my resolve to stay.

"It was at this point that they brought my baby to me, only he was not in the form of a newborn infant, but that of an adolescent male. As we looked at each other he said (mind to mind), "Mom! You promised to do this for me," and complete recollection came back to me and I knew I had. This weakened my resolve to stay, as I knew I had an obligation to this young man and had given him my word. Looking into his eyes, I agreed to go back so he could be born. But I made it perfectly clear that once he was born, I could elect to stay on earth or return to this place. This they all accepted, my son, the Being of Light, my father, and the other beings there.

"The preview of my life, I felt, could give me an edge in coping with the trials I saw. Knowing what they were and when they would occur, I thought I could avoid most, if not all, of them. Knowing what I was thinking, the Being of Light informed me, "Not so. Your memories of these things will be blocked when you go back. You cannot avoid them. You will experience them--every one of them," and I knew He was right. But if I elected not to stay on earth, I would avoid all of them and the pain and suffering associated with them.

But, at the same time, I would forfeit all the growth I could achieve from them. That was fine with me.

"With this assurance I returned to my room where I again found myself perched up in the corner looking down at my body. I was repulsed by that body; it was dead and looked horrible. I dreaded the thought of ever returning to it.

"Then an aide brought in my supper tray and placed it on the table. She turned to leave. My roommate called out to her, 'Someone ought to examine her. She has not touched any of her food all day. I have been trying to speak to her and get no response. And I have not seen her move for hours.'

"The aide returned to the bed and looked at my body. Her eyes got very large. She ran to the nurse's station and two nurses ran into the room. When they looked at my body, they panicked. They pushed my bed out into the hall and ran with it toward the elevators because there was no resuscitation equipment on this ward. I could hear what they were thinking and it was not about me. Their only concern was that they were about to lose their jobs.

"I knew where they were taking me and I thought that attempts to resuscitate me could hurt or even kill my baby and I couldn't have that. So I returned to my body to prevent this from happening. One of the nurses noticed signs of my reentry and said, 'She's back.' Before anyone could discover their neglect they quickly returned the bed to my room and repositioned everything.

"Long before my son's birth, I had made my mind up that I was going to return to heaven and I began preparing my husband and doctor for my death. I told my doctor that no matter what happened, it would not be his fault. I told my husband that he must remarry and to pick a woman who would be a good mother to my three children. I even contacted various friends and asked them to look for a woman who would make a good mother for three young boys and wife for my husband. And every single woman I met I would evaluate as to her qualifications for being a good mother. My husband, physician, and all my friends thought I had taken leave of my senses.

"There were major complications associated with the last few weeks of my pregnancy and my son had to be delivered by C-section. My physician had assembled an emergency team to handle the expected serious problems during the birth of my baby. But the moment my son's face was exposed, he commenced screaming. All present breathed a collective sigh of relief. When I knew that he was here and OK, I started to leave my body. At that moment my son appeared to me just as I had seen him three months earlier. He looked me straight in my eyes and said, "Mom, please don't leave. I need you." Seeing him standing before me and knowing how much he needed me, stopped me. I was torn between returning to the glories of heaven or staying on earth. It was the hardest decision I have ever had to make. But I knew I had to stay."[11]

Bonnie learned that covenants we make with others in the premortal world are taken seriously. She had covenanted with her son not only to have him, but to rear him. Her life and his were so intertwined that she needed to look beyond her own desires to those of her sons. She could have returned to heaven. That was her right. But if she had, many lives would have been negatively affected. However, no matter what she elected to do, it would turn out to be good for her sons. But she discovered she had covenanted with him and she recognized that she had an obligation to fulfill that covenant and did.

Linda Kearl already had four children and wanted more. The fact that she would have more seemed to be confirmed when she felt the presence of a girl who she thought must be a daughter she would yet have. The feminine spirit she felt near her would indeed become a member of her family but not in the way she anticipated.

"I was expecting my fifth child and somehow assumed this child would be a girl as I had four girls already. So I was very surprised when I gave birth to a boy. I had been absolutely certain that my baby would be a girl, because I had felt the presence of a little girl and assumed that she was the spirit of the child I was carrying. Even after my son's birth, I continued to feel her presence and sensed that she wanted to join our family. I knew her name was Shayna. I wanted to have her but medical complications ended my ability to have children.

"Years later I was in the delivery room when my oldest daughter was about to deliver her first child. Just as she gave birth to a little girl, I glanced up to see my deceased father standing behind my daughter's husband. I could see only his face and he was grinning the big lopsided grin that I loved so much. He said to me, 'Linda, here is your Shayna!'

"As they laid the baby on my daughter's stomach, my son-in-law turned to me and said, 'Mom, do you know what we are going to name her?'

"I said, 'Yes.'

"He looked puzzled and said, 'You do?' He then turned to his wife and said accusingly, 'You told her! I thought we were going to announce it together?'

"My surprised daughter said, 'No, honey. I haven't told anyone.'

"He then turned to me and skeptically inquired, 'And what are we gong to name her?'

"I said, 'You're going to name her Shayna!'

"He looked at me, then at his wife who was also stunned, then back to me. 'How did you know?'

"I was so emotional at that moment that I could not say anything. Seeing my father who had passed away some 25 years earlier, was a very comforting and spiritual experience for me. When I regained my composure, I told them about seeing my Dad and how he had identified the baby to me and told me that her name was Shayna."

This female spirit had to wait a generation, but, with her deceased great-grandfather's help, she finally joined the family of her choice and was called by the name she had chosen.

Janice also had four children but she thought that her child-bearing years were ended. Janice had a sister who was caught up in the pursuit of her career and felt that children would be a severe liability. So she had her tubes tied to eliminate any chance of pregnancy. Shortly thereafter Janice had the following experience.

"One night as I was about to drop off to sleep, two adult spirits, a young man and a young woman, appeared to me and told me that they needed to come to my family. They told me that they had originally been assigned to my sister but, given her attitude and the ensuing surgery, this was no longer possible. Would I be willing to have them instead? I told them that I would be very willing to have them, and I did."

While a visit to a dentist is not one of the most enjoyable experiences for the vast majority of people, few have had an experience like Steve's. Steve was having four impacted wisdom teeth removed under general anesthesia when he had a severe reaction.

"The doctor had given me four cartridges of anesthesia, two at the beginning of the surgery, and two later on when I appeared to be waking. I only weighed 140 pounds at the time and had been having problems with my liver. I later learned that my liver was slow to metabolize the drugs.

"I felt a warm, almost hot, bright light shining in my face. It felt very much like closing your eyes while lying on the beach on a warm August day with the sun shining on your face. I felt a hand on my shoulder and turned to see a woman in white. She helped me to sit up. Initially I thought she was a nurse but when I looked at her I could see that she was *not* a nurse. She seemed to be made of white light and was the source of the bright warm light I had felt shining on my face.

"I looked around the post-surgical room. There were no windows and the lights were off. The woman was barefoot and was wearing a long white gown that went from her neck to her ankles. I could see the details of her feet and ankles. She appeared to be about twenty-seven years old and her eyes were blue, and her hair seemed to be a light blond that glowed intensely. Her blue eyes also glowed, almost like a type of fire, with a powerful light of their own. Other than her eyes, all the light was white and gold in color. Her feet and hands were a natural golden color, but her skin was not exactly like skin. It seemed to be illuminated from within as if made of some type of energy and it had no cracks or creases. She wore no makeup or ornaments in her hair. She seemed to be very serious, and her expression showed a sense of urgency.

"She gently helped me sit up and then assisted me to stand. I looked down, and saw my motionless body lying on the couch. This troubled me, and I started to wonder what had happened to me. She intercepted my thoughts, and said, 'Don't worry. You're not dead. You're quite alive.' Our conversation was not in words but telepathic. She continued, 'Your breathing had become irregular. There was too much anesthesia and your body was unable to metabolize it. No one where I live is willing to take any chances with your life, so I've come to make sure your breathing is stabilized.'

"She drew me closer to my body, and pointed to the chest, 'Look,' she said. 'Your heart is still beating.'

"I looked and could see through the chest into the heart, as the flesh was transparent. I watched the chambers filling and emptying with blood. They were moving slowly and somewhat laboriously, but they were all working. I could see the blood moving through the arteries.

"She had work to do so she diverted my attention. I looked around the room. There was a passageway from where she had come. It appeared to me like the entrance to a cave or a tunnel, but it was as if she had torn a hole in the fabric of space and walked through.

"My curiosity led me to want to explore the opening, but she said firmly, 'Don't go in there. If you go through that passage, you will never be able to come back here and finish your life, and there are many people who are depending on you.' She showed me images of four children who were going to be born to me--my future family--and an image of my wife before she was born.

"This woman was a very powerful, multifaceted women with a strong presence who had a very large corona of energy around her. She walked over to my body and placed her hand on my chest, and indicated that she was going to work on it, to change the chemical balance in the blood, stabilize the breathing, and weaken the effect of the anesthesia. Shortly she said, 'You're all right now. It's time for you to go back.' She encouraged me to lay down where my body was, and I began slowly stepping backwards.

"My wife was in the room by then and held my face between her hands as she saw me reviving. She noticed me looking beyond her and apparently talking to someone behind her, like hearing one side of a conversation.

"The light receded, the woman disappeared, and I was back in my body, sitting up, wondering where she went. At the time of this experience my wife was about three months pregnant with our oldest daughter.

"Today, twenty-four years later, my oldest daughter looks just like the woman I saw while I was in respiratory arrest. She has the same facial features, the same hands and feet, and the same personality. I strongly believe that she was the woman who came to save me."

What is unique about Steve's experience was the fact that he was permitted to see a heavenly messenger in the process of healing his body. He not only saw the healing done, but was told by his unborn daughter *why* it was done. Steve feels sure that he was visited by his future daughter to heal him so that she and her siblings could be born. Her words, "No one where I live is willing to take any chances with your life," reveals that those in heaven are definitely aware of what is happening on earth including those who are waiting for their turn on earth.

Sometimes active intervention of one kind or another is necessary to assure that a spirit can be born to specific parents at a specific time. Such was the case of Charlene Hobbs.

Charlene Hobbs was a very unconventional, free-spirited woman who delighted in violating conventional stereotypes. She loved riding motorcycles which was not something women commonly did in 1945. She was out with some friends one day racing down a highway when she lost control of her motorcycle, which then skidded down the highway colliding with a parked car. She had numerous broken bones, a collapsed lung, and massive blood loss. She was rushed to the nearest hospital where they tried to repair her broken body. Their major concern was her collapsed lung and its potential for infection and pneumonia. The combination of drugs given for her lung and other injuries resulted in cardiac arrest. Charlene then found herself out of her body.

"I knew what had happened. I was dead. I looked down at my body. The doctor was on my right and the nurse on my left and they were working frantically. At the time I was not happy with what was going on in my life and so was perfectly ready to leave. I could remember my earth life and all the things I had done, the people that I knew, my family, but I was totally at peace, and it was an incredible feeling. I turned away from the scene before me and began to ascend. As I moved up I could hear beautiful music, and

I found myself in a gloriously beautiful place. I could see flowers of all types with colors so vivid that they actually glowed. I was reveling in the magnificent beauty of the place when I heard someone call my name. I turned and saw a young man and instinctively moved towards him. I did not have to walk as when I thought about moving closer to him, I did. He said, 'You've come too early.'

"I responded, 'That's fine with me.'

"He smiled, and I could actually feel his love radiating out to me. He was a very good-looking man and was dressed in a white robe. The robe had a V-neck and sleeves that came three-quarters of the way down his arms. He said, 'You need to go back!'

"I countered with, 'I don't want to go back. I did not like it down there.'

"He smiled again and repeated, 'You need to go back!'

"I said, 'No! I don't want to return to earth!'

"He then said, 'Your mission on earth is not yet completed and you need to go back and complete it!'

"He had such a beautiful loving smile and when I looked into his eyes I could not resist, so I agreed to go back. I turned and was surprised to discover that I could see my body quite clearly through the roof of the hospital. I descended to the hospital passing through its roof and into my room. I turned onto my back and I reentered my body. The moment I entered it I experienced excruciating pain. Fortunately it only lasted a few moments. But the weight of my physical body was very distressing. I now felt so constrained, so weighed down, so restricted. I found myself longing for the freedom I had experienced when I was out of it.

"This experience changed me completely. I no longer felt the need to twit the nose of society. I settled down, married, and had a family.

"Many years later, I was sitting on my couch reading when I happened to look up. There stood the man I had seen during my near-death experience so many years before--that same handsome, smiling, loving man. I was stunned! He had been with me all these years and it was only now that I realized who he was. It was my son who had sent me back so that I could complete my mission. I now realize that part of that mission was to become his mother."

Charlene's experience reveals some very fascinating information about the interconnectedness of heaven and earth. First of all a spirit can actively intervene in its mother's life so that he/she can be born at the correct time. Second, spirits can appear to their prospective parents as they will appear as an adult which suggests that the physical body takes on the form of the spirit body, given nothing inhibits its physical development. And third, the restrictions placed on the spirit by a physical body are profound and frustrating--as Charlene discovered once back in her physical body. Further, motherhood would seem to be a divine calling in the eternal scheme of things, not a chore or a punishment.

In the next account we meet a precocious four-year old named Andrew Cross who would occasionally tell his parents about events he participated in before he was born. He usually began his various memories with the words, "I remember when. . . ." His mother, Debra shared one such experience.

"On one occasion we had been asked by an extended family member how and where we met. We were just about to tell her when a giggling Andrew spoke up and said, "I remember when Daddy and Mommy met each other. I was watching them. I was really happy. I wanted them to get married so that I could be born." He then proceeded to tell everyone present that I had not wanted to go to the dance without a date, but that my roommates had persisted until I finally agreed to go. Andrew accurately described what I was wearing--a brown sweater and light brown pants--and how I had stood by the door because I so urgently wanted to leave. He described the room in detail, including where the lights were and the area where people were dancing. He then described what Mark was wearing—a green shirt and light brown pants. He said that Mark was watching the girls around him and didn't look over to where I was standing. Andrew said that I wasn't looking at Mark because I was too busy trying to talk my friends into leaving. He said he made one of the spotlights shine on me and a second on Mark so that we noticed each other. Then, using exaggerated facial expressions, he showed us what we looked like when we saw each other and when we danced, including how we looked at each other as we left the dance. He acted so proud that he had helped us meet, thus assuring that we would keep our premortal promise to him and to each other. After everyone left, Mark and I got out our respective journals to check, and Andrew was right in every particular."

Apparently the circumstances whereby some couples meet and fall in love are not accidental or random. Some of those in heaven have such a deep stake in assuring that specific individuals meet, marry, and ultimately give birth to them that they actively intervene.

Amy Cohen is positive that her two unborn sons, William and Richard, will be instrumental in determining who she marries.

"When I need time to think and reflect I go for a walk on the beach. One day I walked for about a mile, climbed up on a lifeguard stand to watch the waves and think. I looked up at the sky and could feel/sense/see two boys who I was certain would someday be mine, floating in the sky off in the distance, holding hands. I thought of them as William and Edward.

"I do not know how much time went by, but it seemed like a long time. They talked to me and, among other things, they told me how wonderful I was, how much they loved me, and that they were watching out for me. They said they were 'getting' my man, their dad, and that I must be patient and have faith. It was so beautiful. I was so happy to be with them. They were so loving and gentle. I asked them when we would be together, and they told me it would be soon and repeated that I should be patient and have faith.

"I have especially felt my boys' presence in the past six months, particularly after I broke up with someone I had been involved with for a year and a half. When questioning myself on whether the breakup was for the best, I strongly felt my boys, in particular the older one, William, telling me spiritually that my former boyfriend was not the one, that they did not want him for their father. At night in bed, crying sometimes, I could feel William almost as if he were there with me, stroking my forehead and hair, comforting me. Those sweet little hands told me everything was going to be okay.

"On the lighter side, I guess I tune into them as a dad meter. When I am unsure about a guy I like, it is like tuning in on something within and having guidance to help me trust what is right and what is not."[12]

We all know that various factors can influence our choices as to whom we marry, but we may never have imagined that little pre-born cupids could be among them. Circumstances just may be engineered so that we can meet the "right person" at the "right time," allowing us to fulfill premortal agreements.

One man noted that before he was married, his unborn son communicated with him on a regular basis. One night his son told him, 'Go get pizza.' So he went to the pizzeria and there met the woman who he eventually married, and who two years later gave birth to their son.[13]

A young woman reported that she felt she should go to a specific night club one evening. While she was looking around she saw the image of two boys standing on either side of a man who was sitting with his back toward her. One boy appeared to be about thirteen, the other about ten. She knew instantly that she was seeing her future sons and that she would marry the man sitting there between them. Sure enough, she is now that man's wife, and they have two sons about three years apart in age.[14]

While most people will agree that a bar is not the best place to find a mate, one time it was.

As discussed in earlier chapters, we must all experience trials and adversity to some degree in order to learn, to grow, and to develop spiritual gifts. Many individuals believe that if they are experiencing adversity, they are being punished. And if they are being punished, they must have done something wrong and are therefore bad. This was Angie Fenimore's attitude. She experienced a life of physical and emotional abuse, and believed that she was bad, and that the world would be a better place if she were dead. She became increasingly despondent and depressed. Sure that death was her only option, she attempted suicide.

The next thing she became aware of was being in the presence of her Heavenly Father. She was awestruck and surprised at the love she felt emanating from Him given that she thought of herself as worthless and bad. It was total love, it was unconditional love, and it was coming to her from Him. All of her life she had thought she was unworthy of love, that she did not deserve love, but here she was in the presence of God and He loved her. She discovered that she was a daughter of God and that she had an important mission to perform on earth. She also learned that all life is important and interconnected.

"I learned that just as there are laws of nature, of physics and of probability, there are laws of spirit. One of these spiritual laws is that a price of suffering must be paid for every act of harm. I was shown my life up to the point where I killed myself. I became painfully aware of the suffering I had caused my family and other people because of my own weaknesses. And I saw that by ending my life, I was destroying a web of connection between people on earth, possibly drastically altering the lives of millions. All of us are inseparably linked, and the negative impact of one decision has the capacity to be felt throughout the world.

"My children, certainly, would be gravely harmed by my suicide. I was given a glimpse of their future, not the events of their lives, but rather the energy, and the character that their lives would have. By abandoning my earthly responsibilities, I would influence my children, my oldest son in particular, to make choices that would lead him away from his divine purpose. Without me, he might well be rendered incapable of completing his assignment on earth.

"The life of my other son, Jacob, was different because he was already performing a sacred errand for God. I was shown that I knew and loved him before I was ever born, and that he had chosen to come to earth as my son. He had knowingly taken a tremendous risk in coming to me.

"I was told that my children were great and powerful spirits and that up to this point in my life I had not deserved them. I caught a glimpse of how deeply God loves my boys, and how I was tampering with the sacred will of God with my callous disregard for their welfare."[15]

Angie learned a very important lesson that applies to everyone. All of us are a part of the great eternal family of God. As family members we have significant responsibilities many of which were established in heaven. We can contribute in positive ways to this great and eternal family or we can detract from it. Like ripples in a pond, our actions can be felt over long distances in both time and space. Angie also learned that we all have worth, that God loves and cares for us, and that we are the real architects of our lives.

### The Appearance of Premortal Beings

Those who have been privileged to see premortal beings have noted that there are no racial distinctions among them such as Caucasian, Asian, or Black. Evidently those distinctions came about because of the families spirits are born into. Resemblances occurring between family members would therefore also seem to be a matter of genetics rather than by virtue of premortal relationships, choices, or covenants.

Roy Mills observed this fact during his very extensive near death experience and commented:

"When I was in heaven, I never saw different races of people, only spirit beings who were filled with love for each other. We are all the same 'race' in heaven. Before we come to earth, God chooses what our earthly race will be. He makes that decision for our spiritual growth and according to His perfect plan. On earth, many people are prejudiced and sometimes even violent toward others who are different—people of color, the poor, alcoholics, and addicts, or those with physical or mental disabilities. But in heaven, it is considered a great honor for a spirit to accept such a difficult life."[16]

What, then, does the spirit look like? The answer is, like its Creator--its Heavenly Father--in general form and likeness. Numerous accounts cited in this book report that mothers, fathers, grandparents, other relatives, siblings, health professionals, and friends have reported seeing the spirit of an unborn child or that of a child who lived only seconds. The spirit they saw was that of a mature, young adult, what the infant would have looked like as an adult had it lived. Others, however, have seen their deceased children still as children and in the care of an angelic being or deceased relative. Apparently the spirit can appear as it would look at any particular time in its earthly development depending on the needs of the observer.

During RaNelle Wallace's lengthy visit to premortality she observed that the clothing worn in that sphere was usually white.

"The clothing that I observed consisted of long flowing robes which extended to the ankle. The material the robes were made of was luminous, light, beautiful, and sometimes had gold shimmers in the weave. Some cloth had golden shimmers, others purple, still others a pink hue. There was the opportunity to chose the type and color of clothing one would wear. But the preferred choice seemed to be material that radiated the most light. The desire was not to pick clothing for its color as such but because it emanated the purest light. Clothing was one of the least significant things that existed on the other side and was not chosen because it made one look attractive but to reflect the likeness of God.

"Neither men nor women wore shoes. I realized that I was not wearing shoes either. I did not feel like I was barefooted nor did I feel the necessity to cover my feet."[17]

Most reports of the clothing worn in heaven generally agree with RaNelle's description. However, on occasion deceased relatives have been seen wearing the type of clothing they might have worn in their earth life which may have been for purposes of identification

### Summary Thoughts

The spirit world is an active, organized, and purposeful place where one of the most important purposes seems to be to prepare spirits to come to earth and perform assigned/chosen missions. During the eons of time we were there, we formed bonds that extended beyond heaven and into mortality. This bond will not end at our physical death but persist into eternity. Birth and death are necessary stages in our eternal growth and what we do in the interim determines the quality of our relationship with God, humanity and especially our immediate family.

Given the sense of urgency and total preoccupation with important tasks that were observed in the heavenly realm, one is forced to question the ability of mediums and psychics to gain access to the deceased at will.

# Chapter Four
## Preparations for Earth Life

There is no way of knowing how long we lived in our heavenly home prior to coming to earth. However, there are indications it may have been a very, very long time. When we had accomplished all we could there, we had to come to earth to continue our progress—like going away to college after graduating from high school. For most of us, the veil of forgetfulness blocks recall of our premortal life thus enabling us to act and learn at our own speed, ability, and motivation. Shocking as it may seem considering some of the appalling tests we undergo on earth, in heaven we understood the importance of these tests and not only accepted them but probably chose them.

### Assignments & Missions

While the vast majority of people on earth will never recall how their earthly missions were determined or what they entail, a few individuals do. Insights into what occurred just before we came to earth are provided by what these privileged individuals saw.

Roy Mills not only remembers his life before birth, but the way he and many others received their earthly missions and assignments. Roy's memories of how he received his were triggered by his near-death experience.

"I was escorted to a building where many angelic beings were teaching others like me. My escorts took me to a male being and left me in his care.

"I looked around the room and discovered it was covered by a huge glowing dome. My instructor taught us that we all have an important mission to accomplish on earth and that this mission is assigned by God who is the father of our spirits.

"I was then taken to a vast room. Spirits were escorted into the room until the huge auditorium was filled. Everyone had a designated place to stand and wait. I was extremely impressed with the aura of peace, order, and harmony. I saw no restlessness, no confusion, no aimless milling around, no irritation, grumbling or conflict of any kind. We faced a magnificent throne that emanated light brighter than the sun but which did not hurt my eyes to look at. I instinctively knew it was the throne of God. Then an even brighter light appeared next to the throne. A feeling of absolute love emanated from that light and permeated my entire soul. There are no words to describe what I felt. I knew that the light surrounded our Father, our Eternal Father in Heaven. The light was so brilliant that I could not see Him clearly. All I could see was his outline and the light that He was emanating. It thrilled and amazed me to realize that I was a child of this eternal glorious being.

"I was filled with great anticipation and watched every move He made. He raised His right hand which extended beyond the blinding brightness and pointed toward someone in the massive crowd. He did not have to specify who He was pointing at. We all knew who it was. When He pronounced the individual's name a bright light engulfed a young man. Our Heavenly Father then explained what the individual's mission was going to be on earth. When He finished speaking the multitude rejoiced. We were happy and pleased for our brother. An angel glided over to him and escorted him out of the room.

"Then the crowd became very quiet as our Heavenly Father pointed to another individual, this time a young woman, and pronounced her name. He explained her mission on earth and, again, everyone rejoiced. It was made totally clear to everyone present that there were no second-class souls and no second-class missions.

We all had a divinely assigned purpose for our lives and a free will. Free will is respected in heaven and we all had the right to accept or reject our assigned earth missions. We accepted our missions because we had divine assurance that we could fulfill them, that our missions matched our unique talents, would facilitate our eternal growth, and would help our brothers and sisters to achieve their missions. There was no jealousy over anyone's mission, only joy and excitement. It was clear to everyone that each spirit was a child of God, a mighty spirit. It didn't matter whether one's mission appeared great or small by earth standards. By the standards of heaven, all missions are important and great. Obscure, poor or handicapped persons or those who suffer greatly, may be some of the mightiest spirits in eternity which is why they qualify for such difficult missions. The important thing is that individuals do their best to complete their missions.

"Then He pointed at me and pronounced my name and I was engulfed in a glorious light. I felt a surge of joy permeate my entire being as He described my mission for all to hear. I was told that I had a special and unique mission to accomplish. As with the two earlier spirits' assignments, all those in the auditorium expressed excitement and joy for me. Then two angelic beings came and escorted me to a room where I was to wait for instruction. As I sat there, other souls passed through the room, each with an escort. I could tell by their reactions as they entered this great room and saw the beings in it, that these souls were just returning from their life on earth. The look on their faces registered awe, wonder, reverence, delight, and joy. I vividly recall two individuals who manifested exceptional joy, even astonishment, at the beauties of heaven. It was clear to me that they had had unusually difficult earth lives and were truly happy to be back home. These returnees were lead by angels to a hall to my left. Other angelic beings came in escorting unborn souls. They exited through a hall to my right. The place resembled a huge railroad station with some individuals returning from earth and others on their way to earth.

"I was also permitted to look at the 'Life Book,' which contained my entire life including things I would do, problems I would encounter, and the role adversity and trials would play in my life. I was told that I could choose my earth tests and trials. I was also shown how each trial and each test could affect me and my eternal life. In my enthusiasm to accomplish as much good and learn as much as possible while on earth, I chose five major tests. I noticed as I made my selections that my escorts seemed concerned. Later, one of them took me aside and told me that the life challenges I had selected had been reviewed and it was their conclusion that the five tests I had selected would be too much for me. Individually they were good and I could handle them, but the specific combination would inhibit my ability to accomplish the mission Heavenly Father had assigned me. They told me that my motives were admirable, but that I had to be more realistic. I was lovingly counseled to eliminate two of the five tests. I was keenly aware of the blessings that accompanied each of the tests and I did not wish to lose any of them but, heeding their council, I limited my selection to three.

"One of the most important questions I remember asking my instructors was whether I would be able to return to heaven once I finished my earth life. I was told that it was completely up to me and depended on how I exercised my free will. Then I asked just what free will entails. I was told that free will is the right God gives to all His children to choose to do good or evil when they are on earth—to love or not to love; to help others or not to help others; to believe or not to believe; to live in the light or in the darkness."[1]

Roy learned that our general earth missions are assigned by God and that we have the right to accept or reject any part or all of the assignment. But we also have full knowledge of what we stand to gain or lose by our choices. In addition to our assigned earth mission, we also have the right to select the type of life we will live and the challenges we will face. So, in conjunction with God, we are joint authors of our lives.

Elane Durham also discovered the degree to which she was an active participant in designing her life on earth. Her near-death experience came about when she suffered a massive brain hemorrhage and collapsed on a public sidewalk. The next thing she was aware of was being escorted by angelic beings.

"I was asked by the angel who was escorting me, 'Would you like to see yourself before you were born?' I was astonished at the question, since the idea of a premortal existence was not part of my religious philosophy, but I said that I would.

"I saw myself sitting before something like a mirror, with five angels/people around to assist me. I was making decisions about my life, including who my parents would be and what trials, emotional and physical, I would experience. As I made my choices, three of the angels conveyed a sense of anxiety, saying, 'You are choosing too difficult a life.'

"I told them, 'I need these experiences because of all the growth they can give me.' I knew that my life would be filled with great pain and adversity, but the increased learning and depth these trials give the soul is a powerful bulwark. I also knew how these experiences would prepare me for the eternities."[2]

In spite of Elane's enthusiasm to maximize her spiritual growth on earth, her angelic escorts convinced her to modify her desires to those she could manage. So like university advisors on earth, our spiritual advisors help us select the experiences that will maximize our spiritual growth while not exceeding our capabilities.

Frances Gomez's near-death experience was initiated by a motorcycle accident. Her experience helped her to understand the larger picture which included her purpose for coming to earth.

"I remembered that I had always been a part of God's plan. In the presence of my Creator, I knew I was accepted unconditionally, and that all that was required of me was to do the best I could to master this physical body and complete my part of the plan.

"I discovered that before we came to this world we existed as magnificent beings of light. We lived in a vast universe with no restrictions. Then one day at an assembly, we were informed that there was a plan to raise up a world. Volunteers were requested.

"The condition was that we would have to take a physical body. This was new to us. It was explained that while on earth we would experience some pleasures with these bodies that we could not experience in the spirit world. We were informed that there were also other feelings, such as pain and fear, which were unknown to us in the spirit world. We would have to master and learn from these new feelings. We were told that we would be allowed to chose the birth parents and siblings that we would have on earth. I was also informed that we chose the challenges and lessons we would experience to help us grow.

"At birth our memories would start to fade until we had complete amnesia. We wouldn't be able to remember who we were, but we wouldn't be alone. We would be born with a spark of God's light within us, to guide us in this world."[3]

Roy and Frances discovered that our general mission on earth is assigned by God, but that we are intimately involved in the types of lives we will experience. All of us have the gift of free will. We can elect to complete our life's mission as assigned by God, in total, in part, or not at all. It is our choice but whatever we neglect to do, we also forfeit those blessings that came with that aspect of the assignment.

Kathleen Pratt Martinez learned first hand that while in pre-mortality she had made serious commitments with her extended family that they took very seriously. This realization came about as the result of major medical complications.

"During my labor serious complications resulted in my being declared clinically dead. I left my body and found myself in a place filled with deceased members of my family. Seated on a throne-like high backed chair was a personage whom I intuitively knew was very important in the spiritual realm. All those assembled seemed to be there to judge me in some capacity.

"At my left side stood my grandfather, who I had never known. On my right side was my grandmother who had died just three months earlier. From what I gathered, the trial was to determine whether I would continue in this life. My grandfather felt that I probably would not carry out the mission I had been assigned and that they would have to select someone else. I apparently was not of strong enough character to follow through with what I was supposed to do.

"My grandmother took my defense and said that she thought that I would, and she said I should be given the chance to prove that I would do this. I was given the chance to come back to life and though I was not told the precise mission I was to perform, I know without doubt that it is very important to my family in heaven."[4]

What is insightful here is the fact that before Kathleen left heaven she had agreed, as part of her mission, to do important work for her family that could only be done on earth. She was the key to achieving these goals and if she would not or could not do them, someone else would have to be sent. So missions would seem to be not only for the personal spiritual growth of a specific individual but for the good of others in the spirit realm.

### Adversity

Angie Fenimore had experienced so much abuse and adversity that she felt her life held no meaning and she and everyone else would be better off if she died. So one day she committed suicide. As she drifted into unconsciousness, her spirit left her body. She eventually entered an indescribably beautiful realm where her understanding was enlarged:

"I had been Satan's puppet. While opposites exist—light and darkness, truth and deception, love and hate—there are also myriad possibilities in between, contortions and distortions of the truth that are made of darkness. To love is the most important thing we come into this world to learn, yet Satan twisted this simple truth to persuade me to perform a terrible act of darkness in the name of love for my husband and children. How could it be love that prompted me to leave them, without ever fully considering how it might affect them to discover my dead body? Suicide was the most selfish act that I could ever have been capable of. It was an act of vanity, stemming from the belief that I couldn't open up to anyone, that I had to solve my problems on my own. These were Satan's lies. God loves us and calls to us but He will not force us to choose light.

"I saw that I was not forced to come to earth. I could see that before my birth I knew what I would face, and that with God I had co-authored the course of my life. I knew that confusion and heartache would be my companions. I chose my parents and even several of my friends before I came to earth. The option to have an easier life was always mine, but I volunteered, I sacrificed, because I loved the people who were to become my family and I wanted to be with them. I knew what to expect, and still chose to come. We all make that choice.

"I also realized that even when I felt I was far beyond God's touch, He had been sending helpers to me."[5]

In addition to discovering that she was a co-author with God of the script of her life, Angie discovered that taking her life was selfish and vain. It was vain because she would not be able to reach out to others, including God, for help and it was selfish because she did not consider what her act could and *would* do to others.

DeLynn (not his real name) had spent his entire life afflicted with Cystic Fibrosis. He had never drawn a breath of air without pain, and he had always had medical problems. While in the hospital to undergo major surgery, DeLynn died. The first thing he was aware of was being free of pain. For a time he stood there just breathing. It was a glorious experience! It was fantastic being able to breath without searing pain. He had not realized how much pain his body had been constantly subjected to until it was gone. DeLynn's story is discussed in depth in Chapter 12—*Why Disabilities and Handicaps?* He asked his angelic hosts why he had been cursed with such a horrible affliction.

"Upon asking the question, I found myself in a classroom in heaven long before I was born. The instructor was explaining the increased growth and progress we would make on earth through accepting certain diseases. On the board was a list of diseases. When the instructor got to Cystic Fibrosis he explained how it could accelerate personal growth. He then asked if anyone would be interested in assuming Cystic Fibrosis with all its implications. Then I saw the most remarkable thing—I raised my hand and volunteered. I realized that, from an eternal perspective, it was a blessing, an opportunity, given in Heavenly Father's wisdom."[6]

DeLynn returned to his body a changed man. He was still afflicted with the disease but he never again spoke of his illness as a punishment or curse. He knew he had chosen it as an important part of his life's experience and from that point in his life tried to make the best of his disease and what he could/should learn from it.

During her near-death experience Betty Eadie also learned the true role of adversity.

"My escorts…took me to a place where many spirits were being prepared for life on earth. They were mature spirits—I saw no children spirits during my entire experience. I saw how desirous these spirits were of coming to earth. They looked upon life as a school where they could learn many things and develop the attributes they lacked. I was told that we had all desired to come here, that we had actually chosen many of our weaknesses and difficult situations in our lives so that we could grow. I also understood that sometimes we were given weaknesses which would be for our good."[7]

What matters is not how long or under what conditions we live on earth, but how well we live with the circumstances, specifically what we learn from them and how well we use what we learn to help others.

### Covenanting With God

During her near-death experience, RaNelle Wallace also saw how extensively she had been involved in the design of her mortal life. She had promised to help others in heaven to succeed on earth, and they in turn had made commitments to assist her. In addition, her Father in heaven promised her that at no time would she be completely on her own. When she needed help, He would let her know what to do and how well she was doing.

"When I knew that I must come to earth to be able to progress, I expressed a desire to meet with God. I was taken to him by my escorts and once I came into His presence, I told Him that I was ready to begin my life on earth. He had me bring my right hand to the square and confirm that it was my desire to go to earth and while there, to use my talents to the best of my ability to complete my assignment. This I did willingly and with no reservations.

The place where I and others made these covenants was a place of great beauty. The walls were made of crystal that reflected a brilliant white light. In front of me was a bar made of pure gold and a square place where I and others stood when covenanting with our Heavenly Father. In my case, He asked me if I had gone over my earthly assignments and if I understood the consequences of the specific assignments I had accepted and the risks involved. I responded that I had thought them out, that I had researched each aspect of my assignment in detail, its consequences and blessings, and that I was ready to take on my assignments.

"Behind him were other supreme beings who I assumed served as witnesses. Once I confirmed that I was ready, He again had me put my arm to the square, called me by name, and asked me to repeat what I had covenanted to do. I remember looking around at the group and I saw that all of the other people there were also putting their arm to the square in support of me and my assignments. They were covenanting with God to support me. I felt overwhelmed, not only by their love and support, but by how absolutely serious my assignments were. As I was thinking about this tremendous outpouring of support, I remembered all the work that had gone into getting to this point. I recalled picking out each assignment, reflecting on how it would help me to progress, to move forward in the eternities. Once I had done this, He said, 'Well done.'

"I was told that all the spirits are brought before Heavenly Father right before they are born to go through this experience.

"I learned that those with whom we have become closely bonded in the premortal realm are also those with whom we will be closely connected on earth. We understood the implications of these connections and that these connections entailed specific responsibilities for each of us while on earth.

"In my case I was present with my children and grandchildren when they accepted their assignments. I was one of their witnesses and I made commitments to them to give them my support. To do this I must live up to the covenants I made before God and my witnesses."[8]

RaNelle's experience illustrates how thoroughly she and, by inference we, are prepared and participate in decisions pertaining to our future life on earth and the degree to which family generations are intertwined.

### Saying Goodbye

A number of individuals interviewed reported that during their near-death experience they witnessed their preparations to come to earth. Just prior to their departure relatives who had already been to earth, met with them. A few of the more intriguing examples follow;

Jodi Sherrill was well acquainted with her grandfather who had died long before she was born.

"I remember a day when I sat upon my grandfather's knee and asked him if I could be born next and go to earth. My younger brother spoke up and said that he wanted to be next. My grandfather looked at the two of us and said that I was to be next and that my brother would follow.

"I remember the day that I left. I hugged my grandfather and cried because I loved him and would miss him. Then I was on my way. The next thing I remember was being held up by the doctor to show me to my mother."

LaNae Clement's experience with her grandmother was similar.

"Just before I was to leave for earth, I was conversing with my grandmother. She said to me, 'I will see you very soon.' We hugged and I left.

"The next thing I remember is the doctor holding me up and saying to my mother, 'You have a baby girl!'"

Monica Wilson's memories of her last moments in heaven also involve her grandmother.

"As I grew older, instead of doubting, I became more and more convinced that I really had a memory of a life before I came to this earth. There was just too much detail. I actually remember sitting on my grandmother's lap in a rocking chair. It was in a large, white room. There were no walls that I could see, but I was aware that the boundary was there. I also remember knowing that I was not an adult. I was what I considered to be a baby spirit. I was not yet born but existed in heaven.

"I know my grandmother was telling me all about my life and some of the important decisions I was going to have to make. She was trying to give me some guidance to make my life a little easier. It worked. I have been aware from a very young age that I have wisdom beyond my years when it comes to making certain decisions."

It seems natural that those who have already been to earth would want to share their knowledge and experience with those about to depart for earth. Encouragement is given, final words are shared, and their love and support go with them. What is especially intriguing is the fact that Jodi and LaNae both remember their births.

### Summary Thoughts

Our lives on earth are part of a much larger picture. Each person born on earth has a divine purpose, a mission to perform. That mission comes as an assignment from our Eternal Father, and it is our choice to accept or reject. It also appears that the individual chooses many, if not all, the trials and tests experienced on earth. While we were premortal spirits, we could clearly see the spiritual growth that accompanied these choices. It is also apparent that part of what we are to accomplish on earth is the fulfillment of commitments we made in premortality. All life, regardless of its length or quality, has purpose. Life is not a hand of cards dealt capriciously, but a carefully designed plan for achieving eternal goals.

## Chapter Five
## The Mission Begins

Once an earthly mission has been assigned and final instruction given, the spirits in premortality are ready to come to earth. However, some parents' priorities do not place having children in a timely manner as a very high priority or even having children at all, so heavenly intervention may have to occur if spirit beings are to begin their mortal experience at the right time.

### Contacts with Prospective Parents

Amy Tenney was eager to start her family but Mark her husband was not. All that changed one quiet summer morning.

Recently graduated from college, Mark was enjoying the challenges of a new career, paying off his student loans, and preparing to buy their first home. In spite of his wife's desires, he did not feel ready for the responsibilities of a family.

Mark and Amy were spending the weekend in a rustic cabin in the mountains. It was early Saturday morning and Mark was lying in bed listening to nature's symphony—wind whispering through the branches of the trees, accompanied by water gurgling musically in a nearby brook. The clean pine-scented air was a delight to the senses. He lay there thinking, "What could be better than this—a lovely wife, an enjoyable job, and this beautiful setting."

As he gazed at the shadows playing on the walls of the cabin, he sensed someone in the room with them. Glancing to his left, he was surprised to see a little girl with long blonde hair and steel-blue eyes. In the crook of her left arm rested a doll. While staring back at Mark, the child stroked a pink ribbon tied around the doll's neck.

At last she spoke, mind to mind, "Daddy, it is time for me to come to you and I need to come now!"

The urgency in her words was unmistakable as she faded from sight. For some time he reflected on the beautiful little girl and her message. At last, he nudged his wife and told her what he had witnessed. Her response was, "It's about time."

About a year later, Amy gave birth to a little girl. Although Mark and Amy have dark hair and eyes, their daughter has blond hair and steel-blue eyes and she habitually strokes the pink ribbon around her favorite doll's neck.

This child, and many others, appeared to one or other of their parents, not as tiny infants, but as adorable small children at an age that would be most appealing to their intended parents. In Mark's case the child was not only very cute, but she clearly informed him that she wanted and needed to be born now.

In the next case, Irene Doucet had decided to have no more children when something happened to make her rethink her decision. Irene remembers the occasion as clearly as the moment it happened.

"Our fourth child was less that a year old and I had decided that our family was complete. In fact, I was quite adamant about not having another baby. Then I saw a theatrical production that made me wonder if I might have agreed to bring additional spirits into my home. What if they were waiting for me now, distressed over my decision, and would have to go to someone else? I could never face my Heavenly Father or those spirits in the hereafter if that were the case.

"Even though I was not ready for another child, I could not let this matter go unresolved. So, fearful of the potential answer, I knelt down and asked God if there were any spirits who were waiting to come to me.

"As I prayed my eyes were opened and I saw a lovely little blonde, who appeared to be about nine years old. As we looked at each other, she clearly informed me that her name was Julie. Behind her, but fleeting and faint, was the vision of a little boy about three years old. There was something very sad and pleading about him but the vision was so fleeting that I could not catch what it might have been. I wondered if my decision not to have any more children--not to have him--had caused his sadness.

"My mind was instantly changed when I saw the sweet spirits of the children which were still to be mine. How I loved them from that instant and how eager I was for their immediate arrival! And how bitter was my disappointment when I was informed that the time for their arrival was not yet but would be in the future.

"Four years went by and I was beginning to have serious concerns when I finally conceived. Nine months later our little daughter was born. She was blonde and beautiful and we named her Julie.

"Then we started looking forward to having the little boy I had seen. Again years went by and after six years I decided that my vision of him had been nothing more than a figment of my imagination and that I must reconcile myself to the fact that I would be given no more children. However I did finally conceive and just before this child was born I had another vision. In it I was sent into the spirit world to bring someone back. I wasn't given a name or any other details just that this person was supposed to come back with me. I stood on the threshold of the spirit world with what seemed like millions of spirits, all dressed in white and all milling about and speaking with each other in joyful and antic-ipatory tones. I wondered how in all this multitude of people I would find the right one, when a young man also dressed in white and seeming to be about twenty years of age addressed me. 'Mother?' This was the one! He was ready for his mission on earth and I was to bring him back with me. A few hours later our son was born. This one would have to have a special name so we called him Michael.

"A few days later, I was holding him. He had his little hand clamped tightly around my finger and his eyes were gazing into mine with what seemed like such an ancient wisdom, when I was taken into another vision. I was taken into the eternities. The tiny hands of my newborn son were now the hands of a man, full grown and glorified. They were held out to the empty and dark universe, and from them emanated beams and rays of glorious light. In those rays a world was turning, and forming, and beyond it, others. And the words came to me, 'Oh Irene, you don't hold a baby. You cradle a God.' Words cannot express the love and humility and gratitude of being given this child, nor the awesome responsibility of teaching him—and all my others—for it became clear to me that this was a destiny not just for him but for all of us."

Irene's experience with her son Michael was unique in that she went to the world of premortal beings to get him. While there she saw the excitement of those waiting to commence their earthly missions. Her concerns of finding Michael were quickly alleviated when he came to her, not as the three-year-old she had seen earlier, but as a vibrant young man. She was permitted to see his eternal potential and realize the awesome responsibility she had assumed when she had agreed to be his mother.

By 1913, Bertha Elder had given birth to thirteen children. She concluded that life was just too difficult for her to have any more. Not long after she made this decision, Bertha became deathly ill. Her spirit left her body and rose up to a point where she could look down at her body. Her initial reaction was not of shock or depression but of relief. All the intense pain she had been experiencing was gone and she was so filled with peace that she had no desire to return to her body.

An angelic being appeared and escorted Bertha into a large room where she was greeted by many of her departed friends and loved ones. She was then taken into another room filled with children. On the far side of the room she saw two little girls, whom she did not know. They were so beautiful that she could not look away from them.

"'Do you want them?' the guide asked.
"'Yes. Oh, yes,' she responded quickly. 'Can I return to earth life and have them?'
"'Yes,' said the escort. 'That is the purpose of this visit, to let you see them. Now we must return.'"

Bertha returned to her body, much to the relief of her family. After recovering from her illness, Berth told her husband she wanted more children. Bertha did indeed, go on to have two more children, both girls, and she stated with certainty that they were the spirits she saw in heaven.

In Bertha's experience the two spirits did not appear to her to ask her to have them. On the contrary. She was taken to a room filled with children where she was immediately attracted to two, and only two, and knew she was to be their mother.

Another woman named Amy also discovered that spirits have an appointed time to come to earth, and that there are specific individuals on earth who can best help these spirits fulfill their missions. Amy learned this in 1968 when she had a very vivid dream.

"I found myself walking in a tranquil place filled with children. As I walked around I saw that some of the children were extremely upset, crying that they could not be born because their parents were preventing their birth. It was very distressing to them as they had to be born on earth to be able to return to their heavenly home. Three of them told me that they were supposed to be my brothers and my sister but my parents, who were also supposed to be theirs, wouldn't have them. I felt very sad because I was an only child. Then I saw a boy that I knew was to be mine.

"At this point my dream ended. I was 40 years of age and at a time in my life when I was sure my childbearing years were over. But shortly after that dream I discovered I was pregnant. This was a total surprise, but I guess that it shouldn't have been, given my dream. I gave birth to the boy I saw and met during my dream. If I had not had that dream, if I had not met him and seen the disappointment of my intended brothers and sister, I might have had an abortion. My son has been a great joy in my life."

Amy was able to see firsthand how the priorities of those on earth can impact the goals and dreams of those in heaven. Heaven will not force those on earth to have children. But when those on earth decline to have them, the affected spirits are disappointed, saddened, and frustrated. Ultimately they will be able to come to earth, but not to those who could have best helped them to achieve their earthly missions. So not only are eternal plans frustrated to a degree when potential parents refuse to have children, but the blessings and opportunities the parents might have received are forfeited.

The discussions in the next segment of this chapter deal with major health and medical problems that make it unlikely for some children to be born. But sometimes heavenly interventions occur resulting in the conception and birth of healthy normal babies. A case in point is that of Nyla Love.

"When I was sixteen I had a cyst that hemorrhaged inside my ovary. The attending doctor explained that there had been a great deal of damage to the ovary. He also told me that the other ovary was only ovulating once a year and my uterus was tipped. Taking all these factors into consideration, he concluded that I had a very slim chance of ever conceiving a child.

"This problem did not really concern me, since my aspirations at the time were largely limited to getting my driver's license and passing exams. Over time, however, and especially when I met a wonderful young man, fell in love, and became engaged, I began to dream of marriage and having children. I confided what my doctor had told me to my fiancée who was disappointed but very supportive and said that we could always adopt. Nevertheless, I did not completely give up hope of having children of my own.

"As our wedding date drew nearer, we decided that in spite of the slim chance of my becoming pregnant, we would use contraceptives for at least a year. We were married on a Friday night and by the following Tuesday morning, I had begun feeling very anxious about using the contraceptives. That night I had a dream.

"In the dream, I found myself completely surrounded by darkness. Suddenly a doorway appeared with an intense, bright light shining from it. I raised my right hand to shield my eyes from the brightness. After a moment I was able to focus. I saw what I presumed to be three young children. The light from behind them created a shadow so I could only see their outline. All three appeared to be boys. I remember noticing the shape of their heads and the way the tips of their ears stuck out. The one in the middle was the tallest and he held the hands of the other two.

"Next, I noticed I was holding something in my left hand. I raised it up to get a closer look and recognized the contraceptives we had been using. At almost the same instant the child in the middle pleaded with me, 'No Mama, please don't!' I never saw his face, but I knew it was he who said it.

"Instantly, I found myself awake in our hotel room. I woke my husband, and told him my experience. We decided not to use the contraceptives, and nine months later our first son was born.

"He was followed by two more boys. Each one has cute little ears that stick out a bit. The oldest has a fetish about holding the hands of his younger siblings which sort of aggravates them. I tell them he cannot help it because he has always done it!"

While heavenly intervention could have caused the contraceptive devices to fail, how much better it was that Nyla and her husband made the decision to stop using them.

Alaine, like Nyla, needed the active intervention of heavenly beings for her unborn children to be able to come at their appointed time. Alaine, at thirty-one, already had two daughters. She also had only one ovary which was partially blocked when the following situation occurred.

"I went to bed one night but had a great deal of trouble sleeping. Eventually my mind started to drift but I didn't seem to be falling asleep as I was fully aware of my body and my thoughts. I saw two men and a woman in white robes that seemed to glow. They told me that it was time for me to have another child and he was waiting to come to me. When I told them that we couldn't have any more children they showed me a baby, a beautiful little boy. I felt rather than heard that part of his name should be Michael—this name came from the baby. They then told me he would be born at home with loving people there to welcome him.

"I wept because I was afraid, afraid to tell my husband and afraid of what people would think. My family would think I was crazy, not to mention my friends. You see, my husband had had a vasectomy and I was not sure that he would want to go through the expense and pain of a reversal. But I knew that a beautiful baby boy named Michael was waiting to join us.

"The next morning through sobs I told my husband what had happened and he asked me if I was sure about a baby boy waiting for us. I said I was and he agreed to have the vasectomy reversed.

"He had the surgery a couple of months later in July. I became pregnant in February of the following year and our son, Michael, was born October 26, 1995, the day before my birthday, at home in a birthing pool surrounded by loving friends. His spirit was constantly with me throughout my pregnancy.

"I became pregnant again in November 1997, but miscarried a few days before Christmas. The night that I began miscarrying I had another vision and was told that this soul was very frightened and needed a lot of encouragement before she would come to this earth. I felt her presence often with me and I am doing what I can to reassure her that she will be loved.

"All my children communicated with me while I was pregnant with them. My eldest daughter had a twin sister who died shortly after birth. Jessica had told me right from the moment she was conceived that she wouldn't be staying and I wouldn't be bringing her home from the hospital and Kristianne, the second twin, assured me that she would be fine even when the doctors told me otherwise. Then my third daughter came to me and told me she was here even after I was told I couldn't have any more children. She also told me to call her Kylie Michelle. The next morning I had a test and it confirmed I was pregnant."

Medical complications and medical procedures apparently made it impossible for Alaine to get pregnant. But with the help of medical specialists, heavenly nudging, and a child's strong desire to be born, the way was opened and Michael and Kylie Michelle were born.

Another couple was definitely not interested in having another child until something happened late one night. Daryl Chansuthus relates what happened.

"In 1988, my late husband and I lived in Bangkok, Thailand. At that time my husband, who was a Thai, had an experience which he shared with me. At the time we had four children, the fourth not being planned but welcomed nevertheless. However, I had a tubule ligation following that birth since my husband and I felt that four children were quite enough. When my fourth child was not quite two years old, my husband woke me up at about 3 A.M., telling me in a voice filled with awe and excitement that we were going to have another child. I told him that having another child was not possible and that he had simply been dreaming. He insisted that his dream was real. He told me that a little boy, dressed in traditional Thai clothing with a topknot on his head, had tugged on his pajama shirt sleeve until he had awakened. Startled by the little boy, he asked him, 'Who are you, little boy? Why are you here in the middle of the night?'

"The little boy told him, 'I came here to tell you that you are going to be my father, and she (pointing to my sleeping form) is going to be my mother." My husband told the little boy that it was not possible for him to be our son, to which the young fellow, with hands on his hips, replied in an authoritative tone that we were, indeed, his parents. My husband then asked him what his name was. The boy replied that his name was Twng, Guman Twng. Roughly translated, these are the Thai words for the spirit of a child. Upon giving his name, the little boy disappeared, and my husband woke me up to give me the news. My husband described the little boy in vivid detail. Two months later, despite all odds, and to my doctor's amazement, I discovered that I was pregnant with our fifth child, a boy, who is now ten, and who matches my husband's description of his night visitor perfectly.

This case clearly demonstrates experiences such as these are not limited to any one culture. I would be very interested in hearing from members of other societies and cultures concerning their experiences with the unborn.

Some parents do not see the individual who wishes to join their family but they nevertheless understand or sense that a spirit is ready and wants to come to them. This news may not at first be received with rejoicing but in time is usually accepted, and eventually even eagerly embraced. Such was Nancy Cohen's case.

"One day I received a very definite message:

"'Yes. A child of light is choosing you. You are her mother. Be grateful. You are loved. You are precious in the sight of God.'

"On another occasion when I was concerned about the awesome responsibilities associated with raising a baby, my unborn child distinctly spoke to me:

"'Fear not. I come to love you. Wipe away your tears. The time has come to put aside the past and begin anew. Rejoice. This is an occasion to rejoice. My light will light your way as well as mine.'

"Two weeks later I conceived. I was very aware of a tremendous sense of peacefulness that descended on the three of us."[1]

Nancy went from being an individual who didn't want the inconvenience of carrying, giving birth to, or rearing a child, to a person who was ready for all aspects of motherhood. But it took a message from heaven to get her to that point.

In another case, Joyce was a mother with two children and had no intention of having any more. She was on a camping trip with her husband, Barry, and her children, ten-year-old Rami and four-year-old Mira.

"On the third day of our camping trip I was sitting alone when I felt the distinct presence of someone beside me. I knew this sensation well, for the same thing had happened to me shortly before both Rami and Mira were conceived. At first I felt in awe of the greatness of this being beside me, whom I could not see with physical eyes but could feel within my heart. Then the message came: 'I am your third child and am ready to be conceived.'

"It was the last thing I wanted to hear at this time in my life. 'No!' I stammered. 'I don't want to get pregnant. I don't want anything different right now. I just want to rest.'

"I felt this being smiling at me, loving me fully and offering the gift of its presence in my life. 'You can conceive me in three weeks. Your family is now ready for my presence in your lives.'

"'No!' harshly echoed through my being.

"My rational mind argued that we were both forty years old, too old to be having more children. Rami and Mira were finally old enough to go with us on adventures or else stay at Grandma's and Grandpa's house while we did necessary air travel. Barry and I had felt long ago that our family was complete and we had given away all the baby things.

"Then I felt this great being stretch out its hands in blessing and in love, seemingly amused by my obvious resistance.

"The next three weeks were extremely confusing. We left our peaceful camping spot and flew east to Buffalo, New York for several talks and workshops. Each morning upon wakening I felt the loving presence of our third child. Each morning I would then sit in meditation and watch my crazy mind resist. The more I resisted, the more love I felt poured upon me. This little soul wanted to be born, to be born soon, and to be born to me!"

The love she felt melted Joyce's resolve, as her unborn child wormed its way into her heart and soul and she accepted the need for his birth.

Some spirits may be scheduled to become part of a particular family but apparently they will not be able to come unless specific conditions are met and if significant issues are not resolved, they will have to come to earth by alternate routes. Richard Dreyfuss, the actor, was one such case.

Following the 1996 Oscar® Night celebrations, Barbara Walters interviewed Richard who had been nominated for his role in *Mr. Holland's Opus*. The interview covered his rise to stardom in *Close Encounters of the Third Kind* and his Oscar® win for *The Goodbye Girl*. Fame had not been easy for Richard and he hadn't handled it well. For twenty years he fought the battle of alcohol addiction which had helped destroy his first marriage. Dreyfuss sought help and was hospitalized in order to detox one more time. During this period he spent a lot of time thinking about his future. While he was so engaged one day, a little three-year-old girl in a pink dress and shiny black patent leather shoes walked in. This was no alcohol- induced hallucination. Her message to Richard was, "Daddy, I can't come to you until you come to me. Please straighten out your life so I can come." With this she disappeared.

The pleading message of her haunting eyes was implanted in Dreyfuss's memory, a constant reminder to reorder his life so that his daughter might come. With this incentive, he maintained sobriety, remarried, and prayed that his daughter would/could soon come. Within three years his wife gave birth to a little girl. This daughter is now his constant companion and the love and inspiration of his new life.[2]

### Birth Order

It is apparent from a number of accounts that spirits are very excited about the opportunity to come to earth and commence the earthly portion of their eternal journey. While it is evident that order prevails in the heavenly realm, sometimes spirits coming to the same family may not agree as to which of them should be born first. I have come across several such cases. One was shared by a professional counselor. She had a near-death experience which affected her entire life and left her with unusual abilities. She requested, for family considerations, to not be identified.

"My near-death experience opened my mind and sensitivities to things spiritual. I do not use my spiritual gifts as the basis of my counseling, but they do assist me on occasion. For example, I discovered that if there is more than one child to be born to a family, which is most of the time, they may be standing in line, so to speak, awaiting their turn to come to earth. Sometimes unborn spirits are so eager to come to earth that they attempt to crowd ahead of their siblings so as to be born sooner. I was approached by a family where the brother and sister argued constantly. I discovered that the primary reason that the girl was upset with her brother was because he had crowded ahead of her and been born before her. As I tried to resolve their conflict, she looked at her brother and said, 'I don't care what you say, I am older than you.'

"I interjected, 'You mean it was your turn to be born and your brother jumped in front?'

"'Yes. That's exactly what he did!'

"Her memory was very clear, and she still felt the frustration of not being able to come to earth when she was scheduled and this frustration carried over and affected her relationship with her brother. As they grow and mature, I hope that the memory will fade and the competition between the two will diminish."

When I was first told about this case, it was thought to be interesting but unique. The chain of events that occurs just prior to leaving the premortal sphere for earth would seem to imply an orderly sequence of events that is determined more by others than the individuals involved. But apparently the desire to come to earth can be so strong that the individual may try to advance his or her scheduled departure time. The following case is  another such example and was resolved in a very unique way.

The year was 1945, and Abby had just rushed to the hospital to have her baby. During the delivery, severe complications set in and Abby died. She left her body and watched briefly as her physician tried to revive her. She turned and found herself moving up and away from the hospital. She was taken to a place where she saw her father and grandparents. They were sitting in chairs and saw her but they did not speak to her because in front of her was a spiritual being and they were listening intently to him. Occasionally her father and grandparents would nod in agreement.

Abby was overjoyed at seeing her father and feeling his love and his assurance that he was okay. Off on her right she saw two individuals in an animated discussion. She could see their faces quite clearly, a blond girl and a dark-haired boy. Their heated discussion concerned which one of them would be able to go to their family next. Both were sure they had a strong case as to why they should go to earth next. These two individuals' disagreement, though curious, distracted her only momentarily. Her attention was drawn back to the man in front of her. He told her many things about her life on earth and of events that would occur in the world, but it was seeing her father that excited her most and to which she paid most attention.

When the man told Abby she would have to go back to her body, she resisted. She did not want to leave her father or the joy and love she felt there. But she was told, and her father concurred, that she must return. Her infant son needed her as she and she alone could help him to achieve his mission on earth. Reluctantly she returned to her body. She did not remember much of what her spirit guide told her but she did remember clearly that the two beings she saw arguing were to be children of her newborn son, her future grandchildren.

Some twenty-five years later, Abby came across two hand-painted plates in a thrift shop which had images of children on them. One had the face of a little blond girl and the other of a dark-headed boy. When she first saw them, she was startled because they so closely resembled the two squabbling beings she had seen during her NDE. She purchased the plates and hung them on her living room wall.

In the meantime, her son grew up, married, and had two children, neither of whom remotely resembled those she had seen. Her son and his wife wanted a large family, but after the birth of their second child, the wife no longer seemed able to carry a child to full term. She had five miscarriages and they reluctantly decided that if they wanted more children they would have to adopt. They had just started the adoption proceedings of a little girl when the wife discovered she was pregnant. They elected to proceed with the adoption; the birth of their third son coincided with the birth of their adoptive daughter.

Abby's daughter-in-law was informed by her doctor that due to medical problems she could not have any more children, but Abby knew that this could not be true because she had seen two more. When Abby shared her experience with her daughter-in-law her daughter-in-law said, "I know, because I have felt them around me."

In spite of dire medical prognoses, Abby's daughter-in-law did become pregnant and after serious problems gave birth to twins. Both of them experienced major medical complications but survived. Abby's son took pictures of them when they were nearly three-and-a-half years old and sent them to her. When Abby looked at the pictures, she recognized the two individuals she had seen in heaven so many years ago. Their pictures brought back that experience so vividly that it seemed as if it had just happened. Evidently the two spirits had never resolved their controversy over who would come first so they came together.

This account is illuminating in that a grandmother saw twin grandchildren over fifty-five years before they were born and witnessed the intense interest of the unborn in commencing their time on earth. She knew who they were, but not when they would be born.

In the next account, there was no controversy over one's birth order or a lack of desire to have children, but a mother-to-be was allowed to see nine of the children she would eventually have and the order of their birth.

From as early as she could remember, Cherie Logan wanted to marry and have lots of kids. She had an experience that clearly informed her that her dream would be fulfilled.

"When I was fifteen, I had a dream in which I saw myself sitting on a park bench with a beautiful young woman.

"We talked about many important things of which I do not remember a single word but I do remember that they were important. Then she stood up to go. Grasping at anything to say to keep her from leaving I declared, 'I don't even know who you are!'

"She looked at me and in a clear and convincing tone said, 'Don't you know? I'm a daughter you haven't had yet.' With that she left and I awakened."

As Cherie grew into mature womanhood, she never forgot this experience and often contemplated what it would be like to be a mother. One day as she was engaged in fervent prayer, she asked if it would be possible to see and speak with her children to be.

When Cherie looked up from her prayer, she was amazed to see nine spirits entering her room.

"I had a clear impression that there were more children than the nine but that they were busy and could not be present at that time. But I also knew that the Lord would show them to me at a later time. Nine! What a wonderful surprise and unimaginable blessing!

"The children were standing before me, not speaking. Clearly they were my children. There was no doubt whatsoever in my mind what the Lord and these children wanted. I could tell by the way they were standing which boy was older than another boy and which girl was older than another girl. However, between the sexes I could not tell the order of birth.

"I saw a boy who appeared to be the oldest with a set of scriptures in his hand, magnificence in his bearing. I was struck with his power. He looked to be about seventeen years of age.

"Next to him was another boy, also powerful in his spirit and beside him another boy of equal ability and strength.

"On the opposite side of the room was a girl, the oldest of the girls, and she was holding a baby girl who I knew would be mine. Next to this girl was a girl who was holding the hand of a younger girl, who in turn held the hand of a boy about her size. Between the grouping of sons and the grouping of older and younger children, was my third daughter. She was the one I had seen in my dream at age fifteen.

"My first baby was a son whom we named Marshall. He was born prematurely and died shortly after his birth. He was the young man I had seen with scriptures in his hand. I knew intuitively that his mission was on the other side and from his bearing that he was engaged in an important work.

"After Marshall's death I so wanted to have another baby but my doctors told me that in all medical likelihood, succeeding children would be born increasingly premature and would be unlikely to survive. But, at this writing, I have ten children."[3]

Cherie's experience is remarkable because she was not only permitted to see the spirits of those beings who were to be her children, but she saw them at a moment in the future at the ages they would be at that time.

### Departure Delayed

Although a spirit may be scheduled to come to earth at a particular earth time, adjustments to the timetable may have to be made under unusual circumstances. Such was the case with Ranelle Kruger. Her spirit was ready to come to earth, but due to concerns and problems in her birth mother's life, it was not the right time for her to be born. This account is particularly fascinating in that Ranelle was actually able to watch the creation of the body she was to inhabit.

"I was having some extremely harsh feelings toward my mother which I was doing my best to overcome when a remembrance of my life before I was born awakened within me. I was in a place of complete whiteness waiting to go to earth. As I was waiting, a woman came up to me and said, 'Father would like to see you!'

"I was a bit perplexed because it was my time to go. She gave me a very knowing smile and said, 'It's all right, you won't be late! Come with me!' She took me into another room where I felt the presence of Heavenly Father and His son Jesus Christ, though I did not see them. Heavenly Father told me that my earthly mother had asked him that I not come at this time.

"I was devastated. I asked him, 'Does this mean that I do not get to go to earth?'

"He said, 'No! You have your agency! You may choose to go now.' I knew that the two of us, my mother-to-be and I, had agreed to be together on earth and now I was told she did not want me.

"I asked, 'Doesn't she know that I am to come to her? Doesn't she remember that we agreed to be together, that I would be a blessing in her life?' As I stood there confused and troubled thoughts flew through my mind. Then I met my brother who was to be born right after me. I told him what had happened and how disappointed I was.

"He said to me, 'Oh, its okay! Don't worry! Everything is going to be all right. Have faith, everything will work out!'

"I thought that he would be extremely upset as he was going to earth after me, and if my departure time was delayed so would his. He tried to assure me that in the eternal scheme of things, everything would work out. As he left, the heavens opened and I could see into my earthly home. Not only could I see what was going on but I also felt my mother's emotions.

"My mother had given birth to seven children and was completely overwhelmed. She could not emotionally or physically manage another child at this time. I could clearly understand her feelings. And as I loved her I knew I could not and should not put more burdens on her at this time. I went back to my Heavenly Father, tears streaming down my face, and told him that I was willing to stay, not knowing if I would ever be able to go to her.

"My Father in Heaven told me that my decision pleased him. Choosing to not place my desires above someone else's needs was what the earthly experience was all about. It was then that he gave me a blessing. He told me that I need not worry about the choices I would make while on earth, I would be guided to the right ones.

"When I had this experience, I was in a place of preparation which was closer to the earth than where I had been living up to this point. As to my appearance and that of my brother, we looked like mature young adults.

"When my mother was finally ready to have another child, I was escorted once more to the place of departure. As I was receiving instruction I was granted permission to go down to earth and watch my conception take place. The sperm did not have to fight its way into the egg but was literally sucked in. I observed the cells beginning to divide and multiply. Once I saw that my physical body was developing properly I returned to my heavenly home for final preparations and instruction."

This account is very informative for a number of reasons. First, the mother was evidently willing to have more children but her physical and emotional state were so fragile that having a baby at that particular time was unwise. Realizing this she petitioned God, pleading that she not get pregnant at that time, and her prayers were answered. At the same time Ranelle's plans and desires had to be considered. God could have told her what had been decided and that would be that, but didn't. Ranelle was consulted and shown the consequences of her coming to her mother. Ranelle's decision pleased God as she did not place her personal desires above that of her mother. Another thing this account documents is that those in heaven have strong emotions as was reflected by Ranelle's tears. Perhaps because of her willingness to wait, Ranelle was given the opportunity to witness her conception and the initial development of her body. I have interviewed other cases where individuals reported witnessing their conceptions so this case is not totally unique.

A second situation where a scheduled birth was changed was that of Doug Bigelow. Initially Doug was to be a twin. But his concern for Teri, his intended mother, prompted him to make a change. Don, the father, explains:

"Terri did not suffer from morning sickness--it was 'around-the-clock' sickness. She was carrying twins and was upbeat and excited in spite of her constant illness. Then one night something happened. Terri, nearly five months along, was sleeping in the bed next to me when my eyes opened to an unusual light in the hallway moving toward our bedroom and growing in intensity. The light reached the doorway forming a conduit through which passed a young man. Although I had no specific recollections of having seen him previously, there was a strong sense of familiarity. He was a handsome young man dressed in a radiant white suit. He communicated not so much in words as in thoughts announcing, to my astonishment, that he was our future son.

"Our unborn son explained that he had originally been scheduled for birth as a twin to his sister. However, in a recent review of their earth mission and the status of their mother's health, it was decided that only one of the two could be born at this time. Our future son told me that he was as excited as his sister for his turn on earth, but that he had agreed that his sister should come first. He would still join our family but in a couple of years. Message delivered, he faded from view, leaving me enveloped in a greater sense of peace than I had felt in weeks. You see, prior to his visit I had been constantly fearful that I might lose my Terri because of all the problems she was experiencing. But after the visit from our son I knew she would be okay.

"I hated to disturb my wife as she rarely had a restful night's sleep but this message was too important to wait. I awakened her and said, 'Terri, a young man in his late teens or early twenties just came to visit me.'

"Terri's eyes widened instantly, 'Right here? In our bedroom?'

"Yes! He called me Dad and told me that he and his sister had talked it over. They had thought that they could be born together, but they have learned it is not wise for both of them to come at this time. He said he would have to leave, but his sister could stay. Then he disappeared.

"The very next day at Terri's doctor's appointment we received ultrasound confirmation that one of the twins had died. You can imagine the grief such a loss would have been without explanation. But whether by divine grace or our unborn son's insistence, we knew the plan. Our doctor, was surprised at our peaceful acceptance of the news.

"Douglas did not wait even two years to join us; his birth came only eighteen months after Jenny's. From his very first breath he has had the appearance of a twin to Jenny. Jenny and Doug not only look identical but they play together with special harmony and closeness. Terri's hair is dark brown as are her eyes. My hair is nearly black, my eyes blue. Our third son is blond with blue eyes. But Jenny and Douglas have red hair and dark brown eyes. There are no redheads in the family on either side for several generations back. Strangers ask all the time if our two redheads are twins."

The loss of a child would undoubtedly have been harder on Teri and Don without the knowledge they received from their unborn son. Although we may not all experience enlightening visitations, we can build hope from those who do. Surely, events so major as eternal souls coming or returning to our heavenly home do not escape God's watchful eye. In His plan, all things ultimately work for our good if we, His children, maintain faith.

In this last account, Colette L's experience reveals one way that heavenly plans can be realized without impinging earthly free agency.

"My husband and I had determined because of family difficulties we were facing, and the fact that we already had three children, that we would not have any more children. I was disappointed but saw the 'logic' of my husband's views. My disappointment came because of an impression I had had about four years previously, that we were to give birth to another girl. However the decision was made.

"As time passed I became increasingly unsettled about it and conveyed my feelings to my husband. I told him if we didn't have another baby, we would always wonder if we had done the right thing. He left for a business trip that took him out of town for several weeks. When he returned home he consented to have another baby. While on this trip he had felt a child's spirit close to him which convinced him that we should have one more baby. It was not long until I discovered I was pregnant. I knew the baby was going to be a little girl. Then I began to feel like I was going to have twins. I asked my OB about it and he ordered an ultrasound and told me that there was only one fetus in my womb. Nevertheless I still had the feeling of twins but in time that feeling dissipated. We had selected the name of Maggie Mae and could hardly wait for her arrival. When the blessed day arrived I was in labor for a very short time. My OB delivered the baby with ease and plopped it on my tummy announcing that I had a beautiful baby boy.

"'A what?' I asked in my somewhat drugged condition. 'Check it again.' Puzzled, the OB looked at my husband, who explained that we were expecting a girl. With no name for this precious child we hastily talked about boys' names and decided on William Anthony. I told my husband that this name is not what the baby wants. I prayerfully put together several combinations of family names and eventually came up with three. I prayed to know what this child's name was. I looked at my list and one name seemed to be highlighted. It was Jacob Daniel. Daniel was the name of my husband's grandfather, but there were no Jacob's on either side of the family. Still, I did like how the name flowed.

"Curious as to the meaning of Jacob and being without a 'baby name' book, I resorted to my Bible Dictionary. The definition it gave was 'a supplanter' and made reference to the story of Jacob and Esau in the Old Testament. I didn't know what a supplanter was, so I referred my question to M. Webster. The definition I found was 'one who takes the place of another.'

"As I contemplated this, information from a heavenly realm flowed into my mind. I could see my precious Maggie Mae on the 'launching pad' so to speak, preparing to come to earth and Jacob running to catch her before she departed. He pleaded with her to please let him go first because he might not have the opportunity to be in our family if she didn't. I felt the great love she had for her brother as she willingly stepped down and allowed Jacob to go ahead of her. This meeting of these two spirits, I feel, explains the feeling of twins that I had early in the pregnancy. I believe that Maggie stayed nearby during the pregnancy. Two-and-a-half years later I found, to my surprise, that I was pregnant again. This time it was Maggie and when she was born, I felt like I knew her already."[4]

To assure that they would not only be born but be born into the right families, two premortal spirits "worked on" their preferred parents. The mother bonded so closely to her daughter-to-be that she willingly became pregnant a fifth time. The spirit must have counted on this if she was willing to let her brother come to earth before her even though she was ready to come at that time.

### Summary Thoughts

In Ecclesiastes, the writer observed that to everything there is a season, and a time to every purpose under heaven, a time to be born and a time to die. (Ecclesiastes 3:1-2)[5] The accounts in this chapter support this observation. For those spirit beings in heaven, there is evidently an optimal earthly time for them to be born to assure they will fulfill their missions successfully although some are so eager that they try to come sooner. Often those on earth need reminders that they have an important role to play if those spirits are to be able to come to earth and on schedule. For some prospective parents a loving voice sets the stage; for other parents, a personal visit by the unborn is needed. Still for others, a brief glimpse into the heavenly realm is the key. It appears that timing is critical and earthly concerns should take secondary place to heavenly needs. At the same time, heavenly desires must and do take into consideration what is happening on earth.

# Chapter Six
## Leaving Home

Our premortal home is a place of love, peace, joy, and total acceptance and it is the *only* place of which we have any experience to this point in our existence. Then it is time to leave home and enter a place that will challenge us to the very limits of our abilities. But we clearly understand that these challenges must be experienced if we are to grow and mature. So it is with feelings of excitement and trepidation that those in the world of premortal spirits approach their sojourn on earth.

### Apprehensions About Leaving premortality

Becky Robb describes her feelings as she prepared to leave for earth.

"I was scared by the thought of leaving heaven. A woman who looked to me to be about thirty came to my rescue. She'd already been to earth and knew what was going to happen because she'd been through it. She reassured me that I would be okay, and I knew that I had known her for a long time in heaven, even before she'd gone to earth. She seemed very close to me, and I knew she loved me.

"She showed me my earthly mother and my being held by my father as a newborn. My angelic escorts then promised me that they would love me and take care of me. After she showed me these scenes I felt better, no longer afraid. I knew my time on earth would be okay.

"A lady approached me with the message that it was time to leave heaven and go down to earth. I was nervous so the lady escorted me, comforting me the whole time, including when I entered mom's womb. Her comforting continued through the birthing process and for a while after I was born. I not only heard her, but saw her while she was comforting me."

On the other hand Roy Mills was excited about his chance to come to earth but at the same time did not want to leave the loving presence of his Heavenly Father and his spirit companions. He describes what happened just before his departure to earth.

"When my pre-birth education was finished and it was time for my mortal birth, my angel guide took me to a very large room the size of a sports stadium. The interior was radiant and beautiful and looked as if it had been painted with sunlight. Inside were large, glowing columns that ran from the floor all the way to the ceiling. My angel guide and I were the only ones in the room at this time. It was called the Exit Room or Holding Room—the final stop for young spirits who were waiting to come to earth.

"As we walked across the floor, my guide gave me last-minute instructions. She had been with me throughout most of my training and I loved her. I knew I was going to miss her kindness and gentle guidance while I was away on earth.

"'Will you come with me?' I asked.

"She smiled, and I knew she would not be coming. But before she looked away, I saw empathy in her eyes, for she knew the experience I was embarking upon. But I also noted that she seemed to know a greater joy in the purpose of what I was about to do.

"She said very tenderly, 'You know I have duties to attend to. But I will check on you throughout your life, and I will see you soon.'

"We walked to the far end of the room and stopped to wait for the angel who would escort me to earth. We continued to talk about the adventure I was about to begin. The more we talked, the more excited I became to embark upon my journey. Then suddenly there was a mighty, rushing wind, and the door appeared in the wall before us. An angel stepped through the door, which disappeared behind him as quickly as it had materialized. This angel had broad, powerful shoulders. The robe he wore was unlike the ones the other angels had. It looked as if it were made of sheep's wool instead of silk. It was long and hung all the way to his bare feet. The escort had a strong, rugged quality about him, and I knew he was a great warrior angel. Yet despite his commanding appearance, I felt great love and tenderness radiating from him.

"When my angel guide saw my escort, her eyes grew wide with surprise and excitement. 'I can't believe he came himself to take you to earth,' she kept saying over and over again as she led me toward him. But she never spoke his name. As I took in his magnificence, I was in awe. He was much taller that even my angel guide. His face was angular, his jaw square and set, and his eyes were confident and kind.

"The two angels spoke with one another for a while, and then the escort looked down at me and asked in a firm but kind voice, 'Are you ready to go?'

"The sound of his voice soothed and reassured me, and I said, 'Yes.'

"Immediately, another door appeared in the wall, revealing nothing but blue sky. I walked to it and looked down. I could see the top of a thundercloud about a half-mile below us.

"'We most go at once,' the tall angel said. He took hold of my left wrist, and we sailed through the open door to the sound and energy of the same mighty, rushing wind I'd heard at his arrival. I turned to look back at the angel guide of whom I had grown so fond.

"She waved and smiled with the same knowing expression.

"I also saw part of the outside of heaven as I looked back. The walls were covered with layers of pure gold, and a brilliant light shone from the door through which we had come. As we departed, I watched the door vanish, and heaven itself gradually became transparent until it completely disappeared.

"I felt a certain excitement for this adventure, but I was also beginning to feel a sense of separation. I knew I must go—I wanted to go—yet I ready missed the warm light of heaven and the calming love and influence of my angel guide. We descended rapidly, headfirst, and there was nothing but open sky. When I could no longer see Heaven, my home, I felt some concern.

"I was filled with mixed emotions as we approached earth. I felt sad I was leaving everything behind: the peace, joy, and beauty of the only place I had ever known. But what I had learned about earth in the Life Books excited me, and I was eager to come and experience firsthand what life here was really like. I looked forward to it like a great adventure, where I would add understanding to the knowledge I had already grown into as a spiritual being. I knew that my knowledge would be tested and that I could grow in my understanding and become a greater spirit for God.

"But the love I felt from the tall angel at my side encouraged me. And when he saw my worry, he said, 'Look straight ahead and don't look back.' I moved close to him and fixed my eyes ahead."[1]

The chance to come to earth is exciting but there is also much concern. Roy needed and received reassurance that he would be able to fulfill his mission.

In the next case, Melissa experienced similar feelings as she faced the prospect of leaving the presence of her Father in Heaven and going to earth.

"I was raised Catholic and went to parochial school for three years. At about the age of eight I had an experience that did not agree with what the sisters thought was correct so I did not talk to anyone about my memories of being in heaven and preparing to come to earth.

"One evening I found that I had been transported to a heavenly world. I was calm, not afraid or hungry or tired, just very peaceful. There was a group of people surrounding me and they were all emanating a bright white light. I had trouble seeing their faces because of their brightness. I was surprised to discover that I was emanating light as well. I could feel their love; it was total unconditional love and I "knew" we had known each other for a very long time. I had never experienced love like that in the eight years that I had been on earth. It felt so good that I wanted to stay there forever.

"Suddenly, at the speed of thought, I was in a very dark but quite comforting place, and I was with three angels who also emanated light and seemed to know each other very well. One of the angels informed me that I was about to be born. As I looked down, I discovered that I could feel the 'sin' on earth and panicked. I told them I wouldn't go. They told me that I didn't have to go, but I couldn't go back to my heavenly home either. I was overwhelmed with homesickness and threatened to tell Heavenly Father. They reminded me that nothing happens in heaven that is not our Father's will. I immediately knew this to be true. I was completely brokenhearted that my Father wanted our separation.

"At this point a female angel came forward. She was incredibly beautiful and full of compassion. She knew me completely including the fact that I could never turn my back on anyone who needed me. She told me that my parents needed me, so while the pain of separation didn't decrease, I agreed to be born.

"I remember waking from that dream and thinking about it for a long time. I had been taught by the sisters that our lives begin on earth, but surely I lived a long time before I was born. As a Catholic I was taught to go through saints and Mary when I prayed so I never felt closeness with God our Father. He just seemed big and scary to me. But now I discovered that He loved me and would protect me!

"I still feel the intense pain of separation even though I understand many of the reasons God thought it best for me to come here. I have also learned that I must ultimately trust Him in all things. I continue to and will always ask his will for me in my life on earth. When faced with obstacles in my life I remember the unconditional love I experienced in my premortal state and know that I need to try to bring this same love to others."

Melissa's experience changed her perspective of herself and her relationship with God. He ceased being a vengeful being who was more concerned with what she did wrong than with her as a personal being. She now knew that she was loved unconditionally, that she had a divine origin, and that her real home is heaven.

### Plans To Meet On Earth

During the long period of preparation for coming to earth it seems likely that deep attachments develop between spirits and that they would desire their relationship to continue on earth. But how would they recognize each other once the veil of forgetfulness falls at birth? Larry Tooley discovered that the eyes are one means whereby earthly recognition occurs. During his near-death experience, Larry found himself back in premortality observing his preparations to come to earth. He saw himself saying goodbye to another spirit being to whom he was very close.

"As soon as he saw her he said; 'I have something to tell you.' Georgia seated herself, wrapping her arms around her knees, leaning forward.

"'I've been informed it's my time,' I said quietly.

"The light flickered in her eyes and they became misty.

"'How wonderful!' she said. 'It's been so long. I can't believe it's finally going to happen. How soon will you be leaving?'

"'Very soon. They said the time is almost at hand,' I replied.

"She looked away, trying to hide her feelings. 'Have they said anything about me?' she asked.

"'Yes,' I said. 'It will be very soon afterwards. In earth terms, probably just a couple of years. Geographically we'll be close, but it will probably be years before we find each other.'

"'Won't there be problems?' she asked, her eyes pleading. 'I'm so afraid we'll never be together again. I just don't think I could accept that. In our altered consciousness on earth, we could forget about each other completely. Why, we'll probably wind up married to someone else and then we'll never find each other,' she said, her eyes going dark.

"'That's why I've made special arrangement here, before we go over. When the time is right, we'll be drawn together,' I said.

"I took her hands in mine. Our eyes met as I said, 'I'll know you. I need only to look into your eyes and I'll know who you are. I could never forget your eyes.'"[2]

And he didn't forget. As he assured Georgia, when the time was right they were drawn together and as soon as their eyes met, recognition occurred.

### Final Instructions

In the next accounts, two women discovered that in spite of their desires for the children they were carrying to be born very soon, medical readiness is not the only factor in determining the moment of birth.

Christine Monsen was five weeks pregnant with her sixth child when John, her husband, drowned. Grief, five fatherless children to care for, a difficult pregnancy—all added up to a heavy burden that was overwhelming Christine. As her due date approached, Christine began to pray that she could "get it over with" and deliver this baby soon. In extreme anguish she called a friend.

"'I can't stand this waiting,' I told her. 'I can't even get a decent night's sleep anymore.'

"'I know it's tough,' she said. 'Do you want me to come over and stay with you?'

"'No. Just pray for me that this baby will hurry up and get here so I can recover in time for Christmas.'

"She said she would pray for me and we hung up.

"'This is too much!' I cried that night in my own prayers. 'Lord, please take me out of this misery. The baby is ready to come and I'm ready to have it. Won't you please let it happen soon? Tonight? I would be so grateful if it came tonight.' But I lay there in agony hour after hour, feeling not even the smallest twinge of labor. It was a difficult, endless night.

"The next morning I awoke with a start. Rays of sunlight fell on the empty crib. I sat up and felt a warm sensation growing in my bosom. Then the walls and ceiling seemed to fade as a light, brighter than the sun, filled the room. The warmth continued to spread through me until I was cloaked in a blanket of comfort and peace. John was there—though I didn't see him. With him, I sensed, was another strong presence, another male spirit, but I didn't know who he was.

"'Chris,' John said in that familiar voice I loved so much. 'Don't rush things. The baby needs time. Its spirit needs to receive final instructions from the Lord.'

"The words rippled through me like crystal waters. 'Have patience. Your prayers will be answered. Just have faith. When the time is right, you will know. Remember, our child needs to receive its instructions first.'"[3]

Though her discomfort did not disappear, this brief experience with her husband helped her bear the pain until her baby's final instructions/preparations for earth were completed.

Melody Davis had made arrangements for a home birth. When consistent, increasing contractions began, she called the doctor, the midwife and designated relatives, some who had to drive quite a distance. A few hours later, with everyone gathered around, her labor suddenly and inexplicably stopped. She was deeply embarrassed and apologized to everyone for the inconvenience:

"All present were gracious and understanding. Offering encouragement that my labor would resume in a day or two, they departed.

"That night I had a vivid dream. I found myself out in the cosmos, midst stars and celestial lights. Gazing in different directions, I detected a child in the distance surrounded by twelve adult spirits. The spirits slowly rotated around the child in perfect harmony, forming a glowing circle reminiscent of a Saturn ring, embellished with twelve distinct twinkles. I knew the child in the center was mine, although the gender was unclear. The scene seemed to represent final preparations for earth birth. I could see knowledge passing as light waves from the luminous spirits, one at a time, to my child.

"Suddenly one of the spirits streaked over to me with a message conveyed directly to my mind, 'We have not completed the teaching of your child.' I did not actually see his form, but I knew he was a male spirit who had already lived on earth and was now continuing his eternal mission back in heaven. As instantly as he came, he flashed back to his position in the teaching ring where the twelve twinkling, advanced spirit beings continued instructing my unborn child.

"I awoke to an astonishing peace. The frustration and embarrassment of the day were gone. I had seen the workings of God's plan. All was in order—eternal order. My child would come when deemed ready and not a cosmic second sooner."

### The Place of Departure

The place where the journey to earth actually begins is a place somewhat distant from the heavenly home. Evidently it is a place where the resolve of spirits can be tested, where malevolent beings can visit and create feelings of anxiety, fear and apprehension. A case in point is that of Holly Draper.

"Once our instruction was completed, we were taken to a place where we received a blessing from our Heavenly Father. He laid his hands on our heads and gave us blessings and special gifts which, if we used them, could help us successfully complete our earthly missions. At that time I knew exactly what my mission was. I still know that I have an important mission to perform but don't remember specifically what it is. It is my impression that part of my earthly experience is to discover what my mission is and to accomplish it. All that I remember is that I knew I would experience much adversity, that my life would not be easy, but that when I needed help, I would receive if I asked.

"After receiving the blessing from my Heavenly Father I went to the place of departure, a place away from heaven much closer to earth where I found myself standing in line waiting for my turn to go. As I stood there, three men came up to me and initiated a conversation. One said to me, 'Well, Holly, are you excited to go to earth?' I said that I was. He then continued, 'I'll bet you are excited! But are you sure you are ready? Aren't you just a little fearful?'

"I replied, 'No! I am not afraid!' When he asked me why I was not afraid, I said, 'Because I know my Heavenly Father loves me and he will never leave me. He will never forget me. He promised me!'

"'Well, Holly, let us show you what you are really in for on earth.' He then waved his hand in an arc and I was shown my entire earth life experience. I saw and felt all the adversity, all the hardship, all the trials, every negative aspect of my life. As I stood there seeing and experiencing these scenes he asked once more, 'Are you sure that you are ready?'

"My excited anticipation turned to dread and I no longer felt the same enthusiasm. Unlike heavenly beings, these three men were not dressed in white clothing but in clothing that was a grayish wheat color. I knew them. They had chosen not to follow Heavenly Father's plan but that of Satan, and had been expelled from our heavenly home. I believe that it was their intent to convince me that my Heavenly Father would forget and forsake me while I was on earth and that I would be completely on my own.

"For an instant, I believed them, and doubt entered my mind. But I still knew that I needed to go to earth, and I remembered the blessing Heavenly Father had given me. Nevertheless, my joy was replaced with nervousness, apprehension, and a little dread. In the life review they showed me only the negative; the trials and adversity were highlighted. Once they knew they had been successful in creating a sense of doubt and apprehension they left me and went to others waiting in line, to those on the brink of birth, attempting to create havoc. Why Heavenly Father and His angels permitted them to do this, I do not know. Since He is always interested in our growth, I suspect it is part of the tests and challenges we need. By remembering truths I'd been taught, plus my blessing from Heavenly Father, I was able to resist those cunning men and come to earth with enthusiasm rather than discouragement and fear."

### Waiting To Leave

Julie had a very unusual experience during which she remembered being in heaven waiting to come to earth.

"I was in a long white dress, and I came through some beautifully carved double doors into a large room. Chairs were arranged on either side of the room. The chairs were empty when I came in.

"The room was like an amphitheater and was slanted down. At the front of the room there was something that looked to be a table or an altar. As I looked at the front of the room I saw three men dressed in white.

"I knew where I was supposed to sit, and I came down the center aisle and sat on the left side, in toward the middle of the seats. All the chairs were padded, and they were hooked together.

"I remember thinking it was going to be so strange to go to earth and forget home. I couldn't comprehend that. I understood exactly what I was getting into and what I had to do. But I couldn't comprehend that I could ever forget this fantastic place. I wanted so much to remember this experience and this room.

"When the double doors to the room closed, I knew that I would not remember what was behind those two doors—a veil would be placed over my mind. But I wanted to remember this room, and I studied it very carefully.

"I also remember it was the three men at the front of the room who would determine when I would go through the door. When my time came I would know it, and I would move down the aisle and go through the white curtains that were across the front.

"The three men were whispering reverently, but I didn't pay any attention to what they were saying. I just kept studying the room—I did not want to forget it. Drapes were over the windows, and the ceiling was very tall.

"It seemed strange to be getting ready to go to earth. And when I thought about earth, it was as if I could see through the walls of the room and see the earth suspended out in space. I was not afraid; I just didn't want to forget."[4]

The individual in the next account is quite unusual because his memories of heaven and his birth remained with him into adulthood. He did not realize that other children did not remember their births until they began to tease and avoid him. Michael Maguire reported that he found himself in a place unlike any he had been in so far and he could see the earth.

"I can remember standing in a dark space, but unlike being in a darkened room, I could see everything around me, and the blackness had dimensions.

"There was another person standing to my right, and like me, he was waiting to be born into the physical world. There was an older person with us who could possibly be a guide, since he stayed with us until we left and answered my questions.

"Behind us was a crowd of people, but they weren't clear to my vision like the two people standing next to me. In front of me and approximately thirty degrees below me, I could see the earth with the facial images of two couples.

"I spoke to the other person next to me briefly, but I can't remember what was said. I can remember talking to the older man. When we communicated, it wasn't with spoken word but with a form of telepathy. We communicated with thought-transfer, but we heard the words clearly as if they were spoken. I asked the older man who the people were behind us and he replied that they were waiting to be born but they were not ready yet. I asked him what was that in front of us and he replied that what we were looking at was earth. I then asked him who those people were whose images appeared on the earth and he replied that they were going to be our parents.

"I didn't know which parents we were going to end up with. The older man conveyed to us that it was time to go. The other person standing next to me walked forward and disappeared from my sight. I was told that it was my turn and I walked forward.

"Suddenly I found myself lying in a hospital nursery with other babies around me. I still had my normal thought processes at this stage. I noticed three people standing near the foot of my bed. I immediately recognized two of them as my parents. They looked exactly as I had seen them. The other person was my older brother, but I didn't know this at the time. I remember lying on my back looking around and thinking this must be earth. I tried to stand up and found I couldn't, since I was now trapped in a baby's body. I can't recall anything before being in the dark space.

"My father, who knew nothing of my experience, often talked about the first time he came to the hospital to see me. He said I stared so hard at the three of them that he thought my eyes were going to pop out. I was born in 1965 and man wasn't able to view the earth as I saw it until they went to the moon. As a child, when I first saw the photos of the earth taken by the astronauts from space, it was exactly as I remembered it.

"As a child I freely told other children what happened, because I thought everyone had this experience. I quit telling others when I discovered that others thought of it as an over active imagination."[5]

Michael's experience is interesting for several reasons. The first is the fact that he was taken to a dark place but unlike the darkness on earth, he could still see distinctly what was happening around him. Next he saw a multitude of people who were still in the process of preparing to go to earth. He then saw the earth and superimposed on it the faces of his parents. At his birth he still felt like the individual he had been in heaven and was frustrated when he could not make his new physical body respond. It must take time for spirit beings to realize the limitations that come with their new bodies and the change is a shock to some spirits. It certainly was in Michael's case.

### Summary Thoughts

The idea that souls exist in a premortal realm where they are prepared to come to earth is neither a new concept nor limited to one culture or religious tradition. For example in early Judaism is described the very chambers (Hebrew—*guf, araboth*) in which the souls dwelled while awaiting their turn to descend into bodies. The Genesis Rabbah even tells of how God took counsel with such spirits before creating the world; and the Tabuma Pekude records a conversation in which God speaks to a soul about to enter a drop of semen. The Carmans in their book, The Cosmic Cradle, recorded numerous such examples. But what is key here is that in premortality, we progressed/developed as far as we could and had to come to earth in order to continue to grow.

# Chapter Seven
## The Journey to Earth

Leaving home for the first time is not easy. But the fear and apprehension of going to a new place, far from home, is easier if you have someone you love and trust accompany you. So it is with the transition from heaven to earth. Our loving Heavenly Father does not send us off alone through a dark and malevolent space, but provides us with escorts. The accounts of thousands of witnesses suggest that no one comes to or leaves earth without one or more escorts. Such was the case of Lisa. One day Lisa was playing outside her farmhouse when she happened to look up at the nearby mountains. As she gazed at them, long forgotten memories were triggered.

"I was about four years old and had been sent by my mother to play outside so she could get some housework done. As I was playing I glanced up and looked at the mountain range near our farm. As I studied the mountains, it seemed that I had seen them before, but from a very different perspective. As I pondered this feeling a vision opened in my mind.

"I saw a group of boys and girls sitting in a circle, on the ground. I don't know how many there were of us, but it appeared to be a group of maybe twenty-five or thirty. I do not know exactly what we were doing, but it seemed as though we were learning, as in a school.

"Suddenly from behind me and over my right shoulder, I could feel my name being called. I say 'feel' because it wasn't a verbal sound. I turned and saw a rather tall slender man standing there.

"As I looked at him, I mentally asked, 'Is it my time to go?' He replied that it was.

"Then the man and I were moving across the sky above the mountain I was looking at. He was on my right side, and we were speaking with each other. Then suddenly we stopped. I looked down and saw a farmhouse, a barnyard with a fence, and a canal behind the house. A small road went down a hill. As I looked down I asked my guide, 'Is this where I am going to live?'

"'Yes!'

"'Will I be the only child?'

"'No you will be one of many.'

"'Will I be happy there?'

"'If you want to be.'

"It was then that a snowflake fluttered across my eyes bringing me back to reality. Yes, I was born on that farm and it looked just as it had from the sky. I was the eleventh child of the family and the last."

Based on what Lisa's angelic escort said, whether we will be happy on earth depends on us. Others can help us to be successful, to feel safe, to feel love and accepted. But it is ultimately ourselves that determine how we feel about ourselves. But knowing where we came from and that we are children of God can give a sense of joy and happiness that can be achieved in no other way.

Jeff was caught in a major blizzard and his wife Roseanne was in the hospital about to give birth to their daughter. She was praying that her husband would be protected and arrive in time to be with her when the baby was born. Roseanne, reflecting back on that tumultuous day, reported some very unusual but inspirational things that occurred.

"My second pregnancy was plagued with serious complications. During my delivery I experienced such terrible pain that I demanded an epidermal. The doctor tried to inject anesthetic into the cavities next to my lower vertebrae so as to deaden the nerves that sensitize the lower body, but he kept missing the target and jamming the needle into the bone. The pain was excruciating. With each misguided jab it got worse, until I discovered that my spirit had left my body.

"I found myself in a kind of a fog that gradually dissipated revealing an older man who told me, 'Be strong. You're doing the right thing. It will all be accomplished soon.' This loving man from the other side of the veil was remarkably consoling. The doctor finally inserted the needle to his satisfaction, but he still fouled it up because I went numb to my arm pits and had headaches for days after, indicating that the anesthetic had punched my spinal cord and seeped up into my brain—a condition that can endanger the life of both mother and child.

"At this point I'm not sure whether my spirit reentered my body or not. I could still see and hear the man comforting me. Melody, my best friend, who was there to support both me and my husband, said I would stare straight ahead, then turn to her and describe what I saw. Melody witnessed the whole thing.

"Suddenly I heard my unborn daughter pleading, 'Mommy, Mommy, I have to come now.'

"I called her by name, Lydia, and encouraged her to wait a little longer for Daddy to return. (He had gone home to relieve the babysitter and find another.)

"At that point I realized about thirty men and women of varying ages had entered the room all dressed in white. Some were coming and going, as though carrying messages. Seven women surrounded the spirit of my unborn daughter. I recognized one of them as my deceased grandmother, Vi. The angelic women expressed their love to my daughter, reassuring her it would be only a little longer until her birth, which she so desperately desired.

"I was increasingly concerned about my husband. A state of emergency had been declared and he was out in one of the worst snowstorms in Indiana's history. The kindly spirit-man next to me gave me frequent updates on Jeff's whereabouts and assured me that he would return safely. I somehow sensed that guardian angels were out in that storm with Jeff, just as they were in the room with our unborn daughter and myself. Jeff found a cousin to watch our son and 'miraculously' found his way safely back to the hospital. Within fifteen minutes of his return, Lydia was born. Just prior to her birth, three older lady angels came to me and emphasized what a special spirit this child was. As they finished their message, Lydia appeared directly in front of me as a beautiful, fully grown woman."

What a gift this very brief appearance was for Roseanne. She knew her daughter would be born, that she would survive her birth, and grow into a lovely young woman. When problems occurred between her and her daughter, she could reflect back on this experience and be assured that they were only temporary as she knew what would eventually happen.

Jean also saw three angelic beings who introduced her to the spirit of her unborn son. They informed Jean just before they departed:

"He is very special and you are to take very good care of him."

As we reflect on Jean and Roseanne's experiences, we can only wonder about the degree to which they are unique. If our eyes were opened and we could see the busy activities on the other side would we see what Roseanne saw? What a difference it would make for a mother to know that the baby that had just been handed to her was a special spirit and also to see what the baby would look like when he/she reached full physical maturity.

While in Jean's and Roseanne's accounts they saw the activities surrounding their children's births, Becky observed the circumstances surrounding her own birth. She remembers waiting to go to earth and the angelic being who served as her escort.

"In the final moments before my birth a lady approached me with the message that it was my time to leave heaven and go down to earth. I was very nervous as I was not sure what I was to do. The lady escorted me, comforting me the whole time, including when I entered my mom's womb. She comforted me again during the birthing process and even talked to me several times after I was born. I not only heard her, but saw her for a few minutes with each visit. There was no question; I knew she was there. Each time she would comfort me briefly, then leave. I don't remember exactly how old I was when she stopped coming, but it was when I was a small girl."

From this account it appears that escorts not only accompany spirits to earth, but may remain to comfort and counsel them while their body is developing in the womb and even for a time after birth.

During her near-death experience Jennifer left her body and traveled toward a bright light. Before reaching the light, she was given an extraordinary vision of herself before her birth. She witnessed her trip to earth and the angelic beings who accompanied her.

"The physical labor was too much for my body because of my weakened condition. My body stayed right there, but my spirit started leaving. I was aware that I was moving through circles and triangles and squares toward a bright light. I was so enthralled by the sizes and shapes of things that I don't remember any colors.

"Before I reached the light, I recalled my life in a sudden flash. It was the most totally incredible thing I have ever seen. I saw the time I was brought from heaven to my body by angels, how I was received at the hospital, and how my parents loved me."

An experience like this could not but help any individual know how special they really are from the heavenly perspective.

In this and preceding accounts, individuals reported seeing angelic beings escorting spirits to earth. In the next accounts, the spirits were escorted by deceased family members.

Kjirstin Youngberg's labor was so difficult that she desperately prayed for help. Her prayers were answered when she saw her son and his escort.

"Most women who bear children notice that each birth becomes physically easier. In my case, each pregnancy became more difficult. Jordan's birth was especially painful and, at one point, I prayed for a "small glimpse" of him, to feel more connected to him, more able to draw upon all my power to push him out.

"In my mind, I suddenly saw a small, very distinctive square ear. I knew it was Jordan's ear, and as I prayed my thanks and continued the birth, I realized we were in trouble. I could not deliver him without medical help.

"My obstetrician ordered an emergency room prepared. Eric, my husband, accompanied me into the emergency delivery room, where Dr. Smith prepared to extract Jordan.

"Eric and I had recently seen the film *Spartacus*. Toward the end of the film is a scene where a huge battle takes place. The hills are virtually covered with the warring armies. A similar scene unfolded above me in the delivery room.

"Hills stretching as far as I could see were covered with people clothed in white. Thousands, perhaps even a million people were thus assembled. All were watching me, and I understood them to be part of my eternal family. I was related in some way to each of those people. It amazed me. As I continued to watch, two men started toward me and the multitude divided, making a path for them.

"As they came closer, I recognized the one on the right to be my husband's father who had passed away six months after our marriage. He looked younger and stronger, but it was definitely Leland.

"The man beside him seemed familiar, but I didn't know him. As they came closer, I realized the man was becoming shorter, smaller, younger. He was a young man, then a boy, then a toddler, and Leland bent down and scooped him up, smiling as he came close to me.

"The toddler became a smaller baby, then as they reached me, a newborn infant.

"Leland broke out in a smile I can only describe as that of a very proud and happy grandpa. It was a smile I'd never seen him give in life, but I saw it now—broad and beautiful. As he handed the baby to me, I heard Jordan's first cry."[1]

When Kjirstin looked at Jordan shortly after her was born, his ears were round. However, the next day as she turned him this way and that to examine his tiny, perfect fingers and toes, she noticed that his left ear had become square-shaped, just as she had been shown before his birth.

Over time, Kjirstin came to understand another aspect of the vision. When her father-in-law started toward her he walked with a man who became progressively smaller until he was handed to her as an infant. As her son grew she realized that she had seen his development in reverse, for as he reached different life stages he looked just as she had seen him at the same stages with his grandfather. Jordan has now reached adulthood and has the appearance of the man who "seemed familiar" to Kjirstin in the vision.

How extraordinary it is to know that thousands of members of our eternal family in heaven may be so interested in our success as to assemble to witness our departure for earth, and to watch over our journey to earth. If they can assemble to observe us then, why not throughout our entire life, or when urgently needed?

While most of those interviewed identified adult deceased relatives who functioned as escorts, others identified their escorts as deceased siblings. In the following case, the sibling only lived a few hours. Lois Hachier, the children's grandmother, reports:

"I have always loved the idea of becoming a grandmother and when my son announced that he and his wife were expecting I was delighted. My son kept me informed on the progress of the pregnancy and called one day to inform me that his wife had gone into premature labor and that the baby was going to be born seven weeks early. He was clearly apprehensive but tried to sound optimistic. I caught the next plane to be with them. Jessica was born at 8:21 in the morning. She had dark brown hair and brown eyes like her mother. She was beautiful. But all was not well.

"Later that day the doctors came in and told us that my tiny granddaughter needed corrective surgery if she was to live because her esophagus was connected to a lung instead of her stomach. During that surgery they discovered that her heart was incomplete and she would need additional surgery to save her life. The happiest day of our lives turned into one of shock and disbelief.

"Before Jessica could recover from her first surgery she died in her father's arms. I was devastated.

"I could not bring myself to accept her death, and in my grief I was no help to my children. One day, about three months after Jessica died, my daughter-in-law asked me out to breakfast. Not only did we have breakfast but we shopped and lunched together. When we arrived home, it was almost dinnertime. It was the first time we had laughed together since before Jessica was born. When she dropped me off at home, she said, 'We had such a good day. Are you going to go into the house and cry because it is over?' I was puzzled by her remark but she continued with much love.

"'Don't you think how this might be affecting Jessica every time she looks down and sees you crying? She must certainly think she caused you all this pain and sadness. How can she help us if we don't give her a chance to be happy in heaven? I miss her too, but I want her to be happy.'

"I knew my daughter-in-law was right but it was so hard to think of Jessica without crying. However I realized that I could not continue to contribute to my children's grief.

"About six months after Jessica's death, I had a dream about Jessica. She had a little boy by the hand and in the other hand she held a small suitcase. On the suitcase was the name Jarrod. As they walked toward a cloud, she told the little boy that she was sending him down to earth to her Mommy and Daddy, and that they would love him very much. She told him, 'Don't be afraid. I will always watch over you.'

"The next morning I was so excited to tell my daughter-in-law about my dream that I thought I would burst. When I finally reached her, I said, 'I have something great to tell you.'

"'I have something great to tell you, too.' She responded. 'I just found out that I'm pregnant.'

"From that moment, we knew that this baby would be a boy. The name Jarrod means, 'descending,' so we knew that he was on his way down on that cloud. He was born nine months later."[2]

How comforting it was to this grandparent to know that she had not lost her granddaughter when she died. She learned that not only Jessica still exists but was helping to prepare her brother for his earth life. And it was Jessica who escorted Jarrod, the name given her brother by her parents, to earth.

The excitement of a birth is not limited to those on earth as is shown in Mary Grace McMenus's experience.

"My unborn daughter told me that she was coming in spite of there being no sign of labor. As I laid down for some much needed rest, two angels descended from above me. They simply said, 'We are here to escort life.' One went to be with my daughter, the other stayed with me.

"I was delighted to see my aunt and grandmother (who had left this earth) were also there. They were tender, nurturing souls on earth and apparently this trait continued in the next life. My grandmother was behind my aunt, jumping for joy like an excited child. Giddiness is nothing that I had ever seen with my grandmother, but she could not contain her joy at this occasion. I rose out of my body, floating in the presence of these angelic beings. I knew that I was not alone, nor was Cheyenne."[3]

Mary Grace witnessed two angelic beings, one was to be her daughter's escort, the second was there to support her during her labor and delivery. Mary Grace was permitted to witness the uncharacteristic unconstrained joy of her grandmother at the moment her grandchild was born, a memory she will always treasure.

In the next case, the spirit's escort was not an angelic being or a deceased relative but the mother herself. Pauline Smith's husband reported:

"When our fourth daughter was born, my wife took a long time to recover from the effects of the anesthetic they had given her. As soon as she recovered enough to speak she said, 'I had to go so far to get her.' She described having to go through an area of darkness and into the light to get her baby."

Pauline's experience is not unique as other mothers have informed me that they, too, left their bodies and traveled into a heavenly realm to get their babies.

Claire reported witnessing the spirit of her daughter entering her body. She saw no escort, only the spirit of her child-to-be. Because of this experience, Claire knew with total certainty that she was pregnant and that she was expecting a girl.

"One afternoon I lay down for a nap. I tossed despite my fatigue until I was in a strange state of consciousness that is neither awake nor asleep, but which bears the earmarks of both.

"Then I saw her. She was at the foot of the bed—patient, not trying to catch my attention. She was perhaps three years old, simply dressed, with long dark hair and a quiet look on her face. She climbed gracefully on the footboard, as though the move was choreographed. She began to crawl toward me, one hand, then the other. Perhaps she grew smaller, or became translucent, I do not know. She reached my legs and kept moving until she faded to become part of my own body. She was inside me."

Claire went on to have a little girl who grew to have long dark hair and the body of a dancer. Says Claire, "I knew her the moment she popped out. We both just smiled."[4]

To witness the spirit of your child enter your body must be exciting to say the least. This experience revealed to Claire that the developing body is more than just a cluster of cells, a fetus, a thing. The physical body is the place where dwells the spirit of an intelligent being, a spirit with hopes, dreams, and an important mission to fulfill.

The concluding experience in this chapter transits nicely to our next chapter in that it describes both the spirit's escorts and provides insights into the nature of the trip itself.

Roy Mill's experience convinced him that in order to travel to earth safely each unborn spirit must have an angelic escort.

"An angel came to me announcing, 'It's time to go.' She reached out and took me gently by the arm. For a time we traveled in light. Then the light faded behind and we flew or glided into darkness. The angel instructed me to stay close and hang on tight. I soon discovered why.

"We were crossing a space inhabited by evil spirits. Almost immediately, three objects loomed up ahead. As we drew closer the objects transformed into human shape, one assuming the form of an old woman, the other two old men. My angelic escort cautioned, 'Do not be fooled by their disguise. They are evil spirits striving to lure you by deception. See how kind they look? It's a facade.'

"Without warning my guide, maneuvering skillfully, detoured around them. This enraged the predators. Emitting the most awful screams I've ever heard, the devils dropped their masquerade and lunged toward us with demonic fury. My angelic escort turned and rebuked them with authority from on High. Instantly a mantle of brilliant light enshrouded us, forming a spiritual shield. The three attackers stopped abruptly, howling the frustrated shrieks of the damned. Repelled by divine power, they slunk back. Clearly the demons would attempt to harm anyone crossing their space en route to earth, but they did not have the power to withstand the light."[5]

This experience of Roy's is not unique as others have also told of similar encounters with malevolent beings on their way to earth. But their angelic escorts had the power to make sure that they traversed the realm of darkness safely.

**Summary Thoughts**

It must be comforting for spirits coming to earth to know that they do not leave the security of our heavenly home alone. It appears that most of us, and probably all of us, are accompanied to earth by escorts. The escorts may be angelic beings or deceased loved ones but they are there to assure that even if we encounter regions occupied by malevolent beings, we will arrive at our destination safely and at our appointed time.

*Chapter Eight*
*Arriving on Earth*

## The Abilities of Those Who Have Just Arrived on Earth

It is generally believed that children are born without the ability to understand and comprehend what happened to them during their gestation or at the time of their birth because they lack the ability to think. Thinking, it is argued, requires a set of symbolic meanings attached to objects, actions, and sounds. Ergo, infants can't be thinking because they have no language. Infants do not know what anything is so they cannot evaluate. Meanings come from experience with the world and from intimate contact with parents, siblings, and other adults. Therefore the prevailing hypothesis is that children can neither think, communicate, nor have a conscious awareness of what is happening around them in the months before and after they are born. This assumption about the mental capacities of the unborn and newborn is being challenged by new and exciting research.

Thomas Verny, a medical doctor, observed that pregnant women could soothe their thrashing unborn babies by singing or humming. This phenomenon caused him to begin a six-year study in which he explored what happens during the gestation period. He summarized his research findings in a book entitled, *The Secret Life of the Unborn Child*.[1] In it he states that the unborn child is an aware, reacting human being who, from the sixth month on (and perhaps even earlier), leads an active intellectual and emotional life. Along with this startling statement he makes the following claims:

- The fetus can see, hear, experience, taste, feel and learn on a primitive level.

- A corollary to this discovery is that what a child feels and perceives begins shaping his attitudes and expectations about himself.
- The chief source of those shaping messages comes from the child's mother. Chronic anxiety or a wrenching ambivalence about motherhood can leave a deep scar on an unborn child's personality. On the other hand, joy, elation and anticipation can contribute significantly to the emotional development of a healthy child.
- New research is beginning to focus much more on the father's feelings. The latest studies indicate that how a man feels about his wife and unborn child is one of the single most important factors in determining the success of a pregnancy.[2]

While Dr. Verny and his colleagues focused on the stage in fetal development when the unborn child begins to take on social and psychological characteristics, Dr. David B. Chamberlain's research also indicates that the ability of the unborn to think and communicate precedes their birth. In the introduction to his book, *Babies Remember Birth*, Psychologist, Dr. Chamberlain states:

"The truth is, much of what we have traditionally believed about babies is false. We have misunderstood and underestimated their abilities. They are not simple beings but complex and ageless—small creatures with unexpectedly large thoughts.

"Babies know more than they have been supposed to know. After only minutes of exposure to its mother's face after birth, a baby can pick her out from a gallery of photos. Babies recognize the gender of other babies, even when cross-dressed, provided they are moving—something adults cannot do. They are mentally curious and eager to learn."[3]

Dr. Chamberlain was surprised when a number of his adult patients spontaneously told him what they recalled about being born.

"My clients kept telling me, in considerable detail, what happened to them at birth, including the ideas they were having as babies. I found an unexpected maturity in their "baby" thoughts. Each person spoke with authority and identity. They knew and loved their parents. Their character did not appear to be age-related or developmental in any simple sense; it was there from the start."[4]

The discoveries of Dr. Chamberlain and Dr. Verney that babies are cognizant of what is going on around them is not at all surprising given the fact that infants do not start their existence at conception or even at some point during gestation. As documented in this book, the spirits inhabiting infant bodies existed premortally. When they come to earth they come as mature spirits, with unique identities, and an acute awareness of what is going on around them. Several examples cited by Dr. Chamberlain and individuals I have interviewed substantiate the facts related in this chapter.

### The Birth Experience

Marianne remembers vividly her mother's contractions and what it felt like to her. The words she uses are words she has learned since the experience but the feelings and emotions of that time are unmistakable.

"They said it's time to be born. I feel the pressure but I don't want to be born. I'm not ready yet. I'm just going to wait; it feels much better in here.

"Now they are coming faster, faster [contractions]; this way, that way. Oh, it's getting intense! It's pushing, pushing, pushing me out. I want to stay right here where I am, but they insist.

"It feels like a tidal wave . . . I can see that I'm attached to the tidal wave. When it's ready to go, I guess I have to go, too . . . Oh-oh, the tidal wave is coming again.

"I'm still not ready. It's pushing, pushing. I'm going to stay right here. I don't want to go any place, but I have to . . .

"Oh-oh, they are putting on gloves. They are getting me. Oh, goodness sakes, grrr, that was a squeeze!

"They are holding my head, but gently; they were gentle. And the next thing I know, they're saying, 'You just lie right here,' and they wrap me up in something."[5]

Marianne felt guilty about not wanting to be born and never told her mother for fear this knowledge would hurt her. She now understands what she experienced and that she had to experience it. Nevertheless, it was very painful and traumatic.

Debbie remembers her mother's womb as a warm safe place that she did not want to leave.

"My first memory is of waking up in a beautiful but totally unfamiliar place. The place was warm and dark but not totally black. I felt like every need I had was being met there. I also knew I could be happy there. The tremendous attraction I had to the place where I was, was akin to the rush of an opiate. It felt like it came from my chest toward the walls of the enclosed place. The initial intensity of the feeling I was experiencing gave way to a sense of peace. I believe I slept, waking intermittently, always comfortable with my new surroundings, and content to spend eternity there.

"Then what had been comfortable became pressure and pain, the feeling of being crushed and suffocating. All along I had been vaguely aware of the distant presence of some beings outside of where I was who seemed concerned for my welfare but whom I initially chose to ignore. Now I began pleading for help from them. At this point a being appeared to me. He was an older white- haired male, not the God portrayed in the Sistine Chapel, but more humble in appearance and demeanor. With him were two others. They seemed to be there to reassure me that no matter what happened, now or in the future, I was safe and would be okay. Without words they were able to convey that I had to learn some things and would be with people I had chosen to learn these things with. During the lulls between the crushing and painful experiences (contractions), I seemed to find acceptance of the process and appreciation for their help. They were so compassionate and helped me to ride out the contractions with an assurance that I would survive being 'crushed.'

"Just as I was about to be born, I 'saw' who my mother was. I don't think I was physically looking at her face; it was more like being shown a video of her. However I did not remember from before I entered my mother's womb why I had chosen her to be my mother.

"Being in the womb was so pleasant that I did not want to leave. I also feared the pain I would have to endure to be born. The entities were almost chuckling with amusement at this, although it wasn't malicious humor--more like there's nothing more we can do to convince you. You'll find out for yourself. Everything's going to be fine. And it was."

While it is not known why all children do not remember their births, those who do remember can help our understanding of the nature of the unborn, what can and does happen at the moment of birth, and when the spirit enters the body.

The birth of a new child is an exciting event in the lives of its parents but it is also a momentous event for the individual being born. It includes all the preparations for coming to earth, the feelings upon leaving the security of the heavenly home, being escorted to earth, entering the mother's body and reactions to the new physical body. The account related by the following man is more complex than most and includes the thoughts and feelings of a spirit at the time of its earthly birth.

"When it was time for me to come to earth I was met by an angelic being. She said that we must hurry because my earthly mother's body was nearly ready to receive me. I was a bit reluctant to leave but my angelic escort insisted saying, 'If you are not born soon, it will interfere with the timing of your mission.' I was aware of the hazards of earth life and wanted some assurance that I would be able to return to heaven. My escort responded, 'I know going to earth is scary, but if you are to complete your assigned mission you must go now! Your earth mother is ready to receive you! We must hurry to the Departure Room.'

"Up to this moment all communications between me and my escorts had been mind-to-mind. But now my escort began speaking to me in the voice of my earth mother. She was speaking verbally, so for the first time my ears as well as my mind were hearing what she was saying. She told me that hearing with my ears would help me to recognize my mother's voice, as well as with earth-style communication.

"I was introduced to the escort who was to take me to my mother. He said, 'Are you ready to go?'

"I replied, 'Yes!'

"My escort replied, 'Then we must depart at once.' He grasped my left wrist and we passed through the door. I looked back in dismay. I was actually leaving heaven. I was excited to be heading to earth but at the same time reluctant to leave the beauty, serenity, and security of my heavenly home.

"I looked over my shoulder at heaven one last time and my escort told me, 'Look ahead, not back,' so I did. We were traveling very fast and I could see the world in front of us. It was beautiful. As we descended to ground level our rate of speed slowed. I recognized the countryside and then the house where my mother lived. We entered the house and I saw about a dozen people, all visiting and enjoying one another's company. I quickly identified aunts, uncles, cousins, grandparents, and above all, my mother. When Mother spoke I recognized her voice. My escort asked, 'Are you ready?'

"I replied, 'Yes.'

"The next thing I knew, I was inside Mother. The feelings I experienced at that moment were not strange or frightening. I felt safe and secure. The time that I spent in my mother's womb was special to me. I had grown very close to my angelic escort and he continued speaking to me, reassuring me, caring for me. This went on for the four months my spirit was in my body growing within Mother. But as time progressed, the visits became shorter and less frequent, a sort of weaning process I guessed.

"Then everything changed and I turned over, bottom side up. I didn't like this change at all. I remained in this uncomfortable and awkward position for several days and then I began to move downward. My spirit left its body and I found myself standing outside my mother next to the being who had brought me to earth. He told me not to worry and that everything was proceeding as it should. He told me, 'You have experienced the womb and now you are about to experience birth. Have courage. Return to your mother with confidence.' He gave me a push and I was once more inside my mother.

"The sliding continued and then I was out and felt an unpleasant sensation that I eventually learned was cold. I could hear people talking and everything was so bright. Then I felt a sharp painful shock. A doctor had slapped my bottom.

"Startled, I sucked in a breath of air. The expansion of my lungs for the first time hurt, a pain that continued for some time. I was aware of what was happening around me and was a bit wary, very apprehensive, and hurting."

The memories of this man reinforces reports that the spirits of the unborn receive specific instructions just before they leave for earth. If this case is typical, it would indicate that the spirit does not enter the body until about the fifth month and also that the spirit is able to leave the physical body for short periods.

Other cases have been reported where spirits left their bodies and appeared to their prospective mothers to give them comfort and assurance during their protracted labor. Some spirits expressed appreciation to their mothers for what they had to endure to provide them with a physical body. These brief appearances provided a sense of peace and created a strong bond between mother and child.

Mary vividly remembers the events immediately following her entrance into this life.

"The doctor has me, and I'm looking at my mother. I'm glad to see her and she's glad to see me . . . She looks pretty. She's all sweaty and frazzled but she looks young, good. She feels good; she's smiling. It's a happy time.

"I hear somebody saying, 'That's my girl' . . . She's happy with me, pleased with me.

"The doctor is talking, giving orders to people, telling them to cut this, get that . . . He has a nice voice; he's a nice doctor, an older man. He's pretty gentle."[6]

While it is quite true that recent arrivals do not have the linguistic tools to communicate with parents, doctors, and nurses, evidently they do understand the thoughts of those around them and what is being said. How long this ability exists for most individuals is unknown but, at least for some, memories persist into adulthood.

**First Impressions**

What is it like to be born, to leave warmth and security and be placed in a hospital nursery bed? Dee is one individual who remembers being left alone for the first time, and for her it was traumatic.

"I'm being put down in a little bed. I feel like I'm left alone. I feel bad because no one is holding me and I'm all by myself.

"Everything seems so big. I feel so small.

"I'm all by myself." [7]

What is it like to switch from being a mature adult spirit to a newborn infant with all its physical limitations and immaturity? According to Emily, it is a difficult transition.

"I can hear her voice and then my father's voice. They're excited and talking about my birth.

"Then he comes and looks at me. But he doesn't pick me up. He just pokes me with his finger. He says something stupid like 'Gootchie, gootchie.'

"He doesn't know I'm a person; to him I'm a thing called baby. He's saying, 'That's all the babies; this one was hard enough.'"

"I didn't think I was that hard.

"I don't think I like these people very well. They give me a headache . . . They don't think I'm a person." [8]

It must be very frustrating to lose the ability to communicate with those around you. You can understand their thoughts and feelings, but they are oblivious to yours.

Dr. Chamberlain reported how Deborah expressed her frustrations. Because her fingers were blue, the staff was very concerned. Deborah was passed around, pulled, pushed, and rubbed in a manner she considered quite unnecessary.

"I knew I was okay. I tried to tell everybody, but they wouldn't listen. I was trying to talk but they didn't understand me... I was crying, trying to talk, but I guess it was just crying to them."[9]

The research of Doctors Varney and Chamberlain supports the conclusion that newborn infants understand what is going on around them including the thoughts of their parents and other health care providers. But they are also frustrated by the loss of the ability to communicate. Crying, in some instances therefore, could well be an uncoordinated attempt to communicate.

### The Physical Body

Dorothy Bernstein explains the frustrations she faced in a tiny physical body that was not yet in sync with her spiritual body. At the time of her interview Dorothy was in her seventies. Nevertheless her memories were clear and her descriptions were animated by lively facial expressions and enthusiastic gestures.

"As a spirit I was intelligent, mature, and in control of my body. I had been taught the language of my future family. I had also been shown the earth, especially the area where I was to be born so I would recognize my earthly surroundings, including the voice of my mother. I continued to communicate with angels for a time after my birth. In the womb and during infancy, I was able to experience both heaven and earth in that I understood both languages. The major problem I encountered as a new mortal was my physical body. My spirit functioned with extraordinary efficiency, but my physical body did not. It takes time for the spirit to learn how to control the body. It is not unusual for a baby to cry for no apparent reason. But there is a reason. Babies become very frustrated when they try to express themselves but cannot. When I was born it was as if I had on a lead jacket. My physical arms and legs were so heavy I could hardly move them. I could see my spirit arms move, then my physical arms would try to catch up to them. I couldn't get my physical body to react to what I wanted it to do. When I would reach for something, my spirit hand would go right to the object but I couldn't pick it up because my physical hand had gone somewhere else. Now that's frustrating and the only way I could express this frustration was by crying. So the first months of life are spent trying to synchronize spirit and body.

"Consider the process of speech. My spirit understood English before leaving heaven. My spirit could formulate words and sentences mentally but it took a long time for my brain, mouth and tongue to develop enough to verbalize those words and sentences. Sometimes I wanted so much to tell Mother something about heaven or about my angel or to warn her of something or to tell her where I hurt, but couldn't. I'd get so frustrated that the only sound that would come out was an uncoordinated one—crying. But gradually I succeed in coordinating the body and spirit and began to walk and speak."

Dorothy next explained the support systems newborns have from heaven.

"We learn many things about the world. At the same time our angel contacts are cut back and eventually eliminated. By the time we are in first or second grade, most of us have filled our minds with so much earth stuff that the heavenly memories get buried and forgotten. Our memory of being sons and daughters of God is veiled. In short, we become 'earthbound' to the extent that mortality may seem to be the whole of existence.

"We are not just dumped on earth without a support system. During the transition from heaven to earth life, angels stay in contact with babies both before and after birth, until they are about two years of age. In my case, the angels talked with me frequently in the womb and during my first couple of years of life. They reassured me, reminded me of how much I am loved in heaven and told me everything was going to be okay.

"Infants understand a lot more of both heaven and earth than most adults realize. The next time you see a newborn, try talking to it telepathically. You may be too earthbound to hear what the infant is thinking, but more than likely he or she will know what you are thinking. If you watch their facial expressions you can see it in their eyes and faces.

"I have many memories of my birth and the first years of life. When I was about two years old I experienced an unusually restless day. I was very tired, but for some reason could not fall asleep. While tossing and fussing, I heard the soothing voice of my angel. She said, 'Just relax and you will go right to sleep.' I did what she said and fell asleep. As I drifted off she announced, 'This is the last time I will talk to you until you get back.' Those were her exact words and I have not heard from her since.

"I remember a time before my mother died when I tested my earliest memories of life on her. I asked her, 'Mother when I was born did the nurse carry me to you in a hospital room near the stairs?'

"'Why yes,' she said, eyes widening. 'How did you know?'

"I responded, 'I remembered it.'"

### Recognizing Mother

Dorothy's experience points out that she recognized her mother's voice. She also knew her mother's face. How did this occur?

"As the time drew closer for me to be born, the lady angel began talking to me in the voice of my mother. She explained this was to help me so I would be accustomed to my mother's voice. She told me all spirits are given training to know their mothers' voices. Certainly when I was born, I could differentiate my mother's voice distinctly from that of anyone else.

"From the first day in my new home I recognized almost everyone's voices and I knew their names. Initially I could see only the face of my mother clearly. All other faces were in a sort of fog. About two weeks after I arrived my angel informed me that she would remove the veils from all the faces, and she did. I have wondered if the reason I could see only my Mother's face during those first weeks was to help me bond with her.

"Perhaps these bonds of recognition help explain the phenomenon of "separation anxiety," when infants become upset when removed from their mothers."

This recognition phenomenon was also experienced by Melanie Harding. Melanie had to undergo an emergency C-section to save her life and that of her baby. When her baby Quin was delivered he was in distress and crying uncontrollably.

"When my son Quin was born, my arms were tied down and I could not hold and comfort him. But when they brought him close to me so I could see him, I said his name. He stopped crying and turned his face toward me. When our eyes connected, we immediately recognized each other. Both of us felt a great joy at being reunited. We embraced each other not physically, but spiritually, and it gave both of us great comfort. As we embraced, it was not as a woman and an infant, but as mature beings happy to be together after a long separation."

Melanie had some intriguing experiences with her young son as he grew. One experience she recalls vividly occurred when Quin was two years of age. She discovered that he had witnessed his birth.

"When my son was about two, he asked me about his birth and who was there. I told him that I was there and so was his doctor.

He asked, 'Mommy, who else was there?'

"I thought and named the nurses and an anesthesiologist. He again asked, 'Who else was there?'

"Racking my brain I mentioned an attending physician and a medical technician.

"He started getting a little frustrated asking again, 'But Mommy, who else was there?'

"Sensing that I was missing the point to his question, I asked, 'Honey, who was there that I didn't mention?'

"He said, 'Mommie! Mommie! My Jesus was there!'

"This really took me by surprise. I looked right into his big blue eyes and said, 'Your Jesus was there?'

"He said, 'Yes!'

"I asked, 'What happened?'

"He said, 'He hugged me and kissed me and said, I love you, Quin. Then the doctor cut your belly.'

"I had never told him any of the details of his birth and I know he had never seen a C-section. I repeated, 'You saw the doctor cut my belly?'

"He could see that I was shocked and took my reaction to this statement as concern and continued, 'But he didn't hurt you, he was very nice.'

"I asked him, 'What happened next?'

"'The doctor grabbed my foot and pulled me out.'

"'Then what happened?' I asked him.

"He looked right into my eyes and said, 'I was crying but when you spoke my name, I stopped and looked at you and we hugged and I was happy to be back with you.'"

### Impact of Parental Actions, Thoughts, and Feelings on the Unborn

Rose Anne had been told by her physicians that she was unable to have children. After three years of marriage, she was assured during a spiritual experience that she would have a child and that it would be a boy. She was given his name, date of birth and birth weight, and told that he would have her large brown eyes and his father's sandy brown hair. She recorded all this information in her journal so it could be verified at his birth.

"I spoke with Benjamin daily throughout my pregnancy. I soon sensed that in the eternal journey of souls, Ben was an old, wise, and mature spirit. I spoke to him aloud and then learned to 'hear' his spiritual responses. Our conversations were in complete thoughts and sentences. For example, he had a love of music long before birth. I would ask him what types of music he wanted to hear, and listen for his spiritual responses. Sometime he requested lively tunes, sometimes soothing melodies. If he requested classical music and I was in the mood for something else he became very restless. When I switched to classical music he would immediately calm down. He was especially upset by heavy rock music, which I soon learned to avoid entirely so as not to disturb or agitate him. We chose not to have an ultrasound to identify gender as I knew he was a boy. When he was born, I expected a son, and that is what I had. Of course it took some time for his spirit to learn to work with his body in coordinated speech, but today at age two-and-one-half, he continues to manifest a maturity beyond his earth age in our 'adult' conversations."

Rose Anne's experience reveals several interesting facts. The first is that an unborn child's spirit is able to be with its mother throughout her pregnancy. Secondly, that a spirit did not have to be in its physical body to be "with" its mother. Thirdly, that infants can and do see their mothers and recognize them. Fourthly, that unborn children have definite musical preferences. In this regard, Rose Anne's experience was not at all unusual as other experiencers and researchers have discovered that the type of music a pregnant mother listens to can calm or agitate an unborn child. One pregnant woman reported attending a heavy metal rock concert and the music so agitated her baby that it kicked violently, causing her internal pain.

Just as surgeons have discovered that anesthetized patients can hear and are influenced during surgery for better or worse by comments, music, etc., we are also learning that the spirits of unborn children are aware—not only of what we say, but also what we think and feel. Unborn children, like Jessica in the next account, know if they are wanted.

One very strong memory Jessica has occurred just prior to her birth when she heard her birth mother say, "I don't want this baby. I would rather that it be dead and, if I could, I would kill it!"

The pregnancy had been neither planned nor wanted because the family was in desperate financial straits. They had other children they were struggling to support and another child at this time would be financially disastrous. The mother did everything in her power to kill the child, short of having an abortion. Nevertheless the child survived.

As a child, the little girl was haunted by the words and actions of her mother and, up to age four or five, she did everything she could to kill herself so she could fulfill her mother's stated desire that she be dead.

Jessica managed to escape abortion, but not the haunting words of her distraught mother.

While this case is unusual, it does document that the thoughts, feelings, and desires of mothers can have significant long term consequences on the unborn.

Tess had had an abortion when she was eighteen years of age. She did not believe in abortions but at the time she felt that it was her only option.

"Because of the abortion I decided that it was best that I never have a baby. It is not that I do not like children, because I do. I was just terrified of giving birth. I married a fine gentleman who already had several children. I enjoyed being a surrogate mother and I was good at it. I had had an IUD implanted to insure I would not get pregnant but it failed. I could not get another abortion as my husband was very pleased that we were going to have a child together. Ultimately, I gave birth to a beautiful but very angry little girl. As soon as she could communicate with me she said, 'Mother! Why didn't you let me through the first time? I had to wait all this time until I could finally get through and then I had to sneak in!'"

That little girl took years to get over her frustration at not being wanted and having to wait to be born. She would stomp around, slamming doors, saying, "I'm here! Why didn't you want me?"

It is not clear how many aborted children have the chance to return to the parents for whom they were originally intended. Why this particular little girl didn't go to another mother is not clear but apparently it was important for Tess to be her mother. She was aware of Tess's abortion and attempts to avoid pregnancy. She was also probably aware of Tess's fears. Evidently none of these factors compensated for the long delay she had to endure.

### Summary Thoughts

The accounts in this chapter definitely contradict society's basic assumptions about the unborn and the newly born. These accounts support the idea that the spirits who inhabit the bodies of babies are mature beings who are entering into a new realm in their eternal journey. These beings need to come to earth to gain a physical body and learn how to control it.

While the prenatal period is generally reported as being pleasant, secure, and warm, it is also apparent that emotions such as prolonged anger, disappointment and unhappiness on the part of their parents, especially their mothers, can have a definite negative impact on children's perceptions of themselves. On the other hand, long-term positive emotions can have the opposite effect.

## Chapter Nine
## Children's Memories of Their Heavenly Home

In what is evidently divine design, most memories of our heavenly home are blocked by a "veil of forgetfulness." And yet, in moments of meditative stillness, or when meeting someone new who seems "familiar," or when out in the vastness of God's creations, we sometimes sense that there is something much greater than what we are consciously aware of. We yearn to know exactly what it might be, to know about our real beginnings. Due to an unusual event in their lives, some individuals have their memories triggered and recall living in their original home and events that transpired there. But very young children often seem to have very clear memories of who they are and where they come from.

To the very young, the spirit beings they interacted with before they came to earth and the events and activities they experienced in heaven are just as real as anything they encounter on earth. With childlike innocence they talk matter-of-factly about what happened prior to their birth including how they came to earth, what happened as they were born, and those they left behind. In this chapter we will examine some of the memories that were shared by children and what they tell us about the connection between premortality and mortality.

### Jesus and God

Darlene and Peter Kutulas were enjoying their son's attempts to talk.

"Brad was just learning to talk and knew only a few words. One was 'Dada.' 'Dada' was not reserved for his father, however.

When Brad saw any man, he would shriek, 'Dada!' in delight. In an effort to encourage him to talk more, we often showed him photographs of people in magazines. Brad would always point to the men and say, "Dada."

"One afternoon I said to my wife, 'Let's show Brad a picture of Jesus.' Brad had never seen one, and given the long hair and flowing robes, we wondered how he would categorize Jesus. But when I held the picture up, Brad suddenly grew solemn, pointed almost in recognition, and said—again and again—a word he had never used. 'King!'"[1]

"King." What an unusual word and application from a child at the "Dada" stage of speech.

In the next account, another child amazed his parents by his claim to a most remarkable experience.

Jim and Ardry were invited to a baptismal service which was to be performed outdoors in a stream in a beautiful meadow. They took their two-year-old son with them hoping that his restlessness would not detract from the sacred nature of the occasion. They were very pleasantly surprised when he was not his usual rambunctious, curious self that day. In fact he seemed mesmerized by the experience. After the baptism they asked their son if he had had fun at the ranch with all his cousins and seeing one of them baptized. He said that he had. Then looking up at his daddy he said, "The best thing was that Jesus was there and I got to talk to him again."

Ardry said that most of the time she had trouble understanding what her son was trying to say but on this particular day, what he said to his parents had been very clear indeed.

We do not have photographs or contemporary drawings of the living Christ so artists have had to use historical descriptions and their own inspirations to portray what they think He looked like. How accurate are these artistic renditions? One young girl was shown a picture of Jesus and her reaction was reported by her mother, Diane.

"Just prior to my daughter's accidental death, she was shown an artist's rendering of Jesus. She pointed at the picture and said emphatically, 'He doesn't look like that at all!'"[2]

Tragically, the girl was killed shortly thereafter, leaving us to wonder what might have been her response to other portraits of Jesus.

That young girl's reaction to a picture of Jesus was different from those of the following two children. Were the pictures shown them more accurate or did they just happen to spark heavenly memories? There is no way of knowing. In the first account the child is my seventeen-month-old granddaughter.

Meg Widdison learned to speak very early, and enjoyed pointing at objects, people, and animals she recognized and saying their names. I was holding her as we walked into a church building, not the one she usually attended. Hanging in the foyer was a large picture showing an artist's portrayal of Jesus and his disciples at the Last Supper, a picture Meg had never seen before. The minute she saw the picture, Meg excitedly pointed at the central figure in the painting and exclaimed, "Jesus!"

In the second case, Robert Banz was reading a book to his granddaughter who was almost two years old. The book had to do with religious topics and activities. Robert would turn a page and point to the central figure or object and say, for example, "This is a church."

Then his granddaughter would also point to the picture and repeat, "Church."

As they looked through the book, they came to a picture of Jesus. Robert pointed to him and told her it was Jesus. She looked at the picture without pointing. He turned the page to a picture where people were all dressed up to go to church only to have her turn the page back to the picture of Jesus. He said, "Yes, that is Jesus," and proceeded to turn the page again. She again turned the page back to the picture of Jesus. It was obvious that she wanted to look at that particular picture so Robert let her look as long as she wanted.

After a long time for an active two-year-old, she looked up at him and said in a reverential tone, "Grandpa, he's my brother." And she reached out to stroke the picture.

Robert was touched by the certainty and sincerity of her words. He gave her a hug and told her, "He's my brother, too."

She said, "I know, Grandpa," and then permitted him to continue to read the rest of the book to her.

Ally tried for years to bear a child. Then one night in a dream her deceased grandmother appeared holding a baby boy. That child became her long awaited son. At age three the boy revealed some remarkable information.

"It was almost eight years after my marriage and I had almost given up hope that I would ever have a baby. Then one night in a dream my grandmother, who had died a few weeks before my wedding, appeared to me. In her arms she carried a beautiful baby boy. She spoke, 'Alili (her nickname for me), don't worry, I am taking care of your little boy. I will know when to send him to you. Enjoy your life.' Then she was gone.

"Three months later I became pregnant, confident the baby was a boy.

"We did not attend church when our son was young, nor give him any religious training beyond telling him stories of Jesus and teaching him to pray. To our surprise, when he was three years old Sergito began telling us things about heaven that he could not have heard anywhere in his short life on earth.

158

"For example the first day I home schooled Sergito, we opened with a prayer and a hymn. As I began the lesson, he interrupted, 'Mom! You're just like Jesus when he taught us! We all sat in a circle and He would teach us really nice things. We wore long white dresses with a rope tied around our waists. We each had different colored ropes. And lady angels would bring us fruit, and it was a lot of fun.'

"When his little sister Alicita was born, Sergito looked at her and exclaimed, 'I remember you from heaven. We used to go every place together and play tricks on the angels.'

"An Amish friend made a white dress for Alicita after her birth. It was plain in the Amish style. To dress it up, I sewed on some ribbons from my wedding gown and made a crown of flowers from my veil for Alicita to wear. When Sergito saw her wearing it he said, 'Oh! Alicita, you look so much like you used to in heaven--a long white dress, flowers on your head and bare feet!' Looking at me he continued, 'You know, Mommy, that's the way we dress in heaven! Everyone goes barefoot, girls have flowers, and boys wear a rope around their waists.'

"He always used to say little things like that but now that he is becoming older, he no longer remembers or talks about heaven. I really miss his remarks about heaven. I learned so much from him."

Since forgetting pre-earth memories is common as children grow, it is important to record their comments as they make them. One wonders what else Sergito might have revealed if asked the right questions before his birth memories faded.

A young father shared the following:

"The other day on our way to the grocery store, my wife drove while our little daughter sat on my lap gazing out the window, speaking nonstop as usual. I have to admit I don't always pay much attention to her childish chatter. But this day I was surprised by her topic. Listening carefully, I realized she was giving warnings of the danger created by mankind's failure to care for each other or for the earth.

"Startled, I looked down at her and asked, 'Honey, where in the world did you hear that?'

"Glancing over her shoulder at me she said something like this, 'Daddy, I didn't hear that here. I was taught by my Heavenly Father before I came to be with you.'"

This child was instructed by God and two things she learned was that we are responsible for each others welfare and the earth and if we abuse either we will suffer severe consequences.

### Heavenly Relationships

Sherry Chiles shared an unusual request she received from her small daughter:

"When my daughter, Jamie was two, she loved to be sung to. On one occasion she said, 'Sing me that song that we sing in heaven.' At that time we did not attend any church and had never discussed religion or heaven with our children, so I was quite surprised by her request. I asked, 'Which song, honey?'

"She replied, 'The one that lady always sang to me, that lady in heaven.'

"I've never forgotten the warm feeling that surrounded us that day!"

In the next account, a child of two-and-a-half years reported having a very close relationship with someone in heaven named Emily. Her father, Michael DeSimone reported;

"My wife and I questioned her about her friend whenever she talked about Emily. Most of her responses were typical of a child her age. She said they played and danced and sang together, things like that. My wife and I wrote it off as a child's imaginary friend and figured it might be her way of dealing with the expected addition to our family.

" Some of Johanna's responses to our questions had become puzzling to us. She started mentioning 'the light' more frequently in relation to her friend Emily. My wife and I began to wonder where Johanna was coming up with all of this and tried to question her more deeply without putting thoughts or words into her mind. In response to our questioning our daughter told us, 'Emily and I were together before,' and 'Emily showed me the light.'

"Now as interesting as this seemed to us at the time, we still blew it off as the imaginary friend thing. Then one day while we were shopping at Wal-Mart, Johanna got very excited and tried to stand up in the shopping cart. She was pointing across the store. 'Over there, there she is, that's Emily!' My wife and I looked to see who she was pointing at. About 100 feet away was a family with four or five kids.

"My wife and I looked at each other and shrugged, 'Why not?' We walked up to the family, whom we'd never seen before, and asked, 'By any chance is one of your children named Emily?'

"Somewhat startled, they answered, 'Yes,' and pointed to their smallest child who was already deep in conversation with our little Johanna. The puzzled parents continued, 'Why do you ask?'

"We explained about Joanna's 'imaginary friend' from heaven named Emily who we were beginning to believe might not be imaginary after all. Not too surprising, Emily's parents appeared to think we were a bit strange. Meanwhile, Johanna and Emily had shut the rest of us out and were excitedly absorbed in each other. We could not help but feel our little daughter had found her friend from heaven."

It is too bad that neither set of parents made an effort to listen in on that animated conversation. It would have been fascinating to learn what these children were sharing with each other, perhaps memories and experiences of leaving heaven and arriving on earth. What is intriguing is the fact that Johanna recognized Emily as her heavenly friend and Emily evidently recognized Johanna even though they were unacquainted on earth.

In the next account, a two-year-old boy reported that his heavenly instruction for his sojourn on earth came from his deceased grandfather. His conversation with his mother, Betty Clark Ruff, came about as she contemplated the best way to tell him about the death of his great aunt.

"Alan was two years old and had learned to talk very early, so by the time of this experience he could speak clearly and express himself with a sizable vocabulary.

"Alan's great-aunt, Lida, had just passed away, and I had been concerned with how I was going to tell him about death. We had taken him to see her once or twice a week so there had to be some explanation for the termination of our visits. Mustering all my courage, I sat Alan on the kitchen stool and drew up a chair. 'Alan, honey,' I said, 'Aunt Lida has gone back to Heavenly Father.'

"But before I could say anything more, he asked, 'Who took her?'

"I stumbled around for an answer, and then I said, 'It must have been someone she knew.'

'Immediately his little face lit up as if he recognized a familiar situation. He said with a happy smile, 'Oh, I know what it's like! Grandpa Clark brought me when I came to you. He'll probably take me back when I die.'

"Alan then proceeded to describe his Grandfather Clark, my father, who had been dead nearly twelve years. Alan had never seen a picture of his grandfather. He told me how much he loved his grandfather and how good he had been to him. He indicated that my father had helped to teach him and prepare him to come to earth. He also spoke of Heavenly Father as a definite memory.

"Needless to say, this little conversation with Alan that I had been dreading turned out to be one of the sweetest experiences of my life. It left me limp with humility and joy. I no longer felt sorry that my father could not see his grandchildren. As each little soul has come along, I have felt that my father probably was better acquainted with the newcomer than I was.

"Immediately following this occasion, Alan's father talked to him and Alan repeated the same account to him. For several months he talked about these things as a happy, natural memory of real experiences. Then, suddenly, the memory was erased and he did not know what we were talking about when we tried to discuss it."[3]

This account shows how early otherworldly memories can quickly fade. But it also reveals the fact that on some occasions, deceased family members are intimately involved in preparing spirits to come to earth and in assuring that they get to earth safely.

### Selection of Parents

In the following two cases, parents' willingness to listen to what their small children were saying helped them realize that family composition is not necessarily random nor in any way capricious.

"I was concerned that my two-year-old daughter, Jennie, had many insecurities. I wondered where they had come from. Jennie refused to sleep by herself, sucked her thumb vigorously, and would go nowhere without her blanket. One night I was trying to settle her down so we could go to sleep—in my bed, of course. In attempting to wean her from her "security blanket" I had purposely left it in her room. Jennie snuggled up close to me, but would not stop whimpering for her blanket. Finally I concluded there would be no sleep without the blanket, so I relented and went to get it. When I returned, Jennie stopped crying, but continued to earnestly suck her thumb. Suddenly she popped it out and said, 'Mommy, you know what? I asked Jesus if you could be my mommy.' She then continued sucking her thumb.

"I was confounded. We are not Christians, but Jewish. Never had we spoken about Jesus or angels or of religious topics around Jennie. I had no idea where my tiny daughter could have heard such a thing. As I lay there contemplating her mystifying comments, she again removed her thumb and said, 'But I was afraid!'

"'Afraid of what, honey?' I asked.

"She snuggled closer, 'I was afraid because of that other baby. I didn't want to have to leave you like she did. I wanted to stay with you. I really wanted you to be my Mommy. I love you very much, Mommy, and I am very happy that Jesus let me come to you.'

"I was stunned. Two years earlier, I had lost a little girl in my ninth month of pregnancy. I was so devastated by her loss that I did not speak about her to anyone. There was no way Jennie could have known about that baby, but she did."

This account is informative for several reasons. The first is that a very young child remembered being with Jesus who is not a part of her family's religious traditions. Second, in premortality she had been aware of the existence of a specific mortal woman and petitioned that she be born to her. And third, she knew about the stillbirth of a previous sibling and was afraid that she might experience the same fate and have to "leave like the other baby did!"

Celestia Jasper had a fascinating conversation with her four-year-old son.

"When our second son Ivan was about eight months old I was having a difficult time with him. I couldn't seem to comfort or nourish him. I said, 'I don't think I'm the right mother for Ivan; I can't seem to do anything right for him.'

"Frank James, who was four at the time, said, 'But Mom, you are. Ivan looked down and picked you out to be his mom.'"[4]

Frank James's memories of his relationship with Ivan helped his mother to realize that her son wanted and needed her. Of all the millions of women on earth he could have been born to, Ivan had picked her specifically. This fact clearly informed her that she and her infant son had a very special bond.

Why would some children prefer particular parents? Hal, the father in the next account, discovered it was how he interacted with another of his children that made one spirit want him as her father.

"When my first son was very young, I used to play cowboy games with him. I would be at one end of our couch, he at the other. We would shoot at each other with our fingers and occasionally we would get shot and fall to the floor. The only thing that 'revived' us was chocolate milk.

"When my third daughter was about three she told me, 'Daddy, I really wanted to be your daughter because of the way you played with Danny.'

"By this time my oldest son was in his teens and cowboy games were long gone so I asked her, 'When could you have seen us playing?'

"She replied, 'I looked down from heaven and watched you.'"

A charming story but certainly not unique. It is not likely that in and of itself this would be the main reason for choosing a parent. Maybe there was a more fundamental and important reason which this child was unable express. Or perhaps this act by the father revealed much of his real character.

### Observing Life on Earth

In the previous accounts and in those that follow, unborn spirits reveal that those in heaven are definitely aware of what is happening on earth.

Ann had vivid memories of observing what was occurring in her earthly home.

"When Ann was no more than three, she would talk about the toys her sisters had played with. She would ask, 'Where's the tricycle my big sisters had when they were little? Where is Lil's doll, Cindy's playhouse, Amy's teddy bear?' She was asking about very specific toys, not general categories of toys.

"When I asked her, 'How do you know your sisters had these toys?'

"She looked up at me with her big brown eyes and said, 'Because I was watching you in heaven before I was born. Mommy, I have always been with you.'

If parents actively explored with their children their memories of heaven and their motives for coming to earth and specifically to them, one wonders what they might say. Denise did try to explore her children's memories of heaven.

My children have given me information and insights about the joys and meanings of life that I shall always remember. One of my favorites is this:

At about age two I asked each one of them where they were before they came to me.

My daughter said, "I was up there (pointing toward the ceiling) waiting in a white chair. Some of us had white chairs, some of us brown chairs."

My son reported, "I was floating above you like a whale in the sea."

Chairs and benches have been described before as existing in heaven. And most people who recall an out-of-body experience, either before or after birth, would agree that when their spirits were not in their body, they "floated."

In the next account, Ann and Paul were out riding in their car with their three-year-old son. As they passed a beautiful Mormon Temple, their son excitedly exclaimed:

"'Mommy, Daddy. That's where you were married!' He then proceeded to describe the altar at which they had made their vows and said. 'You knelt down on either side and you held hands.' He proceeded to describe in great detail the entire ceremony. When we asked him how he knew all this, he looked at us and said, 'I was there! I watched!'"

His parents were both amazed and dumfounded as they had never had any reason to explain to him where they had been married or what had been said and done on that occasion.

While in the preceding cases, children shared with their parents happy memories of what they had seen from heaven, another child revealed that some unborn spirits are also aware of the tragedies and sorrows that plagued various family members.

Andrew, who earlier in the book claimed responsibility for getting his parents together, related his memory of an event he witnessed in heaven concerning his great-grandmother. Debra, his mother tells the story.

"During dinner one evening we spoke of my grandmother and some health problems she was having. Our youngest son, Andrew, interjected, "I remember when great-grandmother was really sad."

"'What do you mean?'

"Andrew chronicled in surprising detail events in my

grandmother's life that were quite personal and unknown to me, even though I'd always been close to her. Since grandma had often confided in me in my adult years, I felt I knew her well and decided that Andrew must have been fantasizing.

"About a week later I had an opportunity to visit my grand-mother. Half jokingly, I told her the 'fantastic stories Andrew had made up.' To my dismay, she began to cry. She then confirmed that everything Andrew had uttered was true. She went on to share several incidents from her life that were so personal and painful she had never before told anyone.

"The sad events Andrew confided in his childish innocence had taken place many years before he was born. We concluded the only way Andrew could have known grandma's secret sorrows was by witnessing them from above."

### Summary Thoughts

Preschool children's memories of what they saw from heaven reveal that heaven and earth are a lot closer than most people think. Parents could learn a lot about their children, their families, and heaven if they would listen to their children tell what they remember before their memories fade as they grow up.

# Chapter Ten
## Unique Qualities Brought to Earth

Evidence presented thus far in this book suggests that our individual identity consists of far more than just genetic and environmental factors. Swiss psychiatrist, Carl Jung, proposed a third factor which he labeled the "collective unconscious," to account for his observations of "memory traces of the experience of past generations."

Could this collective unconscious include memories of our heavenly home? Given the fact that we lived for eons of time in premortality it seems logical that each of us developed specific interests and unique abilities which set us apart from each other and which we brought with us when we came to earth.

### Talents & Abilities

Previously acquired talents and abilities are evident in many ways here on earth. Mozart, for instance, was an accomplished musician and composer at an age when other children were still playing with building blocks. In addition to child prodigies such as Mozart, there are often people who seem to have special inclinations that enable them to develop talents and skills more readily than others. We usually refer to them as "gifted" people or "naturals."

Several years ago the CBS News program *60 Minutes* presented a segment dealing with a unique psychological phenomenon known as the "autistic-savant syndrome." People with this condition possess extraordinary intellectual or artistic abilities even though they are severely mentally handicapped. Often the feats performed by an autistic-savant surpass those of the most brilliant of "normal" people. Scientists are puzzled by this phenomenon and find the achievements of such individuals so remarkable that they defy belief and explanation. In the *60 Minutes* program three men with this condition were highlighted. One was an artist who produced remarkably beautiful and intricately detailed sculptures of horses; the second demonstrated complex mathematical skills and an incredible memory. The third, Leslie Lemke, was a most gifted musician with an amazing story of his own.

Leslie's story is recounted in a book written in 1981 by Shirlee Monty entitled *May's Boy: An Incredible Story of Love.*

Leslie's adoptive parents, May and Joe, had been struggling to help him develop skills that most of us take for granted such as eating with a fork, standing by himself, and walking. Leslie was eighteen years old when his mother saw his finger "plucking" a taut string around a package. Did this perhaps have a connection with music? So May and Joe bought a piano and May spent hours pushing Leslie's fingers down on the keys to show him that he could make sound. They also played music constantly although Leslie gave no indication that he was listening.

Then one night, May was awakened at three A.M. by someone playing Tchaikovsky's Piano Concerto No. 1. It was Leslie.

He had never before gotten out of bed on his own. He had never seated himself at the piano. He had never voluntarily or deliberately struck the keys with his fingers. Now he was actually playing a difficult piano concerto—and with deftness and confidence.

Why the music burst out of him on that early morning hour in late winter is unknown. But it did, like a gale. His repertoire ranges through the classics, rock, ragtime, country/western and gospel.

And he sings. Before learning to speak clearly he could readily mimic a variety of singers. He has a big, round voice and, when he pulls out all the stops, it can be heard a block away. He can do Luciano Pavarotti in two Italian operas, Jimmy Durante in "Inka Dinka Doo," Louis Armstrong in "Hello Dolly!" and both parts of the Jeanette MacDonald/Nelson Eddy duet in *Sweethearts*.[1]

A man whose fingers perform so brilliantly at a piano keyboard yet whose same fingers cannot use a knife or fork indicates that something very unusual has occurred. Where did this remarkable talent come from? Where did he learn to love and perform music so brilliantly? George Ritchie, during his extensive near-death experience, might have seen how and why at least some individuals are born with unique musical abilities. George reports being taken to a place he called the realm of intellectual, scientific, and religious knowledge where he observed individuals engaged in various activities. In one place music was the focus.

"I was taken to an area that looked to me as a musical conservatory. The beings there were playing on all the instruments I had seen and quite a few I had never seen. They were making the most beautiful music I have ever heard. Bach, Brahms, Beethoven, Toscanini, all of the great musicians must have been able, in deep meditation, to have listened into this area and brought some of the music back to our own realm."[2]

Was this heavenly training the origin of Leslie Lemke's musical talent? Joseph F. Smith hypothesized that every ability seen on earth began its development long before birth.

Being subject to [eternal] laws and having their agency, all the spirits of men, while yet in the Eternal Presence, developed aptitudes, talents, capacities, and abilities of every sort, kind and degree. During the long expanse of life which was, an infinite variety of talents and abilities came into being. As the ages rolled, no two spirits remained alike. Mozart became a musician; Einstein centered his interest in mathematics; Michelangelo turned his attention to painting. When we pass from preexistence to mortality, we bring with us the traits and talents there developed. True, we forget what went before, but the capacities and abilities that then were ours are yet resident within us.

171

Mozart is still a musician; Einstein retains his mathematical abilities; Michelangelo his artistic talent—and all men with their infinitely varied talents and personalities pick up the course of progression where they left it off when they left the heavenly realms.[3]

This idea challenges the belief that the newborn mind is equivalent to a blank slate waiting to be filled with knowledge. In fact, the newborn mind may be filled with extensive information acquired over eons of time in our heavenly home. Notice I did not reference the brain. There is evidence that the mind can function independently of the brain, both before and after birth and during a near-death experience when the brain is temporarily "dead." It appears that it takes time and practice on earth for the brain to become a vehicle of physical consciousness and knowledge. Prior to this time, knowledge is spiritual and independent of a physical brain, what is often called the mind.

While in heaven during a near-death experience, Mosiah Hancock was permitted to see spirits being instructed and prepared for their earth lives. He observed that some spirits more readily grasped certain skills and fields of knowledge than others:

"The spirits I observed were clothed in robes of a light color, tied in front. They were being instructed in everything that could be imagined, the finest oratory and everything of literary turn, including astronomy, trigonometry, surveying, and the use of the most delicate machinery.

"Oh, the music of those spheres; I am totally inadequate to touch upon the least of those accomplishments of the Heavenly Characters. Yet they were so orderly and harmonious that it seemed as if one could hear a pin drop. I saw some who became more efficient in science or other knowledge and they were advanced from class to class."[4]

Joseph F. Smith in reflecting on the reason why some people seem to have unique abilities concluded:

"The spirits of men were created with different dispositions and likes and talents. Some evidently were mechanically inclined. From them have come our inventors. Some loved music and hence have become great musicians. We evidently brought to this world some if not all of the inclinations and talents that we had there. The fact that one person finds one bent like mathematics easy and another finds it difficult, may, in my judgment, be traced to the spirit existence. So with other talents and skills."[5]

### Character Traits

Not only do people bring talents and skills when they come to earth, but each also brings unique personality and character traits.

A young woman was busily scrubbing the kitchen floor on her hands and knees when she sensed she was being watched. Brushing a strand of hair from her face, she looked up to see two small boys smiling at her. She noticed that the smaller of the two stood behind the other boy.

She smiled at them knowing intuitively that they had come to express their desire to be born into her family. She agreed immediately. Then, concerned that the smaller boy who hung back needed extra encouragement, she looked straight into his eyes and said, "It's okay, you can come, too!"

She did have two more sons, and they were the two children she saw that day. The second son came eighteen months after the first and is quiet, reserved, and shy just as his spirit self had appeared to be.

In the early 1900s, Albert R. Lyman, a rancher, settler, and cattleman, was shown in a dream aspects of his unborn son's personality, both symbolically and directly.

"I had a dream, and in that dream I was reading a book that had on its front cover an artistic design of a wreath of sharp thorns, two inches long.

"While I read, very much absorbed with the story, a little boy played around me on the floor. Even though I had no son, I was not surprised at his being there. I was more interested in the book than him. Somehow as I read, the sharp thorns on the cover got caught in the pages making them difficult to turn. I couldn't see how they caught, but they did, and it annoyed me. And then one of them caught in the left shoulder of the little boy. That drew my attention to him, and I noticed that he was stooped and thin as if he had been sick. In looking for the thorn in his flesh, I found an ugly black hair, or bristle, growing out of his left shoulder. It was a mean thing as thick as a knitting needle, and it seemed to exude a black, sticky tar. When I tried to remove it, it was thickly imbedded in his flesh and he expressed extreme pain whenever it was touched, so I let it alone. While I studied it, much perplexed, I awoke.

"What could it mean? The mystery thickened as the months passed. We were at that time expecting another baby, which turned out to be a boy. He seemed to be perfect physically, yet on his left shoulder was a brown birth-mark the size of my fingernail. I tried to think that it had no significance, but later when he contracted some lingering disorder and became thin and stooped, he was without doubt the boy I had seen with the bristle in his shoulder. Then I took the dream to be a warning to me. He was a choice spirit but there was something about him that I would have to be very watchful of. I gave him the name of my father, and watched him with great care as he merged into boyhood, taking him with me whenever possible, hoping to keep him free from every dangerous agency.

"As time transpired, the meaning of the dream became apparent. Platte, as he was named, was a strong-willed, rebellious, independent child, who was drawn to activities that alienated him from his parents and family. This thorn, which I had seen embedded in my son's shoulder, dominated his life for over twenty years, until the death of a brother, brother-in-law, and nephew so jarred him that he completely reversed his wild life. Platte became a loving doting father, an active member of his church, and a stalwart in his community. But this did not occur naturally and took considerable effort."[6]

Platte was a rebellious, free spirited individual from the day he was born in spite of the best efforts and good example of a caring parent who had been warned of his problems. It took the deaths of several relatives before Platte reevaluated his life and began living up to his potential.

### Names

Thus far the data reviewed indicates that unique qualities pertaining to our talents, abilities and personalities were brought with us from premortality. Another thing that many individuals reported bringing with them is their name.

Throughout time and across many cultures names are a manifestation of status, rank, and position. Many Native American and African tribes give names to their children that relate to an incident or sign associated with their birth or childhood such as "Running Bear." Further names may be added in response to later incidents in their lives as related in the Academy Awarded film, *Dances With Wolves*, the name given the character who befriended a wolf. In the Bible, names were given to children that related to their current or prophetic missions.

The assignment of a name impacts the individual for the rest of his/her life. While parents might agonize as to what name they should give their child, some are told what their child's name is. The name of the child may come as a pronouncement from heaven, or a growing awareness that a specific name is the correct one. In the case of pronouncements, two of the best known are those of John and Jesus in the New Testament. John's name was assigned by an angel:

... the angel said unto him, Fear not, Zacharias: for thy prayer is heard; and thy wife Elisabeth shall bear thee a son, and thou shalt call his name John. . . For he shall be great in the sight of the Lord . . .[7]

John became famous as John the Baptist. Why his name had to be John was not stated, but Zacharias was told that John was to be his name and who was he to contradict the will of heaven? In the case of Jesus, his name was given to his mother, Mary:

... And the angel said unto her, Fear not, Mary: for thou hast found favour with God. And, behold, thou shalt conceive in thy womb, and bring forth a son, and shalt call his name JESUS. He shall be great, and shall be called the Son of the Highest.[8]

Part of a person's identity is his or her name, and this seems also to be true for at least some premortal beings. Unborn children have been known to inform their parents that they have names by which they wish to be called during their life on earth. In some cases the preferred name is implanted in the subconscious of one of the parents-to-be. In other cases, unborn spirits have appeared to one or other of their parents and announced their names. In still other situations, the name of the unborn child was revealed by heavenly beings such as they were for John and Jesus. Following are examples of parents being informed of the correct/preferred name of their expected child.

In the first example, a first-time mother searches for the perfect name for her unborn daughter.

"I was really concerned about choosing the right name for my baby, and I thought to myself, 'Well, I'll have to go through baby books.' I was sitting on the edge of my bed and all of a sudden I was transported in my mind to a little room, and I was sitting on this stool at a big table like a ledger table. There was this huge book, about two feet by two feet, and it had a jeweled front cover. I was turning these huge pages and it had every name that was ever given to anybody—the name and the definition of the name and all the people who had the name.

"And I was going through the big book and I thought, *Boy, this is going to take me forever!* In walked a young girl about twelve years old, with brown hair that was kind of wavy. She stood very stately and said, 'My name is Cara June.' And so I said 'OK' and closed the book, because that was all I needed to hear. And then I was back in my room at the edge of my bed. I felt very elated and tingly for about three hours after that. When my daughter was born, I knew that it was the same child whom I had seen coming into the room. So I named her Cara June."[9]

A young couple was searching for the perfect name for their son. They had narrowed their list down to three names but when it came time to name their son they knew that none of the names they had considered was the right one.

"When I discovered that I was going to have a baby boy, my husband Mark and I started searching for just the right name for him. I didn't want a trendy name but a name that would fit a mature professional man because I had great expectations for our new baby. We purchased several books with children's names and poured over them. We narrowed the choice of names to Benjamin, Jonathan, and Christopher with me leaning toward Christopher. But when he was born, I looked at him and knew that he was Gregory. Gregory is not a family name, I did not know anyone by that name, and I did not particularly like the name. But I knew it was his name. The name came right out of the blue when our eyes first met. It was almost as if he were introducing himself to me. I heard no voice; I just knew that Gregory was his name."

Margie had decided on a name for her first daughter long before she even met her husband. She did not have to persuade him to name their first daughter Heather as he also loved the name. In fact their daughter's full name was to be Heather Ann, Ann being the given name of her husband's mother. But that was not what the baby was ultimately named and Margie explains why.

"Ever since I was a little girl I dreamed about having a daughter named Heather. There was no question whatsoever that this little baby I was carrying would be that girl. There was no need for long searches, no debate. Her name was Heather.

"But two months before she was born, I got the very distinct feeling that the baby I was carrying was named Natalie. I had known a very stuck-up girl in college named Natalie and detested the name. I tried to reject the name Natalie, but could not get it out of my mind. The closer her birth date came, the stronger the impression became that Natalie was my baby's name. And when she was born, I knew that I held Natalie in my arms."

Tammy was having trouble deciding on a name for her forthcoming son until he intervened.

"When I was pregnant with my third son, we had trouble deciding on names. I'd been through the name book, reading out loud the ones I liked, but couldn't find one that my husband liked. He said, 'Get another book!' as the one we had was a small pocket version.

"I didn't get around to buying another book, as I was only about four months pregnant at the time, so we weren't in a hurry.

"A few weeks after this, though, I noticed that any time I was sitting quietly, the name Nicholas popped into my head. I'd never been particularly partial to the name, nor had I any particular dislike of it. After this happened several times, I figured that the baby was trying to tell me the name he wanted! (And, therefore, I also knew that he was a boy.) I told my husband, and he mentioned that he'd been getting the name Stephen.

"In the end, we decided not to argue about which name would be first, and let our oldest son decide which way the two names would go. So we ended up with Nicholas Steven, and when asked, I tell people he picked his own name!

As do many mothers, Candice "talked" frequently to the child she was carrying:

"Throughout my pregnancy Dannika and I talked. We would try out names, none of which she cared for until two weeks before her birth. I had discovered an ancient Celtic word meaning Morning Star. Suddenly I couldn't remember any of the names I had been considering. Dannika was to be her name and she was born in the early morning, a true morning star."[10]

Why the unborn find it necessary to have a specific name is not clear. But it must be important because some unborn children have actually appeared to their parents-to-be and announced their names. This was so for Myrtle's unborn daughter who appeared to her in a dream and literally spelled out her name.

"She appeared to be about six years of age, had long blond hair, and was wearing a white dress. Looking into my eyes she said, 'My name is Marisa,' and proceeded to spell it out, 'M-A-R-I-S-A.' Then she said, 'I'll be seeing you soon.' Her joyous smile radiated total love. When I woke up the next morning, I could still feel her presence in the room."

Isabelle Kessler's unborn son also spelled out his name. He spoke to his mother when she was only one month pregnant.

"I was sitting in a sun filled room blissfully contemplating the child within me. I was wondering what name I would choose and whether it would be a boy or girl when I heard a powerful voice within me say, 'My name is A-B-R-A-H-A-M,' spelling it out to me.

"My first reaction was to look skyward and think, 'Oh, my . . . I've gone crazy.' Then I realized that this wasn't the case, that this was a communication with my child and that it was good."[11]

Another unborn child appeared to his mother-to-be and announced her name. When her mother repeated the name she thought her unborn child had said, her unborn daughter quickly corrected her and then spelled it out so that there would be no chance of a mistake.

While most such announcements seem to come to the mother, fathers have also been told the baby's name.

"All my children clearly informed their father what their names were. We were driving home one evening, several months before I even got pregnant, when my husband turned to me and said, 'We are going to have a son and his name is Shawn Thomas.'

"I looked at him and said, 'What did you say?'

"He repeated, 'We are going to have a son, and his name is Shawn Thomas!'

"I asked, 'Why Shawn Thomas? Is that the name of someone you know?'

"He said, 'No, that is the name he wants!'

"'Who he?' I asked?

"'The baby. He clearly informed me that he is on his way and that Shawn Thomas is his name.'

"What could I say? When our other children were born, I had to have a C-section and was out of it, so our doctor always handed our babies to my husband. My husband would look into their eyes and their spirits would announce their names. We always had other names picked out but gave them the names they wanted."

A mother had a very unusual experience with her little daughter. One day as they were sitting at the kitchen table her daughter said the following:

"'I know that you really wanted to name me Tiffany, so I let you call me Tiffany. It is not my real name but I can accept it while I am here.' She never did reveal her 'real' name."

It appears that the unborn have names whereby they are known in heaven and at least some of them want to be known by these names on earth. But, as in the case of Tiffany, some children are willing to be known by other names if the hearts of their parents are strongly set on it or if their parents aren't in tune with their children's desires.

Parents frequently go through a book of names and pick out several they like. Others have family names that they select for their forthcoming baby. But when the time comes to name the baby, sometimes the baby vetoes their choice.

When my son Benjamin was born, we had another name picked out. But then he spoke to my mind saying, "No, that is not my name. My name is Benjamin." So Benjamin he became.

All of our children came with their own preferred names and only one was reticent about informing us of this fact.

Ann Wasserman's family had a long tradition of naming their children after deceased family members. Struggling with large numbers of potential choices, their daughter whispered part of her name independently to her and her husband. Her husband recalls:

"I was driving in that semi-dazed state one often gets into when driving in the city. I was thinking about what to name the baby, trying to think of 'K' names, and I suddenly heard, inside my head, 'Katrina.' I smiled and thought, 'I like that.'"

Ann continues:

"We picked 'M' for the middle initial, honoring three of our four grandparents. A few weeks after we settled on Katrina, I heard 'Margaret' in much the same way, while sitting quietly at the table after dinner. It's never been a name that I've liked, so I knew it wasn't my idea. But Katrina Margaret was just right."

As Leigh searched for the perfect name for her second baby, she got stuck. She had narrowed the list to two names but she couldn't make up her mind as to which was the best. She knew that her baby was to be a girl and asked her unborn child which name she preferred:

"I believe that the correct name is very important for a child so I decided to ask her what her name should be and she told me Iris. Iris is not one of the names either my husband or myself had on our lists. It had not even occurred to either of us as a possibility. I looked up its meaning in a book and discovered that it was the perfect name. It means rainbow."[12]

The woman in the next case was told by a voice that she was pregnant and the name of her son-to-be. She shared this experience with her best friend, Kjirstin Youngberg.

"I was in the parking lot, getting into the car after I put in the groceries, and a voice in my mind said, 'It's a boy. His name is Joseph.'

"Kjirstin asked her if the voice had said, 'And thou shall call his name Joseph.'

"'No,' I laughed. 'Nothing flowery like that. Just—it's a boy. His name is Joseph. The funny thing is, I wasn't even thinking about it at the time. It just popped in there.'"

"'Well,' Kjirstin said. 'I think you'd better name him Joseph.'

"'But we want a girl, and we really do not like the name Joseph because it usually gets shortened to Joe or Joey.'

"A few months later, my husband called Kjirstin with the good news. 'It's a boy!' he exclaimed. 'We decided to call him Joseph.'

"'Wise choice,' Kjirstin answered."[13]

Wendy also discovered the sex of her unborn child and what his name should be.

"I had a very vivid dream during which I found myself holding on my lap a little boy to whom I was explaining that 'the trees with the red leaves are maples,' and in the dream he was a sweet, happy child with the name 'Bridger.'"

"I told my husband about my dream and he said he liked the name Bridger, which neither of us had heard anywhere before. He said, 'If we ever have a baby boy, we'll name him Bridger.'

"Two weeks later I found out I was pregnant. Bridger was born two years ago and looks very much like the child in my dreams—same eyes and shape of face who asks about the trees as we drive by them."[14]

On occasion a husband and a wife will share a dream. A couple, not knowing the sex of their expected baby had been looking at a lot of names for both sexes. Then one night their problem was solved.

"One morning when we woke up we discovered that we had both had a dream in which we had a daughter named Sef. We figured that this was no coincidence and that was what her name should be, and that's all there was to it. Being curious I looked up its meaning. In Egyptian [it means] all things that ever were and ever will be."[15]

When twins are expected how can one make sure that the correct name is assigned to each child? Kjirstin Youngberg reported how she was informed who was who and their correct names.

"I heard a voice saying, 'You shall call the first son Matthew, and the second is named Benjamin. If they are taken by emergency Cesarean, Benjamin will be the first born.'"

She mentioned this experience to her physician and he said, "That's right. Due to their positioning, Twin 'B' will be the first out if it's an emergency Cesarean, but in a natural birth or a planned Cesarean, we'll cut lower and Twin 'A' will be the first. To assure that the correct name would be assigned each twin, specific instructions are given to the prospective mother."[16]

In the next case, Fay and Jan were clearly told their names by their unborn babies.

"Fay was a very athletic woman who often ran in marathons. Early in 1981 she began to feel the presence of a spirit hovering around her. Thinking this might be a sign that she was pregnant, she went to her doctor. As he came into her examination room he said, 'Well Fay, what can I do for you?'

"I said, 'Doctor, I think I may be pregnant.'

"He inquired, 'Is that a problem?'

"I told him that I was preparing for a marathon race and was concerned that if I were pregnant, all my running might hurt my baby and this I did not want to do. I needed to know how much running would be safe if I was in fact pregnant. He said, 'Well, let's check you out.' He gave me a test, and left the room. A few minutes later he came back in and announced, 'You're not pregnant so there is no need to cut back on your running.' So I didn't.

"At the time, I had a good friend named Jan, and we shared

everything that was happening in our lives. As we were talking one day I told her about my sensing the presence of a spirit around me. I also mentioned that the only other time I had felt this way was when I was pregnant with my first child. She grasped my arm and said, 'That's interesting, very interesting. I also feel the presence of a male and he has informed me that his name is Matthew.'

"I was surprised but delighted as I did not know that other people also had this experience with their unborn children. I told her that I knew that the spirit hovering so close to me was also a boy and that his name was Benjamin but that my doctor had told me that I was not pregnant and that puzzled me. I asked her what she thought.

"My friend Jan sat thinking and then said, 'Either your doctor is right, or you have a son named Benjamin who wants you to know that he is coming to you soon.'

"We found it fascinating that we both sensed the presence of male spirits and even knew their names. But she was pregnant and I was not."

Because Fay's experience with her unborn son is so interesting and inspirational, the rest of the story has been included here.

"I entered a 10 K race and continued running many miles in preparation. As I ran I wondered if Jan might be right that the doctors could be wrong. On the day of the race even though I was in very good physical condition I collapsed halfway through the race. I was rushed to the hospital where they ran a series of diagnostic tests all of which came back negative. I then asked them to do a pregnancy test. They did and discovered I was two-and-a-half months along. I was not surprised. As soon as I was released from the hospital, I called Jan and told her the news. She said, 'See! Doctors are not always correct. You must trust your instincts and feelings.' During our pregnancies we chatted a lot, comparing notes and were surprised at how similar our experiences were. We even delivered about a week apart."

Fay's experience with her unborn son Benjamin is only part of her story. He appeared to her later on during her pregnancy and helped sustain her when she was faced with almost insurmountable problems.

"Early in my pregnancy my husband left me so I ended up a single expectant mother with a three-year-old daughter and meager financial resources. About eight-and-a half months into my pregnancy I went to a family reunion. I returned home to find that my husband had been there and had taken all of my food, most of my possessions, and had trashed the house. I was devastated. No food! No money! How was I going to survive? I managed to clean up my house enough so my little daughter could go to bed. I was fatigued, extremely upset, and totally depressed. I went out to the back yard where I would not disturb my daughter, threw myself on the lawn, and sobbed uncontrollably.

"It was at this darkest hour of my life that my unborn son came to me. He comforted me, promising me that everything would be okay including my financial affairs. He also told me that all my questions and concerns would be answered and opportunities would open up as I needed them. I was comforted by his assurance and love, but I was still troubled. I told him that I was very concerned about my three-year-old daughter. Because of the turmoil in my marriage she would not sleep at night and fussed a lot. My concern about her and her well being was having a major impact on me. How would I be able to care for her and a newborn and work? My son assured me that he would be a very easy baby to care for. He also showed me in three dimensional snippets what would take place in my life as he grew older. During his entire visit, I could feel his concern and great love for me.

"When I arose from the lawn, I was totally changed. I knew that the food, support, and help would be there when I needed it. But more importantly, I knew that divine beings were actively watching over my daughter and me. This experience with my unborn son gave me strength and hope. I knew I was not alone. I knew that there was a divine presence who I could call on when I needed help. But what really helped me survive was being shown that there was a reason for all the problems I had been experiencing. Though I cannot now recall what the reason is, I know that there is one and that I will grow from it.

"Occasionally as my pregnancy progressed, Benjamin would come to me. During these very brief visits I could see how delighted and excited he was to be coming to earth as my son.

"I was approached by a number of people who offered to help me by adopting Benjamin. But my experience with him, witnessing his excitement at being born to me, and feeling his great love for me made that impossible. Our future was to be together and everything has occurred just as he promised."

In the final account Mosiah Hancock learned how names, at least how some names, were assigned in premortality.

"Oh, such a glorious realm. I saw He whom at that time we reverently spoke of as The Great Eternal. I saw the females at his right side. I have no idea of their number. I saw the Savior; and calling me by name, He said, "Mosiah, I have brought you here that you may know how it was before you went to yonder earth." Thinks I, 'What earth?' For it seemed to me that I had no knowledge of an earth.

"He said, 'As it is written in the beginning, God created man, male and female, created he them.'

"And I witnessed them coming before the throne of the Great Eternal and the mothers named the females."[17]

### Summary Thoughts

Any parent who has more than one child knows only too well that each child is unique. One child might be very sensitive to the feelings of others, another caught up in the love of books, and still another, a natural athlete. Each has a unique personality and abilities and interests that often transcend their family's influence and social environment. Knowing that we existed for eons of time prior to our earthly birth helps to account for some of these seemingly inbred qualities.

Along with these innate qualities and abilities, many spirits come with preferred names—a name that has intrinsic meaning to the spirit. While many parents believe it was they who chose their child's name, others acknowledge that the name came to them out of the blue.

When we came to this earth we came with unique personalities and with distinct talents and abilities. How we develop these abilities and talents is up to us and it seems likely that what we do with them also accompanies us into the next life.

*Chapter Eleven*

*Why Adversity?*

The Old Testament tells the story of Job who was a wealthy happy man until he started experiencing extreme adversity. His house caved in killing his wife and children. He lost his vast flocks and his wealth. And, as if that were not enough, he was afflicted with painful boils over his entire body. After watching Job suffer for a week, his friends suggested that he must have done something to offend God. The truth, of course, was that he had done nothing of the kind.

Things haven't changed much over the centuries. When pain, sorrow, and problems occur in life, we are still apt to view them as punishments for something we did or failed to do and, as in the case of Job, this is not necessarily so. As much as we feel the pain and anguish of adversity, those who have visited the heavenly realm discovered that adversity is not punishment and that it has a definite purpose. They discovered that before we came to earth, we were well aware of the challenges we would experience on earth and looked forward to them. At that point in our existence we could see the long term implications of adversity. We understood that adversity would provide opportunities to grow, help us develop spiritual qualities, and teach us to empathize with the plight of others. Everyone will inevitably experience adversity in one form or another. The important thing is how we respond to it. Handling adversity well will prepare us for life in heaven and, hopefully, qualify us to return to and live in the presence of God.

The individuals whose sufferings are reported in this chapter were shown during their near-death experiences why they were having such serious problems. They were surprised to learn that instead of their adversities being inflicted upon them by an unfeeling vindictive God or even by pure chance, they had personally selected their trials. They had not chosen them because of a masochistic desire for self punishment, but for what they could learn from them. They discovered that they had been instrumental in designing the type of life they would experience on earth. As you will read, some changed their self-perceptions from that of helpless victims subject to the whims of fate, to knowing that they, and these experiences, had meaning and purpose. They now looked for what they should be learning from their adversities/challenges and how these experiences could prepare them to help others.

Elane Durham had had a very difficult life and suffered much physical and emotional abuse. One evening she suffered a series of seizures and her spirit left her body. For a few moments she watched people working on her body, then she was transported to a place of intense activity and beauty. For a time she reveled in the beauty of her surroundings. Then thoughts of what she had endured on earth entered her mind. She inquired of her angelic escorts what she had done or failed to do to experience such a terrible life.

In response to this question Elane was taken to a place and told to look into what appeared to her to be a large translucent stone. In it she saw herself in premortality preparing to come to earth. Elane was surprised to see that the abusive childhood she experienced was one she had personally selected prior to her birth. She discovered that she had not been a pawn on the chess board of life but a key player in determining the type of life she would experience including all her challenges and what she had considered adversity. She actually witnessed herself as she selected the life she would live.

"After I had selected the challenges I would experience on earth I entered into a waiting area, and it was here that I and my angelic escort went over the choices I had made. I understood very clearly the implications of each choice and I also knew that I had chosen what those on earth would consider to be a very hard life. I knew that to achieve the wisdom, empathy, and growth I needed, these challenges were necessary. Don't get me wrong. When I saw that I had chosen a life of adversity, this did not mean that those I met on earth were predestined to abuse me, but I knew that I would be placed in an environment where abuse was likely to occur. I was excited for the opportunity to experience life to its fullest. I wanted to experience it all. I could see how various experiences on earth could help me to grow and I wanted them. So I selected many opportunities. (On earth they would be defined as challenges or adversity.)

"As I reviewed various events in my life, my angelic hosts asked, 'Are you sure you want to go through this?'

"And I replied, 'Yes! Yes! I am sure.' You see, at that time my perspective was eternal. I knew that time on earth is very short and would be quickly over. It's sort of like going to college. ('Yes I know I have a difficult course load, but it's only for a semester, sixteen weeks, and then it's over.') I needed the experience these 'classes' would provide to prepare me for the rest of my eternal existence. When the review concluded I was asked if I had any questions and I said, 'No!' I was ready and eager to go to earth.

"When I stood up I found myself surrounded by bright light. My angelic escorts informed me, 'This light is for your protection. As long as you live your life righteously and live what you have been taught, you will be protected.'

"Then this scene withdrew and I found myself back on earth in severe pain. Recovery was not easy, but memories of this experience in heaven and my heavenly escort sustained me. My perspective of myself and my parents was totally changed. They will eventually have to account for what they did to me, but I now knew that I was not a helpless victim. I was the architect of my life and everything I experienced would help me to grow spiritually. I now know that whatever happens is for my ultimate good and, rather than feeling sorry for myself, I must search for what I can learn from these experiences and how they can contribute to my spiritual growth.

"With this change in perspective came a significant change in my life. I ceased feeling as if I was a victim and became involved in activities to help improve the lives of children, to reach out to the terminally ill, to try and help those experiencing severe emotional and physical pain. I am now able to understand the problems facing those in pain because I have experienced pain. And I can help those who are dying because I have died. I am in a unique position to assure them that death is not the end but a door back to our real home and a glorious reunion with God and our loved ones. At times I am almost envious of my dying friends and patients because I know where they are going."

Elane's experience is typical of many who have had a near-death experience. In addition to the beauty and grandeur of their heavenly environment and the glorious reunion with departed loved ones, they learn that adversity is like a refiner's fire which tests their mettle and purifies them. The empathy, understanding, and abilities they acquire help prepare them for eternity. They stop feeling like helpless, worthless, and meaningless victims of forces beyond their control. They know that God is in control and that everything they go through while on earth has some part to play in the eternal scheme of things. Elane has recorded her experience and the impact of it on her life and the lives of others in a book entitled, *I Stand All Amazed*.[1]

Roy Mills also discovered that he had an active role in choosing the type of life he would experience on earth. Roy found himself in heaven witnessing himself preparing to come to earth as Elane had.

"In heaven we all work on developing unique spiritual gifts. I had received mine and when I compared mine with those my companions had received, I felt a bit disappointed. I asked my angelic escort if I could trade some of my spiritual gifts for others. She looked a bit surprised and said I would have to go before the Heavenly Council to get something as special as spiritual gifts changed. She did not think that such a request would be honored, but I insisted and she hesitantly agreed to take me to the Council.

"She led me to a very large room where there was a tall, bar-like bench, behind which were seated thirteen beings of light. It reminded me a little of what I had seen of the Supreme Court on TV. Many people were there who were returning from earth and appearing before the council in what appeared to me to be a review of their earthly lives. The people were waiting in long lines and as far as I could see, the room appeared to be full. On one side of the room, some beings appeared to me to be very agitated. They were doing everything they could to get out of the lines before they reached the bench. But these people were unable to avoid going before the council. It was as if they were stuck there, as if a giant magnet kept pulling them back in line. It was clear these people were in great turmoil.

"By contrast, people in other parts of the room were calmly standing in line, smiling and looking happy to be there. As far as I could tell, there were many more happy people than those in turmoil. Everyone who went before the council manifested great emotion, either positive or negative. This experience, the review of your life, is a major event. It is where individuals stand before the Heavenly Council and are evaluated as to how well they have completed their earthly mission.

"After reviewing their earth life with the beings of light, it appeared to me that everyone was happy as they withdrew from the bench, even the people who had been fearful and had tried to escape. And all of the people were now glowing with a degree of light. Some were noticeably brighter than others, but all appeared to have achieved some heavenly light reflecting the degree to which they had successfully completed their earthly mission. It was as if the fearful ones had been rewarded better than they expected. This outcome of going before the council reminded me of a saying I once heard that went something like this, 'God cannot condone unrepented evil in any of His children. But he loves us unconditionally as individuals.' So I believe that in the final judgment, He would be perfectly just by assigning the least punishment and the greatest possible rewards earned by each of His children during life.

"When I and my heavenly escort arrived at the council room it was crowded and I was concerned that they would not have the time to speak to me. I implored my angelic escort to help me speak with one of them. She instructed me to wait while she approached the bench. She caught the attention of the nearest council member and explained my concerns, and he had her bring me to him. When I arrived in front of the bench, the council angel leaned over and peered at me with a look of absolute love.

"I knew that this angelic being knew everything about me, both my past and future including my earth mission. He knew what I was going to ask before I asked it. Nevertheless, I expressed my desires concerning my spiritual gifts. The council angel gently chided me for jealousy and doubt, explaining that heavenly gifts are developed and assigned with great care to help each soul fill his or her earthly mission. I was no exception.

"The council angel emphasized that my particular gifts were necessary if I was to complete my mission. After I was born, a key to my success on earth would be to learn how to use my gifts to help others. The council angel promised to speak with me again when I returned from my life on earth, and I knew without doubt at that moment that my gifts were a perfect match for me. He smiled again and returned to his work. As we departed the council room, my mind was at peace. I accepted my spiritual gifts and was excited about learning how to use them in behalf of my fellow beings on earth.

"I also learned while there, that we are actively involved in selecting the types and extent of the trials and adversity we will experience during our earth lives. As we are taught about the purpose of earth life, we are encouraged to begin thinking about the types of trials and tests that will best contribute to our personal growth and best help our fellow beings. In my enthusiasm to accomplish as much good as possible on earth, I had chosen five major tests I would experience while in mortality. When I made the selection I noticed that my angelic escort's face had an expression of concern. A bit later she took me aside and explained that the choices I had selected had been reviewed by the heavenly council and they had concluded that the five major trials I had selected were too great. If I was permitted to experience all of them I would not succeed in my earth mission. My desires were admirable but I was lovingly counseled to be more realistic and select only three of the five tests. I reluctantly did as I was advised."[2]

Both Roy and Elane experienced very hard lives on earth and often wondered why. They were both surprised to learn that they themselves had selected the trials they underwent, and that these trials were a blessing in the eternal scheme of things.

While abuse, heartbreak, and adversity may be tools to help develop spiritual maturity, it does not excuse in any way those who cause the hurt and abuse. The perpetrators will eventually have to stand before the judgment seat of God and answer for their actions. But out of the most appalling of situations greatness can and does occur. This is clearly demonstrated in the next two accounts.

Both Angie Fenimore and CamBria Joi Henderson had been born into very abusive families. They had been conditioned to believe that they were bad, worthless, and deserving of the abuse they received. Both of their lives deteriorated to such a degree that they felt their only escape was to kill themselves. Angie committed suicide and CamBria seriously contemplated doing so.

In Angie's case, she had received so much abuse as a child that her self-image was extremely poor and her self-confidence non-existent. She was absolutely convinced that she was a worthless bit of human trash and that she deserved whatever abuse she received. Things got so bad that she concluded she and the world would be better off if she ended her life. So she tried to kill herself. Then her spiritual eyes were opened and she found herself in the presence of a powerful being of light. She knew that he was her Savior and found herself flooded with His love and the excruciating pain he had borne for her.

"Once my spiritual eyes were opened I saw exactly what it was that He had done for me, how much he had sacrificed for me. He showed me that He had taken me unto Himself, subsumed my life in His, embracing my experiences, my sufferings, as His own. And for a second I was within His body, able to see things from His point of view and to experience His self-awareness. He let me in so I could see for myself how He had taken on my burdens, and how much love he bore me.

"As I watched from my Savior's perspective, I could see that the suffering I experienced in my mortal life was temporary, and that it was actually for my good. I discovered that my suffering on earth was not meaningless or futile. Out of the most tragic of circumstances springs human growth."[3]

Angie's experience testifies that all of us are children of God with great worth. In her case her experience changed her perspective of herself totally. She knew she was loved of God, and that her suicide attempt in essence rejected the suffering and sacrifice He had experienced for her. When she came back she ceased being a victim and assumed control of her life. She appears before many groups testifying to them that God lives and loves us unconditionally, that all of us have important missions to perform, and that suicide is a repudiation of the life and death of Christ.

In CamBria's case, she also experienced severe physical and emotional abuse in her life. She had been raised in a home where abuse was prevalent and love, affection, and God were not. She had been taught early in life that "God" was a myth, a fairytale like Santa Claus or the Easter Bunny.

"No God had ever intervened on my behalf from the violence of an angry parent, nor from their incestuous lusting. No God had ever filled my hungry tummy, nor put his arms around me when I hurt. No God had ever heard my anguished cries at night. All I received was a mocking silence from the heavens. There was no God. Only a fool would believe in such nonsense.

"At age nineteen, life was rough and ugly. My world was crumbling around me. Whether it was work, school, home, health or my social life, everything seemed to be falling apart. No matter what I did, there was no cure for the anger, depression, and emptiness I felt. No matter where I went, ugliness followed. Nothing satisfied. The pain and the ugliness seemed to invade and envelop every facet of my being, growing, gnawing away, and destroying like a cancer.

"When I heard that a friend had taken his life, I suddenly felt I had a viable solution. Suicide. It was so simple. The pain and the ugliness would be silenced forever. I had no God. I had no meaning, no purpose, only hate and anger. The finality of death would be a welcome relief.

"One cold February morning, I boarded a bus heading north. I told no one of my plans. I left no note. I simply disappeared. I took nothing with me, no money, no identification, no second thoughts. My plan was to get as far away from my home as possible, then take my life. The next morning the bus stopped in Ellensburg, Washington at a college campus.

"It was the weekend. Except for an occasional student, bundled against the cold, there didn't seem to be much activity on the campus. Though it was icy cold, I was dressed only in a pair of jeans and a summer jacket. I had no protection against the elements and I didn't want any. I only wanted the pain to go away.

"The campus seemed to be its own small oasis. I could see miles of open, snowpacked land all around it. I began heading across the campus towards an uninhabited area where I would walk until I could walk no more. A brutal death, yet not nearly so brutal as life had been.

"Part way across the campus, I noticed how perfect the sky was. It was a beautiful cloudless blue with an occasional bird. Suddenly, from almost directly overhead, there was an awful crash of thunder and lightening. Immediately, rain poured and I was drenched! Where all this rain came from, and at that very moment, I do not know. I ran into the nearest building, literally dripping wet. My tennis shoes sloshed on the polished marble floor and I left a trail of water and mud behind me.

Someone was coming down the hallway toward me. I could hear the rhythmic tap of high heels. Not wanting to be seen, I ducked into the nearest doorway, only to discover the room was packed with people, listening intently to a teacher. Both they and I were a bit startled by my sudden appearance in the room.

The instructor indicated that it was all right and to have a seat. He even pulled a chair out, front and center, and invited me to 'sit down and dry off for a bit.' It was quite obvious from my bedraggled appearance that I had been caught in the rain. I was mortified but couldn't figure how to withdraw tactfully, so I sat down, totally embarrassed.

"I looked around the room, trying to gather clues as to who this group was, and what they were discussing. Then I saw the title of the subject being discussed written on the board. It was, 'How to

Pray and Stay Awake.' The expression on my face must have spoken loud and clear because the instructor stopped speaking and addressed me personally, 'Do you pray?'

"In angry mockery, I asked, 'To whom? God? That's stupid! Your God is a myth!' I could see that he, and the others, was taken aback by my hostility. I hadn't meant to spew my anger, but 'God' was a senseless joke, especially in light of my impending suicide. The instructor was silent for a very long, uncomfortable minute. When he spoke, it was with a gentleness and sensitivity I hadn't expected.

"'Would you close your eyes for a minute and do an exercise with me?' How could I say no? 'I want you to think about something you did yesterday and briefly tell the class about it.' I did. 'Now, I want you to think back to a year ago, and briefly share something that happened then.' Again I did as he asked. 'Now, I want you to think about something that happened in your early teens. And now something from your childhood. Now, I want you to find your earliest memory. Briefly share that with us.' I did as I was asked.

"Then he said, 'Now, I want to take you back to a time before your birth. Tell me what do you see?' As he spoke, a vision, like a remembrance, opened up to me. I was in awe not only by the clarity of the memory, but by the memory itself. Where did it come from? I had no belief in an existence before birth but here it was and I was sharing it with this group of total strangers.

"In my memory of premortality I found myself standing on a balcony, taking one last sentimental view of what had been my home for eons of time. My long white robe gently rippled in the breeze and the gold railing on the balcony shone brilliantly in the light. I gazed on the fairway below, the river beyond, and the sky above. The scene was as beautiful and as vibrantly alive as it had always been. The city, in the distance, was a pearlescent hue, pulsating with energy and light.

"I was not enjoying the scenery though. I was pacing, back and forth, across my balcony. I was deeply concerned, anxious to the point of distress. Tomorrow I was going to earth. The woman I had chosen to be my mother was preparing to give birth to me and I didn't want to go. I knew what lay ahead. The 'human experiences' I had chosen to have were going to be difficult, and now that my turn had arrived, I wasn't as confident about my ability to rise above them as I had been.

"I knew I could choose whether to go or not. I knew I didn't have to, it wasn't required. And yet wasn't it I who had been teaching and encouraging other spirits who were preparing for their human experience, to go with boldness to earth and to trust that all would be well? How could I be there for them, encouraging them in the greatest experience of all time and not go myself? I knew that I must go, or they would lose confidence, and possibly not go themselves. I knew my actions could either discourage or encourage them in their human experience. I was carrying a heavy burden. My own fears, anxieties and hesitations had grown to the point that I needed encouragement and reinforcement, lest I back out. I needed to speak with Father.

"Instantly, I was with Father, walking on the fairway. We were deep in conversation and I was pouring out my heart to him. I told him of my fears and my concerns. My distress was evident. 'What ifs' plagued me. I had chosen too many trials, any one of which would be overwhelming. The odds were against me and I feared that I might never make it back home. 'Father.' I cried out, 'I can't go. I'm scared.'

"He listened compassionately. I knew He felt my concern. I knew He cared deeply. We came to a beautiful sitting area. Father sat on a marble bench that seemed to be floating. I sat on the ground at His feet, my heart breaking. I longed for the safety of my heavenly home and at the same time, the possibilities that could come with the 'human experience' which was what I had dreamed of for as long as I could remember. I looked into his eyes, knowing that His words would be all the encouragement I needed. All that I was, my entire being, my eternity seemed to hang in the balance of His words. He tenderly looked at me. There was no question as to his love for me. It radiated, not just from His eyes, but from His entire being. I knew he loved me, as if I were His only child. I reached up, putting my hand on His knees, my heart aching, seeking His guidance. 'Father,' I cried. He placed His hands on top of mine, lovingly looking me in the eye and said, 'Peace, my child. Peace.'

"Suddenly, a bell rang, echoing throughout the building. The clanging snapped me out of the experience and back into real time. I opened my eyes, in awe of what I had just witnessed. As I looked into the moist eyes of the instructor, I began weeping and laughing for joy. 'God is real! God is real and He loves me. He loves ME!' I could not suppress the joy of knowing.

"Those in the room sat stunned. No one wanted to move, to lose the moment. There were no dry eyes in the room that day. The Holy Spirit had born a powerful witness to each of us that Father God is real, that His love is beyond measure, and that there was a plan laid out that we chose and agreed to from before our birth, for each one of us individually. This 'human experience' is merely that--a human experience that we, as extraordinary, eternal beings of light, must have to progress on to greater heights."

This beautiful experience changed CamBria's perspective of herself and of God. She was not alone but had a Heavenly Father who loved her and was there for her. She was not worthless flotsam on the sea of life, but a choice child of God. She also learned that she had selected a large part of the trials and adversity she had experienced and would yet experience. This brief experience--the memory of who she really was and where she came from—changed her and those with whom she shared her experience. From that moment on, suicide was no longer an option in her life.

CamBria's experience also reveals that those in premortality are keenly aware of the conditions on earth and that there is a chance that they might not make it back home. For some this possibility is disconcerting if not terrifying, and they are resistant in taking this chance. So they need encouragement and support before they can make the final choice. They will not be forced, only encouraged, but they and their Heavenly Father know that if they are to grow, they must leave the love and security of their heavenly home.

Neddie also discovered this fact. She had been seriously injured when she was hit by a speeding car. Her spleen was ruptured, her back broken in two places and her pelvis crushed. She was paralyzed from the waist down and had lost some muscle control in her arms. Her lungs collapsed and her doctors did not hold much hope for her recovery. But Neddie did recover.

"One night as I was saying my prayers and thanking my Father in Heaven for all the blessings He had given me and for the miracles that had come into my life, a small voice came to me and said, 'It really doesn't matter what your trials may be here on earth. It's how you accept them. That's the real test.'

"I realized my test wasn't the injuries I received in the accident or the hardships I have had to overcome. My test was how I accepted what had happened to me. I believe I had already accepted it (the implications of the accident) before I came to earth."[4]

In the next account, a young fourteen-year-old-girl named Liz also learned that she was unconditionally loved by God. Liz was experimenting with drugs when she overdosed.

"I looked up and saw a very bright light moving toward me. This light was coming from a man who, when he reached me, put his comforting arms around me. Although it was not communicated to me explicitly, I know without doubt that this man was Jesus Christ.

"He then asked me if I knew that what I was doing was wrong. I said, 'Yes.' At this point he was holding me, hugging me like a dad would hug his daughter. This is when the review of my life started. It was more of an emotional type of review than a judgment. I was reliving all the remorse, all of the pain, and all of the feelings I had felt. It was extremely intense.

"Throughout the whole ordeal there was nothing but love radiating from the man whose arms were around me. All the negative feelings and emotions were coming from me. At the conclusion of the review I had to make some decisions. I was shown His kingdom and I didn't want to leave it. But I knew that I wouldn't be able to progress from where I was at the moment if I did not. I realized that the most important thing I had to do was to bring people back to him. It was then that I remember him hugging me again and just holding me. During this embrace I communicated to him that I wished to return to my body.

"Quite a few years later, I was having a lot of health problems and was quite depressed. I was pondering over my health when suddenly it hit me. My health problems were part of the decision I had made—I had decided to accept health problems as part of my earthly trial. I had learned of this trial when I was having my near-death experience and consciously made the decision to return to my body and accept what was intended to happen to me."[5]

Liz's experience helped her to put her health problems into perspective. They were not thrust on her but were part of her earthly mission. She had known this fact and had accepted it, not once but twice, the first time before she was born and the second when she elected to return to earth. She was sustained through all her most difficult and trying days by the knowledge that Jesus Christ lives, loves her, and is waiting for her to return to Him.

Linda had severely injured her leg and had not taken care of it which, coupled with extreme fatigue, resulted in her dying.

"I was suddenly above my body, looking down from the corner of the room above the window. My leg didn't hurt a bit. Nothing hurt. My body looked awful there, so white and uncomfortable. I felt a wonderful warmth with no painful chills. Someone was standing behind me. The warmth seemed to come from that person and spread around me, like a pair of arms. I knew I was dead.

"The Being spoke to me and his communication was so loving and so peaceful, that I knew the warmth and beautiful golden-white light around me came from his love. He knew what I thought, and his understanding and compassion put me at complete ease. He said, 'You're dead, you know.'

"'I know. It's great!'

"'Do you truly want to be dead?'

"'Oh yes! Why not? This is all so wonderful,' as I thought of the relief, the light, and the love I felt.

"I saw my roommate come in and place her hand on my body's forehead. She screamed and tried to find a pulse. It was all so far away, but so clear. The sound of her scream didn't jar me a bit, but the way she was upset immediately impacted me. She grabbed the phone, and called my parents.

"I saw my mother's face. I saw my whole family. They called my brother overseas. An entire network of phone lines with people on the other end spread before my view. I was surprised to find that I felt every emotion they experienced, but my euphoria over-shadowed my empathy.

"Yes, I was pretty selfish not to think of how my family was going to feel, but they would get over it. They were just shocked and surprised. I thought death is the most natural thing and, besides, I felt at home here.

"Then the voice behind me said, 'But look what you're

missing,' and a scene opened up before my eyes and I saw a blond man walking up to a beautiful church. I didn't know who he was, but I knew somehow that he was a fantastic person, and that I was missing out on something significant. Although I only saw him from behind, I knew he had on a suit. He had a boy with fair skin and hair by one hand, and a girl by the other. They were beautiful children and very excited about seeing the church. The little girl jumped up and down and her ruffly skirt and strawberry-blonde curls bounced with every jump. I knew this scene was a promise of motherhood and of being married to this man. It seemed at that moment that nothing could be more desirable than being a mother and a wife. The heavenly warmth was still around me, but the feelings of bliss had left me. I began to question the desirability of staying in heaven without this experience.

"Sensing my feelings He said, 'The choice is yours.'

"Gazing at the still body then at the man and the two children, I said, 'Yes, I want to go back.'

"He told me, 'You are aware that it is not going to be easy. There will be pain and sorrow.'

"Fervently I repeated, 'I want to go back,' and I did.

"This experience changed my life. At times when things get very difficult, I remember that I chose to be here and I welcome whatever comes my way—even the sorrow, because sorrow is necessary to experience true joy. I have no fear of death, but I do fear that I might not accomplish all that I need to do in this life.

"Incidentally, I did marry a blond man who I know was the one I was shown by the Being. The two children I saw have yet to join our family."[6]

Linda's experience in heaven is both typical and unique. It is typical in that the beauty and serenity of heaven are so all encompassing that she did not want to return to earth and the pain and anguish experienced there. But what is unique is why she elected to return to earth. The Being could have ordered her to return and undoubtedly she would have done so. However, he instead showed Linda what she would be missing--marriage and motherhood. She had her choice, and she chose to return. She was allowed to retain some of her experience as a memory which helped her to put her personal problems into an eternal perspective.

One question that plagues many thinking people is, if there is an all-wise, all-knowing, and all-powerful God, why would he permit innocent children to be abused and killed? Howard Storm, during his lengthy experience in heaven, asked his angelic hosts about this.

"Why does God allow suffering, misery, child abuse, and things like that in the world? I was thinking specifically of the Holocaust. If God is so powerful, why would he permit such horrendous atrocities to occur?

"The angelic beings told me that God didn't want wars to happen, but as much help as he gives mankind, as much inter-vention as His angels do in this world to prevent mankind from being harmed, mortals have to suffer the consequences of their actions. They told me that for every war that has occurred, God and the heavenly angels have stopped hundreds from happening. God knows that sometimes mankind can only learn through suffering. But what individuals suffer is, to a significant degree, the consequence of their own actions and the actions of others, not of God's.

"Sometimes the innocent suffer as did the victims of the Holocaust. They were not responsible for what happened to them there. The people who did it to them are responsible."

Howard then asked why God could allow that to happen.

"The beings said, 'Let us show you something.' Suddenly I was at the depot at Auschwitz, watching soldiers unloading boxcars of their human cargo. They were yelling at the people and the people were really dazed as they came out of the cars to encounter German shepherds barking at them, the Ukrainian and Lithuanian guards were pushing them along, and there were doctors and officers at the end of the long line sorting them.

"Although I don't speak German, I understood what they were saying. I heard one guard say to another guard, 'A good batch for the Angel Maker.' He was laughing. What he was referring to was the crematorium. There was literally fire and smoke coming out of the chimneys. All the women, children, the sick and the elderly, and the crippled were being herded in that direction.

"One of the beings said, 'Look up at the smoke.'

"In the smoke, I saw all of these souls no longer suffering, no longer in pain, rising right up into heaven. All their pain and all their suffering were erased, and they were going with perfect bliss.

"Years later, I read a book about the Holocaust, and I found out that the guards at Auschwitz actually called the crematorium the Angel Maker out of cynicism."

Howard's experience has been published in book form. It is entitled, *My Descent To Death*.[7]

The perspective of many of us is all wrong. We think that what we suffer in this world is bad and a form of punishment. But from God's perspective, whatever we suffer in this world has purpose and reason, and the ultimate outcome is always for good, that is, if we choose to use it for good. The adversary, that old devil Satan, and his minions think that they have won when the innocent are mutilated, abused, and killed. Oh, how wrong they are.

### Summary Thoughts

When we experience adversity, it is true that some of it is due to the consequences of our own thoughtlessness, irresponsible behaviors, and poor choices. But adversity is not necessarily bad as many individuals, a few of whom were highlighted in this chapter, discovered. Just what is the role of adversity in the lives of mankind?

- Adversity is not punishment.
- Adversity is an opportunity to grow.
- Adversity is not forced upon us by a vengeful God.
- Adversity was chosen by us in premortality for what we could learn from it.
- Adversity helps develop humility, patience, and empathy.
- Adversity sensitizes us to the needs of our fellow human beings.
- Adversity is a test of our spiritual character.
- Adversity helps to purify and refine us.
- Adversity prepares us to return to heaven with the qualities needed to live in the presence of God.

It is learning from our experiences that is the real purpose of life on earth. Without challenges, we cannot grow, and the more challenges we face, the greater the potential for growth.

*Chapter Twelve*
*Why Disabilities and Handicaps?*

Parents are devastated when their baby is born with serious problems. Their first reactions are those of disbelief, grief, and loss. Once over the initial shock they tend to think in terms of what they might have done wrong, or what they possibly failed to do to prevent this tragedy. I know firsthand what it is like to plan for a much-wanted child, only to discover that his beautiful little girl was afflicted with a severe disability.

For the first six months of her life, Valerie was a perfectly normal baby. Then she started having seizures. Our pediatrician referred us to specialists at a regional medical center where she was diagnosed as having the genetic disorder, Tuberous Sclerosis. We were told the chances were great that she would be mentally handicapped. Her physicians were correct. As she grew she fell further and further behind her peers. While she has been generally healthy, over the years she has had some major medical problems resulting in the removal of a large brain tumor and one kidney.

Her affliction hurt us deeply. My wife and I have tried to make sense of this tragedy by reading everything we could find on the disorder. We discovered that Tuberous Sclerosis is a dominant genetic condition but there is no history of it on either side of our families. We then began to explore what we might have done to cause Valerie's problem. My wife thought Valerie's condition might have been caused by the radioactive iodine she took for an over-active thyroid several years before Valerie was born. I wondered if I might have been exposed to some form of radiation when I worked for the Atomic Energy Commission. But agonizing over the possible causes solved nothing; there was no cure and we would have to deal with Valerie and her problem on a daily basis for as long as she lived.

Relatives and friends, trying to sympathize with and comfort us, made comments such as, "Your daughter is very fortunate to be born to you. You have such incredible patience, understanding, and love. We could not care for such a child." Well, before Valerie was born, we would have thought we couldn't handle it either. But we have had to learn to cope and it hasn't been easy. Valerie will never be able to live on her own, go to college, marry or have children, and our lives will never be the same because of her and her limitations. We have wondered many times why a benevolent and merciful God would inflict such a terrible handicap on our child and, indirectly, on us.

As people were interviewed for this book and related their experiences, intriguing and surprising information was revealed which might explain why our daughter is handicapped. The accounts included in this chapter are only a few of the many which could have been included, that reflect what those afflicted with severe physical problems have learned about themselves and their disabilities. What they shared helped me and my family understand that disabilities and handicaps may impact the physical body but not the spirit. In fact, in the eternal scheme of things, disabilities seem to have a far different meaning than is generally supposed.

### A Choice

DeLynn, introduced in an earlier chapter, was born with Cystic Fibrosis, a severely debilitating genetic disease which greatly limits activities and causes constant pain, impacting on every major system of the body but especially the lungs. Every breath is accompanied by an intense burning sensation. Breathing becomes impossible without extremely painful daily treatments required to clear the lungs. Whereas most individuals born with Cystic Fibrosis die before adulthood, DeLynn lived to be over fifty. DeLynn had a near-death experience in which he discovered why he was born with Cystic Fibrosis.

"I often wondered what I had done to deserve such punishment. I tried to be a good person, but I must have somehow failed although I didn't know when or how. I experienced many medical problems associated with my disease necessitating major surgery. After one operation I was surprised to find myself out of my body. The first thing I noticed was that I could breathe for the first time in my life with no searing pain. I took great gulps of air; it was an exhilarating experience. For a while I just stood there with my eyes closed, breathing and enjoying what it was like to have lungs that didn't hurt. I also noticed that I had no other pain. Pain had been a constant companion throughout my life, and I had learned to accept it as normal. But suddenly it did not exist. Being able to breath without pain was fantastic. Wondering about this sudden change in me, I opened my eyes and looked around. I was in a hospital and in front of me was a hospital bed with a body in it. I focused on the body and was shocked when I recognized it as mine. It was at this point that it suddenly dawned on me that the reason I felt no pain was because I had died.

"I then became aware of a voice. It was a soft masculine voice that kept repeating my name, 'Delynn. Delynn. Delynn.'

"I turned toward the source of the voice and said, 'What?'

"When the voice didn't immediately respond, I asked, 'Why am I here? Why me? I'm a good guy—why did I die?'

"The voice answered, 'You are here because you earned the right to be here based on what you did and what you experienced on earth. The pain you suffered qualifies you to be here. You have suffered as much pain in thirty-seven years as a normal person might have suffered in eighty-seven years.'

"I was surprised. 'It's pain that got me here?'

"The answer was, 'Yes!'

"Still puzzled I asked, 'But why was it necessary for me to suffer so?'

"His answer totally shocked me. He said, 'You chose your disease and the amount of pain you would be willing to suffer in this life. You made this choice in heaven before you were born.'

"When he told me that it was my choice to suffer when I came to earth, I was both astonished and incredulous. He obviously understood my incredulity because I was immediately transported to a time before my birth. I was viewing a room from above and to the side, but at the same time I was in the room. It was a strange sensation in that I was both an observer *and* a participant. About thirty people were seated in the room with me, both men and women, and they were all dressed in what appeared to me to be white jumpsuits.

"At the front of the room was a person who was teaching us about accountability and responsibility—and about pain. Then he said, and I'll never forget this, 'You can learn lessons one of two ways. You can move through life slowly, and have certain experiences, or you can learn quickly through pain and disease.' He wrote on the board the words Cystic Fibrosis, then turned and explained how it would help those with it to achieve the experiences that come with pain and adversity. He then asked if anyone would be interested in the challenges associated with Cystic Fibrosis. I saw myself raise my hand.

"The instructor looked at me, smiled, and accepted my offer. With that, the scene ended. The next thing I knew, I was back in my body once again racked with pain and burning lungs. But my brief experience on the other side changed forever my perspective of myself. No longer did I consider myself a victim. Rather, I was a privileged participant in an eternal plan by my own choice. That plan, if I measured up to the potential of my choice, would allow me to learn what I needed to learn in mortal life the fastest way possible. True, I would not be able to control the inevitable slow deterioration of my mortal body, but I could control how I chose to handle my illness emotionally and psychologically. My choice to inhabit a body with Cystic Fibrosis was to help me learn dignity in suffering."[1]

To realize that disabilities are not necessarily thrust on us and that they have positive long range consequences can be a powerfully helpful shift in perspective. DeLynn lived ten additional years following this interview. Instead of wondering—Why me?—he focused on what he could learn from his disease and pain, and used his knowledge to comfort and help others.

When hearing about DeLynn's experience, it seemed informative and inspirational, but unique. However further research has revealed that DeLynn's situation was not unique at all, as shown by the following scenarios.

The following case of Vicki Umipeg is included for several reasons, but the main one being that Vicki has been completely blind since her premature birth, but during her near-death experience was able to see. It is *what* she saw and the great difficulty she had in explaining her experience with sight, from the perspective of a blind person, that makes her account remarkable.

Vicki was born very prematurely, having been in the womb only twenty-two weeks and weighing just three pounds at birth. As was common for premature babies in the mid-twentieth century, she was placed in a then-new airlock incubator through which oxygen was administered. Unfortunately, because of a failure to properly regulate the concentration of oxygen, Vicki was given too much and—along with about 50,000 other premature babies born in the United States at that time—suffered optic nerve damage that left her completely blind. She has never had any visual experience whatever nor does she even understand the nature of light.

In early 1973, Vicki was working as an occasional singer in a nightclub in Seattle. One night at closing time, she was unable to get a taxi to take her home. She had only one option, to ride in a Volkswagen bus with a couple of patrons both of whom were inebriated. Not surprisingly, a serious accident ensued during which Vicki was thrown out of the van. Her injuries were extensive and life-threatening, and included a skull fracture, concussion, and damage to her neck, back, and one leg. It took her a full year after being released from the hospital before she could stand upright without the risk of fainting.

She has no memory of the trip to Harborview Hospital in the ambulance, but after she arrived at the hospital's emergency room, she revived. She was surprised to find herself up near the ceiling watching a male doctor and a woman (a female physician or nurse) working on a body. At first she was not sure the body was hers, but observed several things that convinced her it was—very long hair that stretched down to the waist, and the rings on the body's fingers. Vicki had always worn a distinctive wedding ring on her left hand and her father's gold wedding ring and a plain gold band on her right hand . . . and there they were.

Vicki had a very fleeting image of herself lying on a metal table and then she was up on the ceiling. She thought, *Well, that's kind of weird. What am I doing up here? . . . Well, if I'm up here and my body is down there, I must be dead.*

Almost immediately she found herself going through the ceiling of the hospital until she was above the roof of the building itself, viewing a brief panorama of her surroundings. She felt very exhilarated during this ascension and enjoyed tremendously the freedom of movement. She also began to hear sublimely beautiful and exquisitely harmonious music akin to the sound of windchimes. But her reaction to being able to see was much more intense—pure shock and awe. She couldn't even begin to describe it and thought, *So that's what it's like! Well it's even better than what I could have imagined.*

With scarcely a noticeable transition, she then discovered she had been sucked head first into a tube and felt herself being pulled up into it. The enclosure was dark, and she was aware that she was moving toward light. As she reached the opening of the tube, the music that she had heard earlier seemed to be transformed into hymns . . . and she then "rolled out" to find herself lying on grass.

Vicki was surrounded by trees and flowers and a vast number of people. She was in a place of tremendous light, and the light, Vicki said, was something you could feel as well as see. Even the people she saw were bright.

Everybody there was *made* of light, including Vicki herself. [Author's note: Vicki saw only light in its different intensities radiating from everything. Light is composed of different wavelengths. The eye sees these different wavelengths being reflected from various objects and are taught as tiny children that particular light intensities are particular colors. As Vicki was never taught what "color" was, she could only speak in terms of "light" and light intensities.]

Vicki then became aware of specific persons she knew in life who were welcoming her. There were five of them—Debby and Diane were Vicki's blind schoolmates, who had died years before, at ages eleven and six, respectively. In life, they had both been profoundly retarded as well as blind. Vicki knew this as she had hugged both girls and was aware of their condition and, from what others had said, what their condition meant. Diane had been somewhat crippled, and had had a lot of trouble moving. Debby had been quite plump, and had had problems with fluid retention. She had a shunt in her neck as she was also hydrocephalic. But Vicki was delighted to see them. They were no longer children and, as Vicki phrased it, "in their prime." They were beautiful, healthy, and vitally alive. Debby's face was light, bright, and happy; Diane was beautiful and her whole being radiated light.

In addition, Vicki reported seeing three of her childhood caretakers, a couple named Mr. and Mrs. Zilk, both of whom had also died and finally, her grandmother, who had essentially raised Vicki and who had died just two years before the accident. Her grandmother, who was further back than the others, reached out to hug her. In these encounters, no actual words were exchanged, only feelings—feelings of love and welcome.

In the midst of this rapture, Vicki was suddenly overcome with a sense of total knowledge.

"I had a feeling like I knew everything . . . and like everything made sense. I just knew that . . . this place was where I would find the answers to all the questions about life, and about the planets, and about God, and about everything. . . It's like the *place* was the knowing."

She was flooded with information of a religious nature, as well as scientific and mathematical knowledge. She came to understand languages she didn't know. All this experience overwhelmed and astonished her.

"I didn't know beans about math and science . . . and I all of a sudden understood intuitively almost all things about calculus, and about the way planets were made. And I didn't know anything about that . . . I felt there was nothing I didn't know."

As these revelations were unfolding, Vicki noticed that now, next to her, was a figure whose radiance was far greater than the illumination of any of the persons she had thus far encountered. Immediately, she recognized the being as Jesus (for she had seen him once before, during her 1963 NDE). He greeted her tenderly, while she conveyed her excitement about her newfound omniscience and her joy at being there with him again.

Telepathically, the Savior communicated to Vicki: "Isn't it wonderful? Everything is beautiful here, and it fits together. And you'll find that. But you can't stay here now. It's not your time to be here yet and you have to go back."

Vicki reacted, understandably enough, with extreme disappointment and protested vehemently, "No, I want to stay with you." But the Savior assured her that she would come back, but for now, she had to go back and "learn and teach more about loving and forgiving."

Still resistant, Vicki then learned that she also needed to go back to earth to have her own children. With that Vicki, who was then childless but who desperately wanted to have children (and who has since given birth to three), became almost eager to return, and finally consented.

However, before Vicki left, she was given one last vision. She then saw everything from her life—birth to present day—in a complete panorama. As she watched, comments were gently made to help her understand the significance of her actions and their repercussions. [Author's note: It would seem very likely that she was probably also shown the role her disabilities played in her life.]

The last thing Vicki remembered, once the life review was completed, were the words, "You have to leave now." She then experienced "a sickening thud" like a roller coaster going backwards and found herself back in her body, feeling heavy and full of pain.[2]

Vicki's account documents the fact that while the physical body may be afflicted with all types of disabilities, the spirit/life force of the person is not. My daughter is mentally handicapped and displays autistic-like behaviors and she cannot appreciate that is done for her. But Vicki's experiences with Debby and Diane testify that trapped inside my daughter is a fantastically beautiful, intelligent, loving child of God. I can hardly wait until I can meet the spirit-child of Valerie.

Neil's experience helped him to understand why he had been severely crippled at age ten. Unlike many people who are disabled in their youth who learn to accept and live with their problems, Neil became increasingly depressed and despondent as time went on. It was during one of the darkest days of his life that he had an experience which totally changed him.

"I belonged to a proud and rather dignified family and was very proud of my heritage, but I also realized that because of my crippled helpless condition I did not present a dignified appearance. People who met me for the first time or saw me on the street were either shocked or repulsed by my appearance. Their reactions wounded my pride and made me totally miserable.

"One day while I was extremely depressed and feeling sorry for myself, a glorious vision burst upon me. It was not a single scene that I beheld but a series of them. The closest thing that I could compare them to would be like watching a movie. I beheld my existence in the spirit world, my mortal existence, and my future rewards. I understood that before I came to earth, I had been given the opportunity to choose the rewards I could receive. I had deliberately made these choices. I could see the rewards I had selected and understood that such a reward was only to be gained by mortal suffering—that, in fact, I must be a cripple and endure severe physical pain, privation, and ignominy. For the first time I realized that I had insisted on having this affliction and was completely aware of the rewards that would accompany it. I emerged from my vision with a settled conviction that to rebel against or even to repine about my fate, was not only a reproach to an all-wise Father, but a base violation of the deliberate promise and agreement I had entered into."

### A Protection

To those with the most severe disabilities, life is difficult not only for them, but also for their parents. These individuals will never be able to care for themselves and will need constant care, supervision, and protection. Why, then, are they born this way? What could their mission on earth possibly be? During an unusually in-depth near-death experience, Elane Durham, whose experience was described earlier in this book, was permitted to see those awaiting birth into bodies with severe disabilities.

"I was informed that all of us are born with handicaps--some are physical, others emotional, still others intellectual. It is not the handicaps that are important in the eternal scheme of things, but how we cope with them and how other people respond to those with handicaps. I was shown that those with quite severe mental disabilities are being protected by those disabilities. They were with our Heavenly Father from the very beginning, His most faithful spirits were totally committed to Him. They had proven themselves in the premortal world and only needed to come to earth to receive a physical body. But because the Devil, Satan, or whatever name you give the author of all evil, knows of the beloved status of these beings and would do everything in his power to hurt them, it was made sure he could not succeed. They would come to earth but in bodies that could not sin because their minds were not capable of understanding the full implications of their actions. Because of this, Satan could gain no hold over them."

This information gave Elane a completely different perspective of the mentally handicapped. They were not to be pitied; they were noble beings who had come to earth in bodies that protected them from the efforts of Satan and his minions to control or destroy them.

"Anticipating my next question, my escort asked if I would like to see myself prior to coming to earth. And I said, 'Yes!' I found myself looking through what appeared to me to be a window that was partially steamed. I could see myself and others, but not distinctly. I was seated with three angelic beings and two other beings were observing us. I understood that I was making decisions for my life on earth. It was much like preparing to leave home to go to college, and I was selecting my major and the courses I would have to take to complete my major. I was given many options and I saw myself choosing what I would like to learn. I was aware of the family I was to be born into, where I would be born, and that my family and location of birth would provide opportunities for me to learn and grow.

"My angelic escort lifted his arm slightly, pointed, and I saw thirty or forty young people who appeared to be in the prime of life. They were conversing as a group, everyone actively involved in the discussion. They were radiant, happy, and enjoying each others' company immensely. But what impressed me the most was the magnitude of spirituality that emanated from each and every one of them. Several individuals in the group stood out from all the rest, two in particular--a woman with shoulder-length brown hair and a young man just behind her. I could feel their unique spirits and knew they were spiritual giants. As I watched this group of excited, happy, loving people my angel escort let me know that all of them would be born on earth into handicapped bodies or would become handicapped after they arrived on earth. I was stunned! I asked, 'Do you mean that they would choose to take these beautiful perfected spirit bodies and enter into bodies that are very imperfect?'

"The angelic being said, 'Yes! Not only that, but you will meet all of these individuals during your lifetime, and three of them will have a profound impact on your life.'

"The group stopped a little way from me. My eyes were opened and I saw the image of a little boy, about ten years of age, and a little girl of about three. Both had the look of Down's syndrome. The little girl was blond, her hair pulled back from her face, and she looked severely impaired. I was allowed to see how these vibrant and radiant spirits would appear with their handicaps on earth so when the right time, came I would recognize them. A woman came up to me with a baby in her arms. I looked at the baby. She had big blue eyes, long lashes, and was gurgling and laughing. She was beautiful. I could see no deformities. The woman holding the baby said without speaking, 'She will live out her life as an infant and, without ever speaking a word, will affect the lives of thousands of people.' I was informed that it would be fifteen to twenty years before I would meet and get to know the three individuals I saw. I was also told that

220

I would recognize them when I met them. I have subsequently met and recognized all three and my life was irreversibly altered by them."

Elane has not led an easy life, but her experience on the other side and her encounter with this special group of spirits has had a significant impact on her. She has become very sensitive to the needs of the disadvantaged and has devoted her life to relieving pain and helping people die with dignity.

### To Help Others Grow

Duane Lucy, the father in the next account, learned of his son's true nature and abilities, thus helping him to deal with the boy's earthly handicaps.

"My wife and I had only been married a few weeks when I had a remarkable experience. I don't know just how to explain it, but I saw myself sitting in my living room. A young man appeared. He was about nineteen years of age. He had brown hair and a big infectious smile. He did not speak to me but I felt I had known him for a very long time. The feeling he projected to me was, 'I appreciate you and I am pleased with you and the life you are living. We have known each other for a long time and I love you.'

"I knew he was a very intelligent, glorious being and I felt honored that he loved me and that I was privileged to be in his presence. Then he disappeared.

"I told my wife that I had seen this individual and how impressed I was with him, but I had no idea who he was.

"Two years later, my son was born and, as he matured into young adulthood, he began to look like someone I knew. Then one day it dawned on me that he was the young man I had seen in my dream. He has the same infectious smile, the same mannerisms, and the same appearance. This dream has been of immeasurable help and comfort to me. You see, my son was born with major problems.

His physicians have not yet been able to diagnose what is wrong with him but he is severely disabled both mentally and physically. I don't know how I would have been able to handle the increasing demands of his disabilities if I had not had this dream. I saw the real him--intelligent, perfect in body and mind. His body may be defective, but his spirit is not. He showed himself to me two years prior to his birth so I would know the real him. He radiated an indescribable sense of nobility, intelligence, and love. This vision has helped me through some very rough times with my son."

Duane was shown that the real essence of a person is not the physical body with all its imperfections and limitations. Our body's age, are impacted by accidents, or are born with serious problems. But the spirit that inhabits the body has none of these defects. If more people realized this fact, what a difference it would make for those with disabilities. I often wonder about the spirit that inhabits our mentally handicapped daughter's physical body. My wife and I both look forward to the day when we can meet and become acquainted with the real Valerie.

Like Duane, Tom received a visitation from an unborn child. This child would eventually become his nephew.

"One day to my surprise, a young man appeared before me. I knew that he was my future nephew. He looked perfectly normal as he searched my eyes. Then he asked, 'Will you love me as I am?'

"I learned the meaning of his question when he was born with severe Down's syndrome. He knew before he was born that he would have a handicapped body and brain, and that many people would be uncomfortable around him. But I knew this was a test, as much for us as for him, because I had seen his real self. I became his most ardent supporter in helping his parents and relatives love and accept him."

During his extensive near-death experience, Roy Mills observed, in considerable detail, the activities of those preparing to go to earth. He concluded:

"It doesn't matter whether one's mission appeared great or small from earth's standards. By heaven's standards, all missions are important and great. An obscure, poor, or even handicapped person on earth, or one who suffers greatly, may be one of the mightiest spirits in eternity. That's why they qualified for such difficult missions."

It is interesting that Roy used the words "qualified for" in relation to difficult earth lives. This description would not seem to bear much relation to those with severe handicaps. Perhaps the mission of these individuals is just as much to test those who will meet and/or care for them as it is to test the afflicted. This is one conclusion that Sandra, the woman in the next case, drew from her suicide attempt.

"I was shown that in premortality some beings had grown spiritually to such a degree that they came to handicapped bodies. These handicaps helped their parents and others develop Christ-like traits as they helped and cared for them.

"If parents elect to abort a baby just because it might be handicapped, they will ultimately discover that it was a serious mistake. The willingness of some spirits to enter defective and handicapped bodies is an act of love. When their sacrifice is rejected and the body aborted, those parents lose a tremendous opportunity to learn, to sacrifice, and to develop spiritually.

"I was told the adversity I had experienced was not punishment or disapproval from God. Rather it was a chance for me to grow. I learned that suicide is not the answer, no matter how severe the problem.

When Delsi was sixteen weeks into her fourth pregnancy, she felt that something was seriously wrong with her baby.

"To confirm my feelings, I had a series of tests—AFP, amino and blood—so I would know what I was up against. When the tests came back they revealed that my baby had Down syndrome. I was strongly encouraged to abort the baby.

"I never seriously considered it. Instead, I determined to learn all I could about the disorder. I read every book I could find and surfed the Internet. At first, I was devastated. I never cried so hard in my life. For a time I wrestled with the feeling that this was unfair, a trial I did not want. And then I would feel guilty for feeling this way.

"I was sad for the limitations of my son's life, but eventually I received spiritual assurance that provided me with comfort and peace through the knowledge that this was meant to be. I was shown that I was chosen to be Jesse's mother even before I was born. And during my pregnancy I felt someone watching over me. I knew that it was my unborn son. He was there making sure that I was okay. On one occasion I saw him, a nice-looking young man who told me that he knew what his body was like and he didn't care—he just wanted to come to earth and be with me. This and other spiritual manifestations provided me with comfort, peace, and a knowledge that this was all meant to be."

It is unfortunate that more parents of handicapped children cannot have this experience. They feel guilt, self-pity, sorrow for their child, and sometimes resentment because of all the time and energy required to care for the child and the restrictions placed on their own lives. But the idea that a child chose them, even if it has to inhabit a less than perfect body, is humbling, exciting, and certainly challenging.

Denise's near-death encounter at age ten was associated with a severe diabetic reaction. The medical personnel at the hospital where she was taken did not expect her to come out of her coma but if by chance she did, they were certain she would be severely brain damaged because Cat-scans had revealed that over one-third of her brain had been destroyed. But she did recover and for her, the veil between this world and the next became very thin. She was able to see and converse with beings on both sides. She also discovered that she could see auras surrounding the people around her. What she saw as an aura was light of different intensity and color emanating from people. For example, people in general had a yellow aura, angry people projected red, healers—purple, and so forth. Very few radiated white of any intensity. This was the color she saw (while she was out of her body) radiating from those beings she saw while with God in the city of light. One day as she and her father were at the mall, she shared with him the various auras she saw. They were sitting on a bench that had a good view of the passing crowd. Her father asked her,

"'See any whites yet?'

"'Nope, but lots of reds. Ooh, she is really red.' Denise motioned toward a woman wagging her finger at her little girl. The little girl was in tears, confused and fearful but the woman wouldn't stop. She vented all her anger on that little girl. I turned away, uncomfortable at the display.

"'Still no whites?' I asked.

"'He is,' She pointed out across the courtyard.

"'What? Which one?' I quickly scanned the area.

"'The one in the wheelchair, over there.' She pointed again.

"'I focused on a middle-aged man seated in a wheelchair. What made him different? The obvious of course; he was in a wheelchair. Anything else? I studied him. Nothing out of the ordinary struck me. So, why was he white? Jesus emanated white and so did that man.

"Sunday arrived. We left for church a little earlier than normal. An outside group was putting on the service. We found our usual pew and sat as a family, Denise right by me.

"Within minutes I could feel Denise getting a little edgy, uncomfortable. I looked around and could see no reason for her discomfort.

"'Who is he, Daddy?' Denise secretly pointed to the back of a man of medium stature that could have been in his late twenties.

"'I don't know. He must be with the performing group. Why?' I bent my head a little so that I could clearly see her face.

"'He's white, Daddy!' She seemed almost puzzled. After three days of looking for whites in the mall, we had found only one, the man in the wheelchair. Now, here was a second.

"'Daddy, they're all white, too.' She motioned to the other side of the chapel where a small group of presenters were finding their seats.

"'They're handicapped, Denise.' I pointed out to her as if that was what attracted her attention and not the auras.

"'Oh.' She breathed a small sigh and settled contentedly back into the bench.

"I turned to look at the man she had first pointed out. As he turned around it became apparent that he had Down syndrome. He, too, was handicapped, and he had a white aura. The handicapped presenters on the other side were not necessarily physically handicapped but mentally handicapped. An idea started to get within my thoughts."

"'Denise, what color are babies?' I whispered to her.

"'White, Daddy.'

"A family sat down in front of us with their handicapped son Erik. Erik poked his head above the pew and smiled at me. His little misshapen head and face quickly melted my heart. There was just something special about him.

"'Denise, what color is Erik?'

"'Duh, Daddy!'

"It wasn't the response I expected but it confirmed what I knew. Those spirits with a body that prevented them from understanding and taking responsibility for their actions, as well as all little children, were white. They truly were heavenly beings. No wonder the penalty was so harsh for harming any of them."[3]

Those with disabilities radiated the light of God and were among his most beloved. Their pure white aura testified of their purity and innocence.

Some time later, Denise was asked to visit Erik on behalf of his parents. One evening she left her physical body and traveled to where Erik lives. While visiting with Erik she learned who he really was and why he was disabled.

"I went into Erik's room. He was sleeping next to his brother. 'Erik, come with me,' I said to him. His body stayed where it was and a beautiful man stood before me. He was like Christ because he loved Christ.

"'Hi, Erik. My Dad wanted me to ask you some questions for your parents.' I smiled.

"'Hi, Denise.' He didn't say that name; he knew my real name that I have when I am out of my body. 'I'm glad you are here. Christ told me you would be coming to talk with me.'

"'I'm supposed to ask you if you are happy,' I told him.

"He smiled. 'Mom and Dad can see me smile yet they still worry. They don't understand the veil that I have, and that it is different from theirs.' (His veil was the inability to communicate in the physical realm and his parent's veil was the inability to see things in the spiritual realm.)

"'I know. Mine's gone and my parents still wonder what it means.' I said.

"'I know my parents are worried about me. They have trouble seeing past my limitations and wonder what I can understand. They don't really realize that I came here because of them and my brothers. I love them. I chose this body because I promised I would help them learn and grow and they promised to guide and protect me. Tell them that the pain and discomfort is but for a short time. It won't last. Let them know that I love them now as much as I did when I first chose them as my parents. I understand their spiritual weaknesses as they understand my physical limitations. Tell them that the time we share together is a glorious gift from Father. I know it isn't easy for them, but when we finish our life on earth they will understand; they will remember.'

"I felt great love the whole time he spoke."[4]

To be trapped in a body that does not permit the spirit to reflect its abilities would seem to most people to be extremely frustrating who do not have the eternal perspective. As Erik and his parents could not communicate, they were projecting the pain and anguish they were experiencing over what he could not do or be, onto how he must feel. But he was not suffering in any way and wanted them to know that this condition and relationship was "a glorious gift from Father."

### Summary Thoughts

There is evidence that at least some and perhaps all of those born with severe disabilities are some of the greatest spirits that existed in premortality. Mental and/or physical disabilities are not punishments or signs of spiritual inferiority. Those afflicted did not have their disabilities forced upon them but willingly accepted them or chose them as part of their earthly mission. For some, their disabilities were a special protection given to them because they had been extremely valiant. For others their mission provides opportunities for individuals to reach beyond themselves and provide service and love. Receiving a body is one of the main reasons we come to earth and even a limited body meets this requirement.

## Chapter Thirteen
## Comfort From Home

Before we came to earth, we understood clearly the extent to which we would experience challenges and adversity. We also understood that these experiences were part of the heavenly scheme of things and would help prepare us for the next phase of our eternal journey. As we left the presence of God we were given assurance that the help we needed to cope with the problems we would inevitably encounter would come.

In this chapter are personal accounts of individuals who have faced what seemed to them to be virtually insurmountable problems. Some lost beloved children, others were severely abused, and still others experienced major medical problems. Whatever the challenge, these people discovered that they were not alone. God was aware of their plight and provided help in one form or another to support and sustain them.

### The Death of a Child

Losing a child can be a catastrophe. Since parents expect their children to outlive them, it violates everything that seems normal and natural when they don't. Parents seem to assume that they have some kind of omniscient knowledge and power which should enable them to identify and circumvent potential hazards whether they be electrical outlets, swimming pools, sexual predators, or genetic disorders. Failure to prevent death causes guilt even when there was absolutely nothing the parents could have done to prevent it. Many parents assume responsibility for their children's deaths to such an extent that it literally immobilizes them. It is therefore not surprising that grieving parents occasionally receive visits from their deceased children. The purpose of these visits is often to make it clear that the parents were not responsible for the death and that the children still exist and are being cared for. In literature, these appearances are often referred to as after-death communications. While anyone of any age might come back after death and for many reasons, in this section the discussion will be limited to children who returned to comfort their parents.

One question that is often posed by parents and others is, why do children die? Elane Durham, whose extensive near-death experience was discussed earlier, asked her angelic escorts, "How could a loving God allow children to die, regardless of the circumstances?"

She was told:

"Children who die in infancy have accomplished what they needed to do on earth, that is, receive a physical body. These spirits had proven themselves before they came to earth. Their missions are back home. These spirits return to heaven where they live in God's presence and are actively involved in His work."

Cindi's experience shortly after the death of her newborn son bears out what Elane was told.

"At the age of eighteen, I had a baby who only lived minutes. My doctor insisted it was not wise for me to see him, let alone hold him, so I didn't. But after his death I began to feel guilty that I, his mother, had not loved him enough to hold and comfort him as he died. As I sat on my bed grieving for my baby, I sensed the presence of someone in my room. I looked up and saw a young man standing in front of me. He said, "Mother, do not be concerned at your actions when I was born. They were not important. I achieved my purpose of being born on earth." He added that he might occasionally be granted permission to come down to earth and assist me and other family members. As we looked into each others eyes,

I could feel great love emanating from him. Then he slowly faded from view."

While this visit did not remove all the feelings of loss Cindi experienced, she was comforted to know that her son loved her and did not resent the fact that she had not held him after he died.

Will also lost a much loved child when he was only a few days old but, because of an experience he had earlier, he was expecting it.

"My oldest child, a boy, was born prematurely. He lived only eight days. Not long before his birth, I had a vivid dream wherein I was in a strange place and feeling very unusual--dead, I think. I was dressed in a white gown or loose robe, which was surprising to me as I normally wear cowboy boots and Wranglers. I walked toward a group of people dressed the same as I was. Drawing near, I was happy to see my maternal grandfather with whom I had been very close as a child although he had died when I was only five. With him were several men I didn't recognize excepting a tall one who was blond and very handsome—him I knew immediately! He was my son! Yet, at the very moment I recognized him, I somehow realized that he would not survive long on earth. I threw my arms around him and wept tears of joy and said over and over, 'My son, my son.'

"I remember that dream as vividly today, fifteen years later, as I did when it happened. The facial features of the young man I met and held are similar to the features of my two living sons. I have since seen pictures of some of my ancestors and realize that they were the other men I met with my grandfather and son.

"I awoke knowing that my firstborn would have but a brief mortal existence, but that we will have a joyful reunion in the afterlife. I know this experience was a gift from my Father in Heaven to help me through one of the toughest times in my life. Even with this knowledge it took me several years to recover emotionally from the death of my firstborn."

This account reveals considerable information about the essence and appearance of an unborn spirit. First, Will's vivid dream introduced him to his unborn son and he saw him as he would have appeared as a mature adult. Secondly, he knew that his son would not grow to maturity. And third, he knew his son was in the company of his much loved grandfather.

In the next case, Amanda had a beautiful experience with her infant son. She, like Will, saw her son not at the age he died, but as a mature young man.

"I was just drifting off to sleep when I became aware that my room was getting lighter and lighter until the entire room was bathed in brilliance.

"I was aware of a feeling of warmth and an overwhelming feeling of love. As I gazed around I began to notice people gathering around my bed, hundreds of people, all wearing white robes and smiling at me. A voice from above their heads called, 'Mammy.' I listened carefully and the voice called again, 'Mammy.' I wondered at the significance of this name. I then remembered the day that my son had died in his cot at just six months of age, I had written his obituary and in my shattered state I had misspelled 'Mummy' as 'Mammy.' Suddenly I realized this voice calling 'Mammy' was my son who had died some six months earlier.

"A light shone above the heads of all the radiant people surrounding my bed, a light that seemed even brighter than they. It floated down until the distinct shape of a young man in his early twenties appeared before me kneeling upon my bed. It was my son, Owen! He spoke to me without words through our minds.

"He identified the people who stood before me as my family, and said they were waiting for the day I could help them. He went on to tell me that he had been given permission to come and visit me. He told me that he was happy for the choices I had made and that he loved me dearly. He assured me that we would be together again one day. He then told me that the spirit world surrounds us and I was to take comfort in that fact, knowing that he was always near. He informed me that he had to die when he did, so he could return to heaven where his mission was to prepare his brothers and sisters who were to follow. He smiled and said that he had to go because he had work to do and was very busy. Before leaving he said that the people standing around my bed would return and visit me. And he would, too, whenever his work permitted.

"I cried at the thought of him leaving me again. Tears began to roll down my face rather quickly. He reached out his hand to wipe away the tears. I could not feel his hand, but I did feel something. He began to rise upwards. I reached out for him, my grief reborn. I did not want to be without him. It was then that I felt the most amazing feeling of love. It was the most glorious feeling I have ever experienced. At that moment I thought, *If this was what it felt like for two spirits to be united, then what rapture we must feel when reunited with God and all our brothers and sisters in heaven.*

"My son continued ascending slowly, until he became a little light and then disappeared. I shall always remember the beautiful face of my infant son as a grown man. The people surrounding my bed smiled at me and slowly the room became hazy until I could see them no more."

Wouldn't it be wonderful if every parent who lost a child could have this type of experience? It would certainly remove much of the anguish surrounding the loss. What is intriguing about this account is the fact that the death of this newborn was necessary to facilitate something of such great importance that it superseded all other priorities, that is, the preparation of his brothers and sisters for their earthly experience.

Patricia had lost twin daughters within moments of their birth. She was so upset by their deaths that she seriously contemplated ending her life. One night she was especially depressed and had cried herself to sleep. She had just dropped off when she had a miraculous vision in which a radiant being appeared to her with her twin daughters.

"The escort put his hand on my left shoulder and I felt a sense of peace and comfort radiating from his touch. My twin daughters were with him and told me that they were all right. This experience literally saved my life."

While the anguish of losing even one child is indescribable, imagine what it would be like to lose many children which was all too common in the days before modern medicine. Between 1869 and 1898, Joseph F. Smith buried nine of his children. Below is recorded the grief he felt at the time he lost his first, fifth, and ninth children and the comfort he received that helped him to accept their deaths and know that he had not lost them forever.

"God only knows how much I loved my girl, and she the light and joy of my heart. The morning before she died, after being up with her all night, for I watched her every night, I said to her. 'My little pet did not sleep all night.' She shook her head and replied. 'I'll sleep today Papa.' Oh! How those little words shot through my heart. I knew though I would not believe . . . that it meant the sleep of death and she did sleep. And, Oh! The light of my heart went out. The image of heaven graven in my soul was almost departed . . ."[1]

On 6 July 1879, Joseph wrote in his journal of the death of his daughter, Rhonda.

"I took her on a pillow and walked the floor with her, she again revived but only lingered about an hour and died in my arms at 1:40 A.M. Now God only knows how deeply we mourn. This is the 5th death in my family. All my little ones most beloved! O! God help us to bear this trial."[2]

At the death of his daughter, Ruth, on 17 March 1898, the ninth of his children to die, Joseph was allowed to see his family in the next world:

"O my soul! I see my own sweet mother's arms extended welcoming to her embrace the ransomed glorious spirit of my own sweet babe! O my God! For this glorious vision I thank Thee! And there too are gathered to my Father's mansion all my darling lovely ones; not in infantile helplessness, but in all the power and glory and majesty of sanctified spirits! Full of intelligence, of joy and grace, and truth."[3]

This vision was without doubt a great comfort to Joseph. He had not lost these daughters or any of his nine children. He saw them not as tiny infants but mature young men and women. He also witnessed that they were with his beloved mother who had died when he was only thirteen years of age.

### Stillbirths and Miscarriages

Far too often physicians, relatives, and well-meaning friends discount miscarriage as an unfortunate but correctable event. They do not regard a miscarriage as the equivalent of the death of a baby and think it should be easy for the mother to recover. But the mothers who carry these babies bond with them, love them, and grieve for them as much as they would for a living baby who died. Such was the situation with Christa Marsee when she miscarried.

"Even though we had three wonderful boys, we had always wanted a larger family and had been trying for some time to have another child. Because I was in my thirties, I wondered if this had been my last opportunity to bring another child into the world. It was sad to think there was nothing we could do to prevent our loss.

"This was one experience where no one else could help or comfort me, I recall thinking that day in the doctor's office. A great sense of defeat weighed heavily on me, and I prayed, 'Heavenly Father, give me the courage to get through this day.' I lowered my head as tears came to my eyes. Then, in the midst of my sadness, these peaceful words filled my mind and heart, 'Heavenly Father is pleased that you tried.'

"My tears of sadness suddenly seemed transformed to tears of joy, for Heavenly Father was pleased—pleased that we desired to have more children come to our home. The joy I experienced in this knowledge is one of the sweetest blessings I have ever known."[4]

Although Christa never saw the spirit of her miscarried baby, the fact that she knew that God approved of her wanting to have more children gave her great comfort.

Charles and Rachel (not their real names) suffered first a still-birth then a miscarriage. They had wanted a large family but after the miscarriage, Rachel was informed by her physician that she would no longer be able to conceive because of serious medical problems. The loss of the much anticipated baby and the news that they could not have other children sent Rachel into a deep depression. It was during this very dark period that Rachel had a remarkable experience that changed her life.

"I had given birth to a stillborn son who we named Carl, and fourteen months earlier I had miscarried at five months a little daughter who we had named Sarah. After losing Carl I went into a deep depression feeling that I was being punished and not understanding why. Then one night I experienced an extremely vivid dream during which I found myself in a meadow filled with exquisite flowers. As I stood there absorbing the ethereal beauty of the place I saw an angel walking toward me. The angelic being, a man, told me, 'I have something special to show you.' In his right arm he held a baby who looked to be six months old, and his left hand was being held by that of a little girl. She was tiny, just a toddler, but she could talk. She looked up at me and said, 'Mommy, I am Sarah, and this is my brother, Carl. We are fine. We are very happy. We love you very much, and we don't want you to be sad anymore. We will all be together someday.'"

Rachel noticed that both children were dressed in white robes. Little Sarah had on sandals, but Carl was barefoot. Both of them were glowing. She asked the angel if she could hold them and the angel nodded yes. Rachel sat on the grass holding Carl on her lap and with her arm around Sarah. She could not contain her emotions. Tears of joy and love coursed down her cheeks. She told both of them how much she loved and missed them. She also told them that their father loved them deeply. She stayed with them as long as she could. When it was time for them to go, she hugged and kissed them. As they walked away with the angel, she told them one last time, "I love you." When she awoke, she was no longer depressed but filled with a deep sense of peace. Rachel knew that she had not failed as a mother. Her children still existed and loved her. There had been no mistaking who they were; Sarah looked like her father and Carl like her.

Rachel's experience with her two children changed her belief in what she had been told and believed about the status of stillborn and miscarried children. Despite the general opinion that the unborn are fetuses with no identity, she now knew better. She had thought that she had lost two babies but discovered that she had in reality not lost them at all. She knows with a complete certainty that they are still hers and will be waiting for her when she passes to the other side.

The next experience is that of a young woman (initials E. B.)

with the spirit of an unborn child she would someday have.

"When I was very young, I think about nine years old, I had scarlet fever. When I was in the worst part of my illness, I realized that it was becoming very hard for me to breathe. Everything in the room was fuzzy and the walls started shimmering and a kind of mist floated into the room.

"Just when I thought I was smothering I looked at the foot of the bed where the mist was centered. There I saw the outline of a little girl with long blond hair. The little girl didn't say anything to me and since she was still in the mist I wasn't able to see her face clearly but I could tell that she was very pretty.

"At the same time I noticed that I was breathing normally again. All the congestion in my chest was gone, as if by magic. I almost couldn't believe it, but I had to because it was true. I put my hand on my chest and looked down at my body in disbelief. When I looked up the room was clear and the mist and the little girl who had been inside it were gone.

"I was married at age seventeen. My health was very fragile and my doctor told my husband that he did not think it would be wise for me to have children. But I wanted children. We waited until my health improved and four years later, at age twenty-one, I became pregnant. It was a very difficult pregnancy from the beginning and by the third month I was confined to bed. Finally my health deteriorated so much that I had to go to the hospital.

"I had been at the hospital for about three hours and was feeling very weak. My doctors were giving me a lot of medication and I started feeling very ill just as I had when I was nine. I was lying in the hospital bed and the whole room began to mist up. Then, just like twelve years had never passed, the little girl was standing right in front of me at the foot of the bed. I blinked my eyes as memory flooded back. This time I could see her a little more clearly. She was blond, about seven years old, with fair skin and pretty delicate features. I could even see a dozen or so little freckles scattered across the bridge of her nose. I spoke to her and asked her who she was. For some reason, I guess because she was silent the last time I saw her I didn't really expect her to answer me. But she did. In the softest of voices, she said, 'I'm sorry, Mommy, but I can't be with you this time. You're not strong enough yet. But don't worry, I'll pray for you to be stronger.' Then she smiled at me and was gone.

"After that, in spite of all the doctors could do, I had a miscarriage.

"When I returned home from the hospital, both my husband and I were very upset and depressed. From that day on I set about to improve my health. Six years later I had a successful pregnancy and gave birth to our daughter, Jennifer.

"During this time I had forgotten all about the little girl I had seen in the hospital but one day when Jennifer came in from playing she stood in the doorway with the sun shining behind her and I was shocked by what I saw. With her long blond hair back-lighted by the sun, she looked like a younger version of the little girl who had come into my room. As she matures she looks more and more like her, right down to the freckles on the bridge of her nose."[5]

This woman was visited by her future daughter twice. Once was to heal her from complications relating to her scarlet fever and the second was to inform her why she had to leave. But she told her mother she would be back once her mother got stronger. While this assurance did not totally remove the pain and anguish of miscarrying, the woman at least knew why it had occurred and was assured that she would still have that daughter someday.

### Suicide

The suicide of a much-loved child is an incredibly difficult thing for parents to accept. Feelings of responsibility, of not being there when their child desperately needed them, of missing all the obvious clues, so plague many parents that they are unable to accept the death and move on with their lives. They suffer intense feelings of failure, guilt, and self-recrimination. In addition, many religions teach that those who kill themselves have violated one of God's commandments and will therefore go to hell. Fears that their child has been consigned to hell make coming to terms with the death even more difficult. But Robert and Martha Ohlms discovered that in spite of their son's suicide, he was not in hell. This assurance came from an experience their ten-year-old daughter, Martha Lynn, had with her deceased brother.

"I was in my room thinking about my brother, troubled that he might be in hell. Reverend Jones had said during one of his sermons that those who commit suicide would go to hell and burn forever. I could not imagine why my brother would go to hell and burn forever if God truly loved us. I loved my brother! I didn't know why he had hung himself, but I knew he wasn't a bad person.

"While I was crying, I noticed the room getting brighter. I looked up and saw the wall at the end of the room glowing with a golden-white light. As I stared at the light, the wall disappeared and I could see a beautiful place. It was like looking at a TV set, but this was real. I could see people, glowing people in white robes. They were in a beautiful park with trees, fountains, and wonderful flowers. The light was warm and peaceful. I could actually feel it.

"Then I saw Jim. He wasn't in hell! He was in this beautiful place. As I stared at him with a mixture of wonder and joy, Jim turned and walked toward me. He was smiling and looked very happy. With him were several persons who I somehow recognized were relatives who had died. Jim stopped in front of me, looked into my eyes and said, 'Jen, I want you to know that I am not in hell. What I did was very foolish and thoughtless. I did not know how much what I did would hurt you, Mother, Dad, and my friends. I want you to tell them that I am sorry and that I love them. I did not do myself any service by killing myself as my problems came with me. But I am with loving friends and relatives and I am slowly overcoming my problems. Tell Mom that Grandpa (her father) is working with me and that when it is her time to come over, we will be there for her.'

"In my excitement and joy I reached out to hug my brother, but he stopped me. 'Jen, you are not permitted to touch me yet. But when it is your time to die, I will be there to greet you and be with you.'

"With that, he stepped back and the light began to fade. Within moments the window into heaven had closed and I was looking at my bedroom wall. But the feeling of peace remained, filling my room. For nearly an hour I just sat there thinking about what I had witnessed. At last I burst from my room and rushed up to my mother shouting, 'Mom! Reverend Jones is wrong. Jim is not in hell! I know because I saw him and he is in heaven with Grandpa John.'"

In the Bible it clearly states that we are not to judge others. We do not know the hearts and souls of others but God does. He is all compassionate, all loving, and all understanding. He knows his children and loves them unconditionally. This was truly manifested in Jim's case. Jim was with loved ones, not burning in hell. Jim was acutely aware of the pain he had caused others and was deeply remorseful. He also knew that he had not solved his problems by committing suicide. But he loved his family and needed to let them know where he was and that he was all right. This account does not justify suicide as the solution for earthly problems. As Jim told his sister very definitely, what he had done was a foolish and selfish thing because you cannot escape your problems just because you die. Part of our mission on earth evidently is to confront adversity and rise above it. But at least some who take their own lives are able to make amends for their foolish and impulsive action. Several excellent books written by individuals who committed suicide but were sent back to complete their earthly missions are Joyce Brown's book, *Heavenly Answers for Earthly Challenges*[6], Sandra Rogers' book *Lessons from the Light*[7], and Angie Fenimore's book, *Beyond the Darkness*[8].

### Messages to Parents And Others

In the following account, a young man who had been killed in an automobile accident appeared to his ten-year-old sister and to several total strangers.

Quin McEgan was in a car driven by his older sister, Kelly, when they were involved in a freak accident. Kelly lost control of the car and hit a split rail fence. A pole from the fence punctured the radiator, passed through the engine compartment and into the passenger area striking Quin in the head and killing him instantly.

An extremely popular and gifted athlete, Quin loved and was loved by everyone. His death shocked the entire community. Not long after he was killed, Quin appeared to his ten-year-old sister, Stacy, to assure her that he was all right. He told her to look closely at his face as he pulled his hair aside so she could see his face. It was not damaged. He then said, "Stacy, tell Mom and Dad to quit crying. Everything is okay. I am fine. It was my time to go."

With Quin, was his grandfather. He had died many years before she or Quin were born, yet there was no question in Stacy's mind as to who he was. After their visit, she ran to her parents with the message, "Mom! Dad! I saw Quin and Grandpa. Quin showed me his face and it was not hurt. He said it was his time to go. They were dressed in white and just before they disappeared, they waved and smiled at me."

During a candlelight vigil at the crash sight, Quin's friend, Nancy, saw him being escorted by two angelic beings. She reported that he looked at her, then surveying all present at the vigil asked his escorts, "Where is Kelly?"

One of the angels replied, "Don't worry about her. She is fine.

She needs to carry on your work now. We have to leave!"

Quin later appeared to another young woman who had heard of him but had never met him. She reported that he had spoken at length with her and that he had also shown her his face so she could see that it had not been permanently damaged by the accident. He told her, "My body is perfect. Please go and tell my Mother and Father what you have seen and that I am OK. Tell them that they have a lot to learn and do before they will be ready to join me."

About this same time a third woman named Lisa had an unusual experience which she shared with Quin's family.

"My husband and I had just gone to bed and the tragic death of a fine young man was on my mind. I was lying on my right side when I noticed a movement out of the corner of my eye. I jerked my head up and there stood a young man. Somehow I knew immediately who he was. It was Quin, the young man who had just been killed in the tragic automobile accident. He was about two feet from me, perfectly visible and three dimensional.

"He looked at me for a few minutes, staring into my eyes. I could see the separate strands of his hair and they glowed with the luster of diamonds. His face was not injured in any way and he had this huge smile on his face. He tried to touch me but his hand passed right through me. He exuded a sense of excitement, of exuberance, of complete joy. While we looked at each other he slowly ascended up toward the ceiling then stopped. At that moment a Being of Light appeared next to Quin and I received the distinct impression that we would all be together some day in heaven.

"I felt their appearance was for all who were grieving for Quin and the way he died. The message I received from him was that he was okay and that all of us in the community needed to accept that he had moved on and that we must now get on with our lives. If we would do this, we would eventually be able to go where he is and be with him."

"A few weeks later I felt an overwhelming need to contact Quin's parents. I had never met them, but I knew I needed to tell them of my experience with their son and the Being of Light. With trepidation I called them up and they invited me to come over. They were very receptive to me and Quin's message. Through their tears I could see the joy his message brought them."

Quin was extremely popular at his high school. He was an outstanding athlete who reached out to all his classmates and teachers in ways that touched them deeply. When he was killed, many of his classmates were devastated and piled flowers and other mementos at the accident site. Some even built a memorial to him at the spot. Why did Quin appear to so many people? Apparently Quin was allowed to return and appear to a number of people so they could testify that he was OK, that people should not grieve his death, that he was busily engaged in important heavenly work and they should get on with their lives. His appearance not just to his sister, but to a friend and two total strangers helped his family, classmates, and the community come to terms with his death.

Another family also lost a child unexpectedly and tragically. As with Quin, comfort was provided to a family by a direct visitation of the deceased child although not to a member of the immediate family.

The Jensen family had gone to a popular amusement park. The family was having a great time until their twelve-year-old daughter, Adrienne, suddenly died. There was no warning. She had no known health problems. She just died.

In spite of the outpouring of sympathy and support from their church and friends, the parents could find no relief. The sudden and totally unexpected nature of Adrienne's death and the lack of any apparent reason for it, plagued them. Even with assurance from their physician that there was nothing they could have done, they were sure that somehow they had missed something. Thus they suffered not only grief, but a haunting guilt that they should have been able to prevent her death.

About this time, a young girl named Becky, paralyzed from the neck down, was at a swimming pool with friends when her wheelchair slipped, pitching her into the pool. Emergency personnel rushed to the pool's edge and were able to resuscitate her. When Becky recovered sufficiently to speak, she made a surprising request. She asked to see the family of the girl who had died at the amusement park. She did not know them, but had seen them on TV.

The grieving family was contacted and agreed to visit Becky. When the Jensen's arrived, Becky excitedly said she had a message for them. "When I drowned, I was taken to Heaven where I met Adrienne. She asked me to tell you that she is with loving relatives who are taking good care of her. She particularly wanted me to tell you that you are not to worry about how she died, because it is not important!"

This message from their deceased daughter enabled Adrienne's family to release their guilt and begin the healing process necessary for them to continue their lives. They thanked Becky and departed with a sense of peace that they had not known since their daughter's death.

Meanwhile Becky had yet another message, this time for the Bishop of her church. She insisted that she must see him now! When he came in, she grasped his hand and explained, "When I was dead I met your father. He wants you to know he is very proud of you and the good work you are doing."

Her Bishop was shocked. How could she have known? Since his father's passing he had been grieving and seriously questioning if he was being successful in his ministry. Becky's message helped him not only to accept his father's death but gave him the assurance that he was succeeding in his ministry.

It is intriguing how those in heaven let us on earth know what we need to know. In this case, messages were relayed to two grieving families through a third party. The paralyzed girl did not learn why she was paralyzed. What she did learn was why another young child had died and that a man's efforts were approved of by his deceased father.

When five-year-old Sandy was bitten by a mosquito she contracted encephalitis and died. This is her story.

"I found myself drifting into a safe place where I felt right at home. Off in the distance was a very small light and I felt myself rushing toward it with great speed. I was not frightened at all. When I came to the light I felt peace and joy, but most of all, a deep unconditional love. The light was a sparkling, glowing cloud. From inside I heard a voice in my head and I knew it was God. Since my parents never discussed God or took me to church, I really don't know how I knew, but I did. Furthermore, I felt like this place was my real home.

"Another beautiful light, only smaller, joined us. It was a girl about ten years old and she looked a bit like me. I could tell she knew me. We hugged and she said, 'I am your sister. I was named after our grandmother, Willamette, who died a month before I was born. Our parents called me Willie for short. They were waiting to tell you about me when you were older and could understand death.' We were talking to each other without words. She kissed me on the head and I felt her warmth and her love. 'You need to go back now, Sandy,' she said. 'You need to save mother from the fire. This is very important, you need to go back and you need to go back now.' She said it with compassion and sweetness as she smiled at me tenderly.

"'No, I don't want to,' I said, 'let me stay here with you.'

"'Mother needs you to save her from the fire,' she repeated, still in a soft and gentle way. Like a selfish little brat, I cried and threw a temper tantrum of the worst kind. I fell on the ground and sobbed and thrashed around and made everyone, I am sure, feel very uncomfortable, and I could see through the look in their eyes that they were extremely worried.

"I was then shown a type of movie in which I saw my parents who were back on earth sitting beside my hospital bed. They touched my body pleading that I not die. I was very sad for them but I was not ready to give up the beauty and awesome feelings of this place, which I assumed was heaven. My escort gave a chuckle and looked at me with great compassion.

"He then pointed a finger at another light forming in the distance. To my delight and surprise, my dear friend and next door neighbor, Glen, appeared and shouted at me in a loud voice, 'Sandy! Go home! Go home now!' He said it with such authority that I immediately quit crying and was suddenly back in my body.

"I opened my eyes to see the joyful and relieved faces of my parents. I told them about my experience as soon as I could, which they at first called my dream. I only learned of my neighbor's death after I told my story to my parents. They told me that our neighbor, Glen, had died from a sudden heart attack the day after I went into the hospital. He was a kindly old man who would always invite my brother and me and all the other kids in the neighborhood into his back yard to play with his five dogs. He loved kids and would give us food, gifts and treats. His wife would eventually tire of us and tell us to go home. He would scold her and say, 'Rose, never tell Sandy she has to go, she can stay as long as she wants.' I was his favorite of all the kids who came to his home to play. It was because it was such a shock to have him yell at me that way that I felt embarrassed at my behavior and stopped fighting to stay. I also recall feeling a little hurt at the time.'

"I drew a picture of my 'angel sister' who had greeted me and described everything she had said. My parents were so shocked that they got up and left the room. After some time they finally returned. They confirmed that they had lost a daughter named Willie. She had died of accidental poisoning approximately one year before I was born. They had decided not to tell me or my brother about her until we were able to understand what life and death were all about. About the need to rescue Mom from the fire, she told me, 'I cried for months after Willie left us. If I'd lost you too, it would have been like a living hell, fire and all, and I would probably have had a mental breakdown.'"[9]

In this account, a young child met a sister who she did not know existed and a beloved elderly neighbor who she did not know had died. Both of them told her that she needed to return to earth. Why? The answer was to save her mother from "the fire." While at the time Rose did not understand the significance of "the fire," much later she realized that it referred to the potential for her mother's total emotional/mental breakdown. So not only did she save her mother's sanity, she also was able to comfort her parents by assuring them that their other daughter still lived and was with protective heavenly beings. It is interesting that neither the encouragement of God nor her sister convinced Sandy to return to earth. But when her neighbor who unbeknownst to her had died during her illness commanded her to return, she responded immediately.

### Abuse

Abuse, whether it is physical, emotional, or sexual affects an individual long after the abuse has ended. If children grow up in fear, they go through their life experiencing strong feelings of insecurity, depression, and unworthiness. Being told that they are ugly, stupid, and bad is far too often accepted by children as true, thus handicapping and even destroying them for life. Psychological and physical abuse may be so severe that heavenly intervention becomes necessary if a child is to grow up and complete his or her mission. Jim Halloran's case is one such example. Jim was the youngest of four boys and different from his three brothers in many ways.

"I have an IQ that is above average, whereas my brothers are exceedingly average and mentally lazy. From an early age I was very athletic, whereas they were clumsy and uncoordinated. I rarely became ill as a child, but it seemed they continually passed their various sicknesses back and forth to each other. To this day I remain the only member of my family who has never been chemically dependent.

"As a small child I had to survive a regular round of beatings from my brothers. My alcoholic parents seemed to feel that it was okay for me to serve as the whipping boy for all the wrongs, real or imagined, they deemed society had dealt them.

"During these early years of dreadful abuse, my guardian angel would speak with me. He would tell me that I was worthwhile, that I was loved by God, and that I had talents and abilities that my family would never be capable of understanding.

"I never went to Sunday School or church as a child so no one could ever say that I was projecting my hopes and my religious faith onto a kind of imaginary friend.

"I am totally convinced that I was able to mature into a balanced person because of the communications I had with and the love I felt from my guardian angel.

"Knowing that he was always there for me enabled me to succeed. I was a straight A student in both high school and college. I worked three part-time jobs and put myself through college. I received my degree in education, and after five years of teaching, married a fellow teacher. We have two daughters on whom I shower love and affection. I tell them about the eternal goodness of God and the love of their guardian angels that will always surround them."[10]

These interventions from home helped Jim to realize who he really was--a child of God. His experience of unconditional love from his guardian angel enabled him to rise above his abusive family. What is unusual about Jim's account is not only the fact that he had a guardian angel, but the extent to which his guardian angel was with him throughout his youth.

Many new parents-to-be are almost overwhelmed by the responsibilities that come with parenthood. Not only must they provide all the things that are needed to sustain a child, but they are also expected to help the child to develop a strong sense of self worth, be intellectually stimulated, and become socially responsible. But most parents do not have any formal training in child development and worry that they will fail in some significant way. This concern is particularly acute for individuals raised in dysfunctional families as was Cynthia, the woman in the next account. She, like many raised in similar environments, was very concerned that she might have inherited abusive tendencies and that these tendencies would impact on her ability to be a good and loving parent. Because of this concern, Cynthia was afraid to have children.

"As a child I promised myself that I would never treat children as Dad had treated me. But I had a violent temper and feared that I might abuse a child should I ever have one. So for years I strongly believed that it would be very unwise for me to have children.

"Then I married and discovered that I was pregnant! My husband is very good with children and was overjoyed. He patiently and lovingly convinced me to go through with the pregnancy although I still had strong reservations.

We decided to move back to the Midwest where we had both grown up to surround our new child with as many relatives as possible. So we packed our stuff, sent it on ahead, and spent four weeks during my second trimester seeing the Southwest on the way to our new home.

"That's when my son made his appearance. We were in Bryce Canyon National Park, a very beautiful place! We pulled in late in the afternoon, set up camp, saw the sights, and then settled down for the night. As I slept peacefully, I had this vision of a young boy of about three, who stood before me, smiling and radiating love. He introduced himself without speaking or gesturing as Bryce, and he let me know that he was very pleased that I had had enough faith to accept my pregnancy. He expressed excitement at being a part of our lives, that we were very special people and he had specifically chosen us and waited for us. This vision/visit lasted all night, and was such a strong experience that I can still picture it clearly three years later!

"The next morning I told my husband, Kurt, about it and explained that for the first time in my pregnancy I felt relaxed and at peace. As my due date approached, we made all the necessary arrangements, but we never did consider a girl's name 'just in case.' We knew it would be a blond-haired little boy named Bryce!

"Through my unborn son's love and assurance I was able to break the cycle of abuse. I discovered that I could be a good mother and would be able to provide my son with a loving and healthy home environment.

"Bryce is now three years old, full of wonder and love. And he is the spitting image of the boy who visited me so long ago!"[11]

There is a vast body of research documenting the fact that abused children tend to grow up to become abusive parents. So Cynthia's concerns were not unrealistic. But her experience with her unborn son helped her to realize that she could break from her abusive past and be a good mother. Bryce's words that he had chosen her and had waited for her and that she and her husband were special people, made her feel that it was right for her to have children. She knew without any doubt that her pregnancy was not an accident but something long anticipated and planned for in heaven.

Sexual abuse at any age can't help but have a devastating effect on the victim. It certainly did with the young woman in the next case. Being raped at age three had a horrendous impact on this child, especially as the child's parents were cold and distant.

"I was almost three years old in 1960 when I was raped by a neighborhood teenage boy. This was such a traumatic experience that I became terrified of men. I also experienced times of great depression and feelings of being worthless. I felt extremely vulnerable, my future seemed hopeless, and suicide often crossed my mind.

"When I was nearly thirteen, I was unusually depressed, desperate, and concerned about what kind of a future I could possibly have. In spite of all my problems, I believed that there was a God and I prayed to Him. I asked, 'Why am I here? Is there anything special for me to live for?'

"There were always a lot of people in our house, but one place I could withdraw to, where I could have privacy, was the bunkbed in my bedroom. It was closed off on three sides, and with a cloth drawn down from on top, I felt like I was in a safe and secure place. I lay there crying, the tears running down my cheeks and into my ears, when I felt a presence enter my room. It scared me at first then I felt an incredible peace. I kept my eyes closed and felt that more than one person had entered my room.

"I asked God, 'Who are these people in my room?' I could feel that they were standing above the floor right next to my bed and were looking down at me. I knew that I could reach out and touch them but I was afraid to move, to even breathe. I thought they might leave if I opened my eyes. The experience was so wonderful and I felt so peaceful, loved, and accepted that I did not want to break the spell. So I kept my eyes tightly closed. But I wanted to know who they were and what they wanted.

"I felt this experience was something very important and again asked God, 'Who are these spirits?' Even though I had my eyes closed, I could see them. They were young adults and it was made known to me that these were the children I would have. I knew that this was true and I cried tears of great joy because all I ever wanted to be was a mother. Not just any mother, but a great mom, who would have one of the best families, full of all that was good that I had been denied. Up to then, I had had doubts that I would even survive my depression let alone become a mother.

"Here I was lying in my bed with my future children standing next to me. Each individual child was unique yet they all were united in thought and purpose.

"The first child stepped forward and spoke to me through telepathy. She was vivacious, outgoing, bubbly and overjoyed that I was to be her mother. She let me know that she was excitedly anticipating her chance to come to earth. She had so much joy and enthusiasm for life that she could not contain it.

"The next child slowly became known to me in a more subdued fashion. He was quieter but yet I could feel him totally and thoroughly. It was as if we touched hearts, spirit to spirit. He was sweet, kind, and loving. I felt a great sense of gratitude emanating from him that he would be my son. I also saw a second little girl. These three I saw distinctly but I also sensed a fourth child. I then knew that I could and would have four children.

"I was excited and thrilled and felt so special that the Lord had allowed me to meet these children, my future family. All my life I wanted to be a Mom. Even in the first grade when we talked about what we wanted to be when we grew up, I would always say, 'I want to be a mom, a really great mom.' I was teased a lot about this, but it was true. That is what I really wanted to be. My Heavenly Father had just revealed that I would have my wish. I would be a mother if I would only hang in there. This experience was to be such a comfort and joy to me in the future. It helped me to try harder, to persevere even on the worst of days.

"I know that Heavenly Father wanted this to happen to me so that I could have comfort when there didn't seem to be any hope. I am very thankful to Him for this experience.

"When my first child was born and handed to me, I looked at him and recognized him. I said, 'I know you. You are one of those who appeared to me.' This scenario repeated itself with each child at its birth. I clearly recognized each child and there was an immediate bonding.

"I was surprised that my first child was a boy as I had expected my children to show up in the order I had seen them. But I now realize that the exuberance of my first daughter, her excitable nature and intense desire to meet me resulted in me seeing her first. My son who was born first is a lot more reserved and easy going. Their personalities were well-established long before their births.

"When I first saw my future children I was nearly thirteen and they were anxious to see and converse with me. But I was so overwhelmed by them that I backed off, cut our visit short. I knew I was to be their mother. They expressed joy at this fact, and it astounded me. In fact it overwhelmed me. Please remember that I was but a child and these beings appeared to me to be far older, wiser and more mature than I.

"I came from an abusive, inexpressive, unemotional family. I felt unloved, unlovable, and very insecure. So this experience with my future children of unconstrained, unconditional love and appreciation was unbelievable. This was the first time in my life that I felt important, desirable, loved, and that I had everything to live for. It was fantastic.

"A number of years after this experience with my family-to-be, I was still terribly afraid of men. In fact I feared that it would be impossible for me to get close enough to any man to be able to fall in love and get married. I had been consulting with the Lord about my concerns and fears when I received a vision in which I was shown my future husband. I saw every feature of him, the color of his hair, the shape of his head, his body build, mannerisms, everything but his face. I knew that I would recognize him when I met him and I did. I knew without doubt that he was safe to get close to and that he would not hurt me.

"Childhood abuse is devastating. It is extremely difficult to get over. Your whole life is so affected that even with the marvelous experience I had, it still intrudes into and impacts my life. For example, one day I was reflecting back over my childhood and all the horrible things that had happened to me. I looked up into the heavens and asked, 'Why? Why, oh God, was I born into such a terrible abusive family?' In response I received such a jolt that I was thrown to the floor. I looked up and there stood my father's father. I said to him, 'How could you have been so mean and cruel to my father that he would be so cruel to me?'

"He responded, 'My father beat me so severely that I bled from my mouth. He kicked me out of his home when I was but a child of seven. I survived, but it was not easy. I didn't know how to be better. I was better to your dad than mine was to me.'

"I thought about this, and said, 'Well, okay.' Then I saw my mother's mother. I asked her, 'Why didn't you love my mother? Why did you hurt her so?'

"She said to me, 'Men hurt and abused me so much that I didn't know how to love, cuddle, and show affection.' She told me that her parents sold her to her first husband, and he treated her like a piece of furniture. 'But,' she continued, 'I was a better mother to your mother than mine was to me!'

"I was first surprised, then disturbed by what they had told me. Who they were was part of an abusive legacy. It was then I realized that if they had been better parents than their parents, I could accept this and forgive them. Their legacy was in part, my legacy and I now understood my parents' actions and treatment of me better.

"About a year later, God again appeared to me. He said, 'I have given you this experience with your children and ancestors not to keep to yourself. I let you have that experience because you are of a choice generation. You were chosen to come to earth at this time to stop these generations of abuse. You must go to your family and share this experience. It is through you and this generation that the abusive chain reaction in your family will stop.'

"This rebuke and command from the Lord was not an easy one. I was afraid of how my parents would take it but I was much more concerned about possible repercussions from the Lord. I was very surprised and elated by my parents' reaction. They both knew that my experience was legitimate and real. My sisters also accepted the experience and are attempting to be better parents. I told my children of my experience and the statement from the Lord that they are a chosen generation and that it is through them that generations of abuse will terminate."

This woman discovered that she had been chosen—might even have volunteered—to come to her family to end a legacy of abuse. Although abuse had persisted for generations, at least members of succeeding generations had tried to be better. But it was she whose specific mission it was to bring about the ending of this deadly pattern.

### Medical Problems

Anyone who has suffered through serious medical problems doesn't soon forget them—or wish to repeat them. Beth certainly didn't. Her first pregnancy had been fraught with major complications and her recovery had been slow and painful. When she discovered that she was pregnant again she became depressed.

"Though I love my daughter deeply, my pregnancy had not been a pleasant thing. I wanted children but was very fearful of pregnancy, labor, and the recovery period.

"When I discovered I was pregnant I went into a deep

depression. My fears were realized as the pregnancy was indeed difficult and became more difficult as it progressed. During my eighth month I was forced to get up and go to the bathroom eight or more times each night. I got very little sleep and was totally miserable. One night as I got up for the tenth time, I noticed that it was only 3:00 A.M.

"I returned to my bedroom and gingerly lay down. I was trying unsuccessfully to find a comfortable position when I felt someone enter the room. I was not frightened because whoever it was radiated a warm, comforting feeling. I didn't want to sit up or open my eyes for fear the person would go away and I would lose that wonderful feeling. But when the presence got right in front of me, I did open my eyes and saw that it was a young man in his late teens. He was enveloped in a white light, so white and bright that it lit up the whole room. He communicated to my mind that his name was Jonathan and that he was the baby I was carrying.

"He said very simply, 'I have come to let you know I will be with you soon--very soon!'

"I realized that he was there to comfort me and to assure me that all my misery would soon end and that I and my baby would be fine. He then walked away from me and disappeared. The baby was born soon after and everything went well."

Beth's very brief visit from her unborn son did not eliminate her problems but it did calm her, reduce her fears and anxieties, and make her whole ordeal seem worthwhile.

Rebecca Todd was expecting a baby and had some serious concerns that her very busy lifestyle might have negative conse-quences for her baby.

"My husband and I lay in bed one night talking about the future. 'I wish I could stay home with the baby' I worried. 'I don't know how I'm ever going to manage the pressure of work plus all our plans for fixing up the house.'

"'You'll do fine,' John reassured me for what was probably the hundredth time in the eleven weeks I'd been pregnant.

"Still, I was anxious. I had no role model for this—my mother and grandmother had been stay-at-home moms. It seemed as though everything were on my shoulders.

"Around midnight I felt a warm but disturbing sensation inside me. I hurried into the bathroom, John close on my heels. Blood flowed out of me. I fell into his arms, crying. "I know I said I had doubts, but I didn't mean I couldn't handle a baby! I was just afraid.'

"John tried to tell me it wasn't my fault, yet I couldn't stop sobbing. He went to call the doctor.

"'Take it easy.' My doctor calmed me. 'Try and get some sleep and come in first thing in the morning. If you feel any pain, give me a call.'

"John and I returned to bed and prayed together for our baby. Sometime after John fell to sleep I made my own silent plea. *Please God, don't let me lose my baby. I know you'll be there to help me after it's born.* I dozed off.

"It was not yet morning when I opened my eyes. At the foot of my bed was a woman who looked startlingly like my beloved grandmother, smiling down at a tiny baby cradled in her arms. My worries eased and I slept soundly the rest of the night.

"The next morning John squeezed my hand as the doctor examined me and then listened for the baby's heartbeat. Finally, she looked up and smiled.

"'Sounds great, Becky. You don't have to worry about the bleeding last night. Your baby's going to be fine.'

"Six months later I delivered a healthy girl. John and I gazed in wonder at her through the nursery windows. 'Let's name her Megan,' I said, 'In honor of her great-grandmother—and the angel that looked like her.' Giving me that quizzical glance, John nodded."[12]

In the concluding account, a woman experienced severe

complications during the delivery of her child. Not only had the placenta separated from the lining of the uterus, but the obtuse angle of the child's head in the birth canal made delivery difficult. When the child was finally delivered, he was found to have had a severe brain hemorrhage.

The child spent months in the intensive care unit of a small community hospital because the mother did not want to transfer him to a large city medical center where she could not spend full time with him. Her doctors also decided not to move the infant because they felt his injuries were so massive that any subsequent treatment would be unsuccessful. The doctors informed the mother that there was no chance the baby would survive. But she would not give up on her baby and prayed that some miracle would occur.

"Late one night, a being of light came into my hospital room. The being had the shape of a person and glowed with a cold gray light as though the light were being beamed through an ice cube. The being said, 'Your son will be all right.'

"I felt as though love was being poured into my body from the being of light.

"The next day I shared my experience with my medical team. I was especially excited because the being had assured me that my son was going to be normal. 'Would they please do another EEG to see if anything has happened,' I asked?

"They repeated the brain wave test and came up with startling results--normal. The child had made a full recovery."[13]

### Summary Thoughts

This chapter illustrates many things about the relationship between heaven and earth.

1.    Those on the other side are acutely aware of what is occurring in the lives of their families on earth.

2.  The message of those on the other side is that you are never alone. You are of worth. Look to God and He will comfort you.

3.  Parents who have had a child die take heart. That child still lives, is aware of them and their sorrow, and sometimes is able to come to comfort and console them.

4.  For those parents who desperately want children but cannot, it is their desire that is really important to God.

5.  Contrary to the belief of many physicians and others, still-born and late term miscarried babies are children with distinct personalities and identities and they consider themselves to be members of their parents' families.

6.  People who commit suicide have not done themselves any favor, but they are in the care of loving beings and a completely compassionate God.

7.  Abuse of any of God's children is a great wrong, but the pattern of abuse can be broken.

*Chapter Fourteen*
*Protection From Home*

While doing interviews for this book, many individuals told of situations where their lives had been preserved by angelic beings. There are also numerous accounts of people who were saved from death or serious harm by heavenly intervention. In a few cases angelic beings were actually seen.

Protection from our heavenly home can come in many forms. In some cases angelic beings are sent to protect and preserve individuals from serious harm. In other cases a deceased relative has received permission or was assigned to help a family member. In still other cases, the protector is an unborn spirit who is watching out for members of the family he or she will eventually join.

If it is possible to draw any conclusions from the experiences of people who have seen into the pre- and postlife realm, a most basic one would be that there is order there. Neither angelic beings, deceased family members, nor those yet to be born can just take off and travel to earth without permission or assignment. Take John Monsen, for example, who drowned and left a pregnant wife and five little children. These were his exact words:

"I can't always be with you. This is a rare privilege, Chris, for me to speak to you like this, to warn you, and to give you guidelines to follow."[1]

### The Deceased as Protectors
The spirits of those who once lived on earth occasionally have the opportunity to return to earth and intervene in situations that are threatening to family members. It does not matter

whether they lived on earth a short time or a long time, recently or in the far past, on specific occasions and under special conditions they have the power to protect those on earth.

Janette Whetten was heartbroken when her third child was stillborn. Knowing the child was a girl, she had called her Kayla throughout her pregnancy. Kayla has appeared to Janette a number of times, explaining that one of her heavenly assignments is to watch over her brothers and sisters as a guardian angel. One example of her protection occurred when her twenty-one-year-old sister and some friends were in an automobile accident. A truck hit the side of the car not once, but twice, breaking her sister's collarbone and shoulder blade. Witnesses and rescue personnel testified that something or someone had to have been holding the victims in the car or they would all have been killed.

Janette also observed Kayla engaged in other activities which caused her to change her perceptions of those in heaven.

"Once I saw Kayla marking papers on a clipboard near lines of people, as if she were keeping a record of those going to and coming from earth. Another time I saw her in church sitting on the arm of a chair. I asked her why she was sitting on the chair's arm and she cheerfully replied, 'Oh, it's my Dad's house and He lets me.' What a thought! Even though we refer to God as our Father in Heaven, I had never thought of the Supreme Being of the Universe as my 'Dad.' That simple reference has helped me so much. Yes, He is my Dad and he loves me as His daughter. Jesus is my Savior, and also my protective big brother. I have taught our children these concepts and it has made all of us feel much closer to our heavenly family."

Janette's experience with the spirit of her stillborn daughter is interesting for several reasons. The first is that a stillborn infant has a spirit and it survived in the post-mortal world. Second her stillborn daughter's spirit appeared to her mother as a mature young woman. Third, Janette observed her daughter busily engaged in some important work. Fourth, her daughter has a very close relationship with her Heavenly Father. And finally, and most importantly, Kayla assured her mother that she was happy, thriving, and loved. What a sense of peace this could give any grieving parent.

This is not an isolated case of stillborns functioning as guardian angels. A number of individuals informed me of similar events some of which are included elsewhere in this book. But regardless of the length of time spent on earth, connections between those in heaven and on earth are strong and abiding.

In the following accounts, those who had lived into adulthood before they died returned from heaven to protect the living. For example, a young child was saved from serious injury or death by a great aunt she never knew.

One day six-year-old Rachel and her mother (Elizabeth) were assembling a family photo album when they discovered a dog-eared picture of a woman dressed in a business suit.

Rachel grabbed the picture and excitedly exclaimed, "its Aunt Betty! She's the one that saved me."

Elizabeth had no idea what Rachel was talking about. Great Aunt Betty had been the independent woman of the family. She had taken a job as an employee of a bank that had a home office in Chicago. She wore a suit most days, unlike the majority of women of that era. Betty was killed in a train accident before Rachel was born. Elizabeth could not remember ever telling Rachel anything about her Great Aunt Betty.

Rachel said she remembered wandering off alone away from the other children during a family reunion. Elizabeth and all her cousins had gathered with their children for a reunion at the home of Elizabeth's mother. There was lots of homemade food and everyone had brought their favorite dishes to pass around. Elizabeth became so absorbed in getting caught up on all that was happening with her cousins that she forgot about Rachel. Rachel recalled exploring the big house. She saw an open door to the basement stairway and headed toward it. But a lady wearing a blue suit caught her, pulled her away from the door and into her arms. She then sent Rachel away from the stairs. The woman told Rachel she was Aunt Betty and that she didn't want Rachel to get hurt. Rachel said Aunt Betty told her that only she could see her and that she had come just "to save Rachel from an accident."[2]

While in many cases, angelic protectors are dressed in glowing white robes, Great Aunt Betty was dressed in the type of clothing she had customarily worn when she was alive which enabled Rachel to identify her photograph and her mother to verify Betty's identity.

In the next case, heavenly beings intervened to save the lives of many children when David Young and his wife took over an elementary school in Cokeville, Wyoming, May 15, 1986. The Young's entered the school carrying a small arsenal of weapons and pushing a cart containing a large bomb. The Young's herded 156 children and teachers into a classroom. While authorities attempted to negotiate with the Young's, their hostages huddled in terror. In late afternoon, suddenly and without warning, the bomb exploded, destroying the classroom. As the dust settled, frantic parents broke police lines and rushed to the school. To their astonished relief, all the children were safe. The only casualties were the Young's! Bomb expert Richard Haskell observed, "To say it was a miracle would be the understatement of the century."

Many of the children gave a simple explanation for their miraculous escape--they were saved by people dressed in white. For example, sisters Katrina and Rachel told their parents that just before the explosion "people" came down through the ceiling and stood about two feet above the floor.

"They were standing there above us. There was a mother and a father and a lady holding a tiny baby, and a little girl with long hair. They were a family of people. The woman told us the bomb was going to go off soon and to listen to our brother. He was going to come over and tell us what to do. She said to be sure we did what he told us. They were all dressed in white, bright like a light bulb but brighter around the face.

"The woman made me feel good. I knew she loved me. She sort of smiled at me with her voice."

Travis, brother to Katrina and Rachel explained:

"I didn't see anyone, nothing! I just heard a voice. It told me to find my little sisters and take them over by the windows and keep them there. I did what I was told. I looked around and found them and told them to stay there and not to move. They were playing with their friends and I knew they had to come with me. They got their coloring pages and I took them over by the windows. I was told to help them through the window when the bomb went off."

In the days following, Katrina and Rachel recalled that the man in white seemed familiar, as if they knew him, and the woman as having hair like their mother's. Out of curiosity, the family looked through old photos of living and deceased relatives. Katrina examined a picture in an old locket and told her mother, "She looks like that woman, except she didn't have glasses. Then Rachel looked at the picture and excitedly exclaimed, "That's the woman, except she didn't have glasses."

Their mother identified the lady in the locket as her mother, the children's grandmother, who had died when their mother was only sixteen.

None of the children seemed startled or surprised to see people all dressed in white hovering above the floor. Six-year-old Nathan reported:

"A lady told me the bomb was going to go off very soon. She told me how to save myself. She said to go over by the window, then hurry out when I heard the bomb explode. She told me that I would make it if I did exactly what she said."

Nathan did not recognize the lady whose directions saved his life until later when he identified her from a picture in his family photo album. She was his deceased great-grandmother.[3]

Just how many guardian angels came to Cokeville, Wyoming, that day is not known. It is clear that some of the guardians were family members, anxious to protect their loved ones on earth. This would certainly seem to show that family connections and concerns are eternal and extend well beyond death. These concerns and interventions resulted in 156 children being saved from serious injury or death at the hands of a deranged couple. This protection came because some of the children had fervently sought help from God and their prayers were answered.

The fact that eternal family connections exist is also evident in the next case. Marie Bottini's deceased father helped her survive severe injuries when she fell off a cliff.

Marie was thirteen when she fell from a cliff and fractured her skull so badly that slivers of bone were driven into her brain. She lay in the ravine for more than thirty-six hours before being rescued. When her rescuers arrived, she was conscious, calm and rational. She told her rescuers that as the night fell, her father had appeared to her and told her to be patient as she would be found and rescued the next day. She was found the next day and her physician tried to tell her that her father was dead and could not have been with her. But Marie knew otherwise. She knew it was her father who had stayed with her and given her courage that long and painful night.[4]

Being trapped in a ravine is frightening enough, but to be alone and severely injured as well must be terrifying. But Marie was not alone. Her beloved father was there, comforting her, protecting her, and sustaining her until help could come. She felt no need to struggle thus avoiding additional complications to her fractured skull and enabling her to conserve her strength.

In the next account, five-year-old Jennifer was run over by a truck. How she survived and why was miraculous—as far as worldly understanding is concerned. But to Jennifer it was not a miracle. Her story was reported by her mother.

"I had been having premonitions that something bad was going to happen to my little daughter. So when the phone call came from a neighbor that Jennifer had been run over, I said, 'I knew it.'

"I ran to my neighbor's and found Jennifer. Her bloodied body was being held in my husband's arms. Her stomach had been mashed flat, and she was horribly scratched. She looked up at me and said, 'I'm okay Mommy, I didn't die.' Her assurances caused me to break down completely.

"I was told that a one-ton truck with dual wheels on the back had run over her. Jennifer was riding her Hot Wheel and was behind the truck when the driver started backing up. The driver was high on marijuana and had not been paying attention to what might have been behind him. He said he felt his truck hit something he thought was a child's toy, so he stepped on the accelerator to back over it, stopping only when he heard a muffled scream. When he got out and looked at the back of his truck, he saw a small child under the rear wheels. He hurriedly got back into the truck and drove it off her body. Then he ran back to where the child was lying, picked her up, and put her on the grass thinking she was dead.

"While he was desperately searching for help, Jennifer jumped up and started yelling at him. He was shocked but relieved that she was still alive and brought her to my neighbor's where my husband found her.

"The doctors at the hospital told us that Jennifer would not live through the night. But she did. She was in Intensive Care and in great pain and she kept calling for her Grandpa Lemmon. We initially thought that she was calling for her living grandfather, but she insisted she wanted Grandfather Lemmon—who was actually her great-grandfather on my husband's side—who had died many years earlier.

"Two years later, when Jennifer was seven, we went to a family reunion in Idaho. Great Grandmother Lemmon was still alive and would be at the reunion, and this would be the first opportunity for Jennifer to meet her. In Great Grandmother's house an entire wall was devoted to pictures of relatives—grandchildren, great-grand-children, children, spouses, and others. Great Grandfather Lemmon was active in athletics during his life. He had been a professional ball player when he was young and his wife had pictures of him on the wall amongst all the others.

"When we arrived my son took Jennifer to the wall of pictures which she examined with great interest. Then she excitedly pointed to a picture of her great-grandfather Lemmon and said. 'There's Grandpa Lemmon. That's how he looked when he came to me while I was under the truck only he was all dressed in white.' We were astonished and queried her further about the incident. We asked her if Grandpa Lemmon had said anything to her, and she said: 'Yes, he told me that he loved me and everything would be okay, and to tell Grandma that he loved her.'

"The picture that she had selected was taken when Great-grandpa Lemmon was thirty-five years of age. He was in coveralls with the farm as backdrop. I showed her some other pictures when he was older, but she said he didn't look like that."[5]

Jennifer was comforted and saved by her great-grandfather. She had never met him but she knew who he was, even his name. The grandfather she saw was not an old man but a young man in the prime of life. Not only had he sustained her through the accident and her long and painful recovery, but he also told her that he loved her and assured her that she would be okay, which she accepted without question. He was also able to convey through her his love for his beloved wife. So through an innocent child the bonds of love were extended between generations and worlds.

In the next account an adventurous young woman was saved from certain death by heavenly intervention.

Bonnie Brimley has always been the sort of person who likes challenges so when friends suggested that they go skydiving to celebrate their high school graduation, she was all for it. It was arranged that a group of them would go on June 7, 1980. However by the night before their scheduled jump, all of her friends had backed out. Bonnie decided to go anyway.

To make a jump you have to have intensive training. Bonnie was taught how parachutes work and what to do in an emergency, such as how to deploy her reserve parachute. This was quite difficult for Bonnie as she had to reach her right hand across her body and pull the lever that was located near her left hip. After the lever was pulled you had to twist your body forward and to the left. This maneuver would allow the chute to expand and to open. Bonnie felt compelled to listen to this part of the class very intently and she memorized all the steps necessary to deploy the emergency chute.

After the six-hour instruction session on the do's and don'ts of skydiving, it was time for the jump. This jump was called a static line jump because one end of a static line is attached to the plane with a clip and the other end of the line to the jumper. As the jumper leaves the plane, the static line pulls tight and automatically deploys the chute then detaches from the jumper. A telecommunication device connected to an instructor on the ground for monitoring jumpers is required for all first time jumpers.

As they boarded the old World War II plane, Bonnie began feeling a sense of unease. She prayed to her Father in Heaven to let everything be okay and to keep her safe.

The plane took off and before Bonnie knew it, it was her turn. She jumped without hesitation. Her parachute deployed but she didn't feel like she was slowing down. She looked up and saw that her parachute was in a position called a streamer. It had come out of her bag but had not deployed properly. It was in a long stream twisting tighter and tighter as she fell.

Over the radio she heard, "Number six, number six--you need to pull your reserve parachute. Number six, pull the lever for your reserve parachute!." She was number six.

Hearing the voice jarred Bonnie into action. She reached across her body and deployed her reserve chute. But it went straight into the air and tangled with the other chute.

Bonnie could not believe what was happening to her. She again prayed to God for help. She could hear the ground instructor tell her to untangle her two chutes. She looked up and tried to reach the cords but could reach only about a foot over her head. Suddenly she saw a man appear above her. He was dressed all in white and he told her that everything was going to be all right. He then went about untangling the cords of her reserve chute. As she watched him, she realized she knew him. He was her paternal grandfather who had passed away six months earlier. As soon as he finished untangling the two chutes he turned to her again informing her that she was going to be okay. Then he faded from sight.

Bonnie's descent slowed after her reserve chute came undone and opened. As she neared the ground, her main chute also opened and she landed safely and without harm. It wasn't long after she landed that her instructor from the plane landed near her. He had seen both her parachutes fail and jumped hoping to catch her and help get her parachutes untangled or to catch her and use his parachutes to carry both of them to the ground. He was very surprised and relieved when he saw her chutes open.

Bonnie was told that her survival was a miracle. There was no possible explanation for her chutes opening by themselves; the fact that her two parachutes came untwisted and opened defies the laws of gravity because in order to untangle and open up, the parachutes needed to stop twisting in the direction they were turning and reverse themselves, which never happens. But it did happen and Bonnie knew that it was because her grandfather had been sent by God to save her life.

In the following account, RaNelle Wallace witnessed an angelic being protecting her husband from serious harm when their small plane crashed.

Ignoring several foreboding premonitions, RaNelle boarded a light plane with her pilot husband, Terry. In spite of her fears, the weather looked fine and she knew that her husband was an excellent pilot. For about twenty minutes they flew through blue skies and sunshine. Then, with no warning whatsoever, they were seized in the swirling fury of a blizzard. Disoriented, Terry misjudged their elevations and they crashed. RaNelle was terribly burned, but Terry was relatively unscathed. After a tortuous trip down the freezing mountain, an ambulance was summoned. That's when RaNelle collapsed and her spirit left her body. She was taken to heaven where she was shown how and why Terry was not seriously injured:

"When our plane crashed, my husband's life was saved by one of his ancestors. That ancestor stepped in and prevented the fire from consuming or even seriously hurting him. This ancestor had petitioned the heavenly counsel and had been given permission to come to earth and save Terry. However the intervention was not just for Terry. It was also for Terry's unborn children, his grandchildren, and those children who were already here. I was shown how his life was interconnected with those of many other people and without him, their abilities to complete their missions, which he agreed in premortality to assist, would have been compromised."

One might ask why RaNelle was not equally protected. She learned it was because the tests she was to endure on earth were different than Terry's. The growth plan for each individual is customized by ourselves and by an all-wise Father.

RaNelle Wallace's experience is but a small fragment of a very complex and beautifully written book entitled, *The Burning Within*.[6] She learned that heaven and earth are very close, and that what we do or fail to do impacts both those on earth and those in heaven. Without her accident, she might never have acquired this knowledge.

### The Unborn As Protectors

In the preceding sections, the beings sent to intervene and protect were deceased relatives. In this section the intervening protective spirits are those who have not yet been born.

Cathy did not like driving in the snow, especially at night. Her husband usually drove under these conditions, but this night she was driving. Her car went into a skid, left the road, and landed on its wheels in a river.

"I tried to paddle the car with the snow shovel but we were in a small whirlpool and just went around in circles. My husband climbed out the window and got the spare tire out of the trunk for me to float on. He swam for shore and I tried to push off from the car on the tire. Unfortunately the tire was somehow attached to the car and I could not use it for flotation as it was going down with the car. By this time I was ready to give up. Death seemed a treat, as I would get to see my deceased mother again. My husband hollered at me from the shore and then seemed to disappear as I sank under the ice. I resigned myself to an easy death.

"Then I heard, 'But I haven't even been born yet!' This didn't seem relevant at that time, but a hand or force or whatever seemed to grab me by the collar of my jacket and much as a cat carries a kitten, propelled me to shore. We found and broke into a cabin. At the time I was so cold that I was dropping in and out of consciousness. Then I heard the voice again, 'I'm not born yet.' We were rescued in the morning.

"Three years later my son was born. The first night I was home with him I had a vision in which I saw my mother, my grandmother and all the women that preceded me nursing their children, and I felt connected to this pattern or plan. Then I knew it was my son who had spoken the night of the accident."[7]

Cathy had to live if her son was to be born. To insure this could happen, he intervened to save her. Her vision of all the women in her past, nursing their infants, helped her identify who her infant son was and realize that motherhood is part of a divine plan.

In the following account, Heinze Bernstein, a German engineer during World War II, discovered that this world and the next are a lot closer than he had ever imagined. He was stationed on a massive battleship, the 'unsinkable' Von Trippets. This ship posed a serious threat to Allied shipping and had been under heavy bombing attacks for over a year. Finally, thirty-two Lancaster bombers managed to penetrate the Von Trippets' defenses and scored multiple direct hits.

The huge ship immediately begins keeling over. Lights flicker. Explosions, the screech of buckling steel and cries of frantic crew members are everywhere. Heinze Bernstein, the chief electrical engineer, works feverishly to save the ship's failing electrical supply. Then comes the Captain's order through the emergency intercom, "Evacuate the below decks."

Before he and his crew can evacuate, all the lights fail and the ship turns completely upside down. Bernstein and his mates find themselves disorientated in pitch blackness. The water level is rising fast . They must find a way to the bottom of the ship—which is now the top and the only portion above water—or they will drown.

Then the incredible happens. There in front of them appears a small boy radiating light. Bernstein's first reaction is to ask, "How did you get here?" but then he recognizes the boy. It is his son, his only son who had died months before. As Bernstein stares in disbelief, the boy points to a hatch, now visible in his luminescence saying, "This way, Father."

Bernstein's three colleagues also see the boy clearly and ask aloud, "How did he get here? How can he glow?"

"This way, Father," repeats the boy.

Uncertain whether he'd heard the words aloud or in his mind, Bernstein concludes this is a time for action not questions. Quickly he slips through the hatch pointed out by the boy and climbs the inverted ladder. As his three colleagues catch up, Bernstein recognizes where they are and knows that they must keep moving for any chance of escape. By this time his deceased son has disappeared along with his light, but Bernstein knows the direction to go.

Feeling their way along, the men reach a large compartment where emergency lights still flicker. Bernstein knows that just above them is a large fuel oil compartment that should be empty. It is the last compartment next to the double hull and their final refuge where they could bang on the hull until someone hears them and cuts them out. That is if the boat is not totally submerged. Bernstein forces open a manhole cover and hauls himself through into pitch blackness. The stench is sickening with oil slime everywhere. It is pitch black; how can they reach the top?

Then light again pierces the pitch blackness. Bernstein looks to the source, expecting to see his deceased son, but this time the light is radiating from a small girl with long blonde hair and blue eyes. She speaks, "You will get out of here." Two of his three companions also see her as they climb into the oily chamber. Then she vanishes.

The men, too astonished to speak, are confined in darkness so thick they can almost feel its weight. Their wonder is broken by a knocking, a pounding sound to their right. It is other survivors who have found their way to other compartments in the "bottom-up" of the ship. "Thank God," Bernstein utters, "We are not alone."

They attack the double-thick hull with frenzied pounding in hopes of attracting attention of those on the outside. Time passes with no return response. The sailors' furious banging subsides to periodic tapping as fatigue mingles with despair. The oppressive darkness is difficult to bear and breathing the thick fumes adds to the confusion. Bernstein is sure of the bombs, the explosions, the screams, the sinking of the unsinkable ship—these are all real. But what of his deceased son and the blond girl who illuminated their way to safety? Were they real or the hallucinations of a traumatized and chemically-affected mind?

Bernstein's musings are disrupted by a change in the tapping. This time it is directly above—from the outside! Soon the hiss of cutting torches can be heard. They *will* be saved. The little blonde girl was right.

Six years after the war the Bernsteins were celebrating the birthday party of their four-year-old daughter. They invited to the party several survivors of the sunken Von Trippets, along with their wives and children. While the children played, the survivors viewed photos of the ship in a scrapbook and exchanged memories of the war.

After a time, the birthday girl entered the room and snuggled up to her father looking at a photograph of the battleship Von Trippets. In a soft matter-of-fact voice, the four-year-old remarked, "I saw you on the boat. It was so dark. I wanted you to be my daddy and I knew you would be saved." With that, the blue-eyed girl with long blonde hair turned and skipped out the door to rejoin her friends.

Bernstein and his companions were stunned. They had been

there. They had seen her. She was the glowing child who had showed them where to go and assured them, "You will be all right."

As for Bernstein, chills of recognition coursed through him as the memories came hurtling back. In pensive thought he contrasts the face of his four year-old daughter with a face aglow in the black bowels of an unsinkable ship—they are one and the same. Not just one, but two of his children had lighted the darkness of the doomed ship as guardian angels, the first his deceased son pointing the way of escape, and the second his unborn daughter assuring not only their rescue, but that Bernstein would be alive to become her father.

This story is part of a much larger narrative located in the London War Museum and it clearly documents that good men existed on both sides of that terrible war. Bernstein had thought that he had lost his son when he died but discovered that this was not true. His son still lived, was aware of the perils faced by his father, and had safely guided him and his shipmates through a critical area of the capsized ship. At that point he turned them over to his unborn sister. Their actions were coordinated, purposeful, and saved their father. This experience absolutely demonstrates the interconnectedness of premortality, mortality, and postmortality.

In the final account in this section, an unborn daughter saved her mother-to-be.

Tess was home late one evening when several men broke into her house and viciously assaulted her. As they bludgeoned her she felt excruciating pain but suddenly it disappeared and she felt the reassuring presence of a woman. This woman assured Tess that she would survive and that everything would be all right.

"Several years later I gave birth to a tiny little girl. One day when she was just two weeks old, I was holding her and studying her when she opened her eyes and looked at me. I peered deep into those big blue eyes and suddenly I recognized her. I knew without any doubt that she was the woman who had sustained and protected me during that horrendous attack."

The woman Tess sensed did not stop the attack, but assured Tess that she would survive and be okay. I have been told by many people that while the beings seen during near-death experiences may not look like those they knew or were to know on earth, it is the eyes that reveal their true identities. This was certainly true in this case since it was the eyes of Tess's infant daughter that confirmed her identity.

### Angelic Beings as Protectors
In the preceding accounts, the protectors were either deceased or to become family members. In the next section, individuals found themselves being protected by unidentified angelic beings. While is it possible that the angelic beings might have had some family connection to those they helped, no specific connections were identified.

In the first account, a young child and her mother were severely injured in an automobile accident.

"On our way to church a big luxury sedan came speeding through the intersection hitting us broadside. We were rushed to the hospital where, after considerable effort, they were able to stabilize both of us. Over a week later when we were finally able to go home, I was in my bedroom resting when I sensed that someone was in the room of my three-year-old daughter. During our accident she had been thrown against the windshield and suffered severe head injuries.

"I painfully pushed myself into a sitting position, slowly slid my legs over the edge of the bed, and managed to get myself into a standing position. I headed for the door of my daughter's bed-room as quickly as my injuries allowed and was reaching for the doorknob when a voice said, 'Holly! Go to bed!'

"Without thinking I replied, 'But there is someone in her room. I must check on her.'

"The voice repeated, but in slow deliberate words, 'Holly! Go to bed. Everything is okay.'

"I reluctantly went back and struggled into my bed. I lay there on my back crying as fearful thoughts raced through my mind.

"Was she in trouble? Was she dying? Was the individual I sensed in her room there to take her?

"Then I felt a heavenly peaceful feeling emanating from my daughter's room and I heard a voice saying, 'There are three angels in her room, and they are there to bless her, to help her heal, not to take her.'

"I really wanted to be in there with her but I thought that if I burst into her room, I would in some way disrupt the blessing. So I stayed in my bed and prayed.

"As soon as I woke up the next morning, I rushed into my daughter's room (as much as my pains and bruises would allow) and peeked in. She was awake, sitting on her bed quietly playing. When she saw me she said, 'Mommy! Mommy! There were three angels in my room last night. But don't worry! They were just here to bless me!'"

It would have been most informative to know just what the three angels did and how the little girl was healed but this, unfortunately, didn't happen.

Next, two Jewish children, Jakob and David Bronski, were protected by angelic beings during the Nazi occupation of their small Polish village. The boy's mother had a dream in which an angel told her to send her sons to the home of a woodcutter she knew who lived in the forest. She paid the woodcutter a lot of money to care for her sons. But as the days passed the woodcutter became increasingly concerned that someone would find out that he was harboring Jews and he became fearful that he and his family would be arrested and possibly executed. So he told the boys they would have to leave. His wife felt sorry for the two little boys and gave them a package containing a loaf of bread and some cheese. She told them not to go back home as the Germans were there and would kill them. She suggested that they should find a place to hide in the forest. For five days the boys hiked deep into the forest using up all their food. As hunger mounted, the younger of the two boys began complaining and pleading that they go back home. Knowing the danger, the older brother refused.

Late one day they saw in the distance a large country house surrounded by spacious lawns. Behind the house was a small barn in which the older brother thought they might be able to get eggs and milk. They waited until dark and then sneaked into the barn. Jakob did not want to risk going to the house because the farmer might turn them over to the Nazis.

In the barn, food was scarce. All they could find were a few small potatoes. But because they were so hungry, the potatoes tasted wonderful. Then they tunneled into the warm hay and fell into a deep sleep.

When Jakob awoke, the sun was shining. They had overslept. He poked his little brother and said, "Come on! We've got to get back to the woods before anyone sees us."

"I already see you," someone said.

Jakob sat bolt upright. His heart pounded in his chest. A teenage girl was standing above them with a milk bucket in her hand.

"I'm sorry," Jakob started to say.

The girl smiled pleasantly, "You're Jewish aren't you?"

"I am," said Jakob, "but my brother isn't." Then he realized how silly that sounded. "I meant to say my friend, not my brother."

The girl's smile was even bigger. "It's all right. You're safe with me." She reached out her hand to help him up from the hay, but Jakob still wasn't sure if he could trust her.

"I think you should have some breakfast," the girl said. "Don't you?"

"Breakfast?" Little David had awakened and had heard that beautiful word.

"Yes, breakfast. Let's see, how do some eggs and toast sound? And of course a big glass of milk?"

"That sounds wonderful," David said. He looked at his brother, but Jakob didn't seem very eager to accept the offer.

She said, "Look, my name is Anna and I work for the owner and his wife."

Jakob asked, "Who are the owners?" When she told them, Jakob's blood ran cold. The man she named owned the bank in town and hated Jews almost as much as the Nazis did. When she saw the frightened look on his face she said, "Relax! My master will be gone for another two hours. By then you will have had your breakfast and be well on your way. You will be all right, I promise. After all, you are very lucky children to have so many guardian angels."

Jakob stared at her. "What do you mean?"

The girl laughed, and then noticing that his expression hadn't changed, hurried to explain. "Last night the owners were having a little too much wine with their supper. The Missus thought she heard a noise coming from the barn—sometimes foxes do get in, you know—and she made the mister go and see what the problem was. In a minute he was back, his face as white as a sheet.

"Well," she asked, "What was it?"

"I saw angels," he replied. "A band of them, standing shoulder to shoulder, surrounding the barn. And each of them was holding a flaming sword. My mistress thought her husband was drunk and made him promise to go to church today and that is where they are right now. But he was not drunk last night."

"What do you mean?' asked Jakob.

Anna's face became very serious. "There really were angels surrounding the barn. I saw them myself, and I hadn't been drinking at all. When I heard what he was telling his wife, I looked out the kitchen window and there they were!"

"Angels with flaming swords?" Jakob asked. It sounded crazy to him.

Anna nodded, "Well, I didn't see the swords. And I didn't see the angels. Not really. But when I looked out the window, at first I thought the barn was on fire. I mean, there was such a bright light around the barn, that it was all I could see. I helped her to get him upstairs to bed, and when I looked out the window again, all I could see was the barn—looking like it does now."

Anna gave them the address of a cousin of hers who lived in the next town and who would help them to find a safe place to stay. They never saw their parents again, but because of the divine protection of angels, the two brothers survived the war.[8]

The way in which guardian angels manifest their presence varies tremendously. They can reveal themselves through a voice, in person, or as glorious glowing beings with swords. These two boys were given the protection they needed--a spectacular visitation of angels standing shoulder to shoulder with drawn flaming swords-- of which the two boys were completely unaware. Evidently these two young boys had some important mission to perform so their lives were preserved.

Nearly 100 years earlier, five-year-old Samuel Rutherford was saved from certain death by an angel.

In Scotland in the 1800s Samuel, a five-year-old boy, fell into the village well. His frightened playmates ran to the nearest house for help. Several men and women rushed to the rescue, fearing that the boy had already drowned. When they arrived, they were astonished to find the bedraggled Samuel, dripping wet and sitting on a mound of grass, not far from the well. "A bonny white man came and drew me out of the well," the boy told them. The well was far too deep for the boy to climb out by himself. The "bonny white man" was an angel. That shining figure saw to it that Samuel would live out every one of the days that God had allotted him.[9]

In many accounts, angels are described as being dressed in white (mostly robes) and both the angel and his or her clothes glow with a brilliant white light that comforts and emanates a sense of peace such as did the "bonny white man." The same description fits the protective beings in the next three accounts related by Brad and Sherry Steiger in their book, *Angels Over Their Shoulders*. This book is filled with fascinating and inspirational accounts of angelic rescues.

Myrna Martinson was awakened from her sleep by a beautiful spirit being who told her to pray. She did as she was bade and continued in earnest prayer for an hour or more. At last a feeling of tranquility came over her and she fell back to sleep.

A few hours later, she was awakened from her sleep once again—the second time by a startling telephone call that informed her that at the very time she had been praying, her nine year-old daughter, Tammy, who was away visiting grandparents, was trapped in their burning home.

The fireman who rescued the girl said that he had found the child's bedroom completely enveloped in flames—except for the corner in which Tammy crouched. Standing protectively over the girl, the fireman swore, was "an awesome being, all white and silvery," who withdrew at his approach and seemed to turn over the rescue of the girl to his professional firefighter's skills.

Later, after she had spent some time breathing from an oxygen mask, Tammy corroborated the fireman's perceptions of the "awesome" silvery and white being.

"He was my guardian angel," she said simply. "And he protected me from the fire until the big fireman came."[10]

The mother's willingness to do what a spirit being told her to do, demonstrated her faith and her faith helped save her daughter. It was not clear if the being who appeared to the mother and the being who saved the daughter were one and the same; the important thing is that Myrna obeyed the instruction to pray and a miracle occurred.

Phyllis was five years old when she was saved from certain death by an angel.

"I was busily playing with my friend when my mother called for me to come home. I ran out into the street not noticing the traffic. Too late I saw the oncoming truck and, trying to stop, I fell into its path. An angel in a white robe pulled me away just in time. He told me that it was not my time yet."[11]

In the following account, both casual observers and the two children involved were able to witness who saved them. While it is not unusual for young children to see angelic beings, it is more unusual for adults to share their vision as they did in the case that follows.

Two sisters aged eight and four, fell into a river. While the hysterical mother screamed that her daughters could not swim, a man who had been fishing from a boat set out at once on a rescue attempt. Although the fisherman was determined to make a valiant effort, in his heart he felt that there would be no way that he could reach the little girls before they drowned. He truly feared that his efforts would be futile.

When he pulled alongside them, however, he found the little girls floating calmly in an "unnatural manner," as if they were "somehow supported from underneath."

The men and women who had watched the rescue from the shore stated that they had seen a beautiful person in white supporting the girls until the fisherman overtook them. The girls themselves insisted that an angel had prevented them from sinking under the water, and they described their ethereal rescuer in vivid detail. [12]

Most people would give credit to the man in the boat for saving the two girls. But he and everyone there knew that he had played only a small part in their rescue. It is unfortunate that the children did not share the description of their rescuers in more detail.

### Summary Thoughts

A question always arises as to why some children are saved through divine intervention while others die. I do not have an answer to this question but believe there is undoubtedly a reason. I have a daughter who is mentally handicapped, a nephew who suffers from a severe case of cerebral palsy, a son-in-law who died of AIDS, and a father and stepfather who were killed in automobile accidents. I have asked "why" many times. I sincerely believe that there is some grand purpose which I will someday understand.

Meanwhile there are several things of which I am certain. The first is that death is not the enemy. Second, death does not destroy relationships. Third, death is but a door to our heavenly home. Fourth, when we cross through the portal of death, we will have a grand reunion with all our departed relatives and friends. And fifth, we should never seek out death but actively work to complete our missions on earth until it is our time to return home.

From the foregoing accounts, it is apparent that the connection between heaven and earth commences long before birth and continues long after death. Throughout this process a heavenly order prevails and there is an eternal plan that supersedes the personal desires of individuals in heaven or on earth. When a crisis occurs on earth, beings may be sent from heaven to intervene if the crisis could impact negatively on eternal plans. Whether these beings are deceased family beings, children yet to be born, or have no known connection, these protective beings certainly are guardian angels.

## Chapter Fifteen
### Assurances That a Child is on The Way

As we enter the new millennium, diseases that once decimated the world have been virtually eliminated. We live in a time of medical marvels in which new treatments and cures are being discovered every day. Certainly we have much for which to thank doctors and medical scientists. But medicine is not an exact science and cannot fix everything. This chapter is not intended to question or discount the expertise of doctors although it does demonstrate that medicine doesn't have all the answers. Some parents were told by a voice from heaven, or by visions, still others by the unborn child itself that their baby is normal in spite of adverse medical diagnose.

An apparently infertile couple who desperately wanted a family were informed by a total stranger that they would have at least three children.

Until that particular Sunday, Sue had never met Alice, a near-death survivor who returned to earth life with unusual spiritual gifts. While visiting Sue's church, Alice glanced up from her prayers to see three children hovering above a couple seated a few pews ahead of her. It was clear to Alice that these souls desired to join the couple. Sue continues the story:

"Long before I married I wanted to be a mother. One of the things that attracted me to Bill was his strong desire to have a family. We believed and expected that children would naturally follow once we married, but they didn't.

"Doctors assured us there was no medical problem why we could not conceive, but it did not happen. Bill and I both came from large happy families and could not imagine marriage without children. We tried many physicians including fertility specialists but nothing worked. After years of trying, our hopes of ever having children were fading. Feeling very depressed we decided to go to church with a two-fold prayer in our hearts: If I could not bear children, might we be comforted by knowing why? And was it time for us to consider adopting?

"While we were praying a stranger approached, introducing herself to us. Then she said, 'Heavenly Father has permitted me to see your three children.'

"Shocked we asked almost in unison, 'What did you say?'

"'Heavenly Father has permitted me to see your daughter and your two sons. They are keenly aware of your desire to have them, and they will be yours in due time.'

"Her calm certitude brought us to tears. This was the answer to our prayers. 'Thank you! Thank you!' I exclaimed while vigorously shaking her hand.

"Alice returned to her home, which was not in the same state where we lived. We maintained occasional phone contact for several months. Then came that joyous day when I called Alice to announce I was pregnant.

"Alice was unable to visit at the birth of our babies, so I sent her pictures of the children as they grew. Alice recognized each of them as the children she had seen clustered around us that day.

"Having children did not come easily to me. I suffered from a wide range of medical problems which made each pregnancy extremely difficult and increasingly complicated. My first child was a girl and later a boy. Childbearing took a severe toll on my health and my physicians expressed escalating concern for my health and even for my survival, should I become pregnant again. But I was resolute. Knowing without doubt that a second son desired to join our family, I conceived a third time against all medical advice.

"Soon I was confined to bed with multiple complications. This pregnancy was extremely difficult but I endured it knowing that a son awaited. Finally, and to our great surprise, I gave birth to a beautiful blonde blue-eyed girl. Bill and I were delighted to have a second daughter but both of us were certain that Alice had said that she saw two boys and a girl hovering about us. Could we have misunderstood? Nevertheless, Bill and I had a distinct impression that this baby was somehow a special gift from God.

"I called Alice with the great news that we had a second little daughter. While we were chatting I inquired, 'Alice, when you told us that you saw three children clustered about us, what were their genders?'

"'I saw two boys and a girl,' she confirmed.

"'Alice, we now have two girls and a boy. What does it mean?'

"Alice said, 'I really don't know but let me inquire of the Lord. I will let you know what He tells me.'

"Later that day Alice called back with a remarkable answer to our question. She said, 'Sue, your newborn daughter is indeed a very special gift. She was intended to be the child of your sister, but she is now given to you. This child knows she is blessed to be born into your loving and devoted family. She has come willingly and gratefully to you and Bill. She will always show love and appreciation to you as her parents. Your unborn son is still waiting his turn to join your family. You will have him and regardless of what others might tell you, he will arrive safely and live.'"

"While Alice was speaking I was overwhelmed with emotions and was temporally unable to speak. I thought to myself, *How could Alice have known?* Once back in control I said, 'Alice, my sister committed suicide. She was a beautiful blue-eyed blonde. As you know, neither Bill nor I nor our two children are blonde or have blue eyes.'

"Eventually I conceived and give birth to Tommy, in spite of my doctors' warnings of permanent disabilities for me and my child, including a high probability I would die. Some of my physicians even withdrew from my case because I refused to follow their medical advice. I was undeterred. I knew without any doubt that I had a second son waiting to be born and if I had to go down into the very shadow of death to bring him into this world, I would. And I did.

"With Tommy's birth I knew that our family was complete and let my greatly-relieved physician tie my tubes."

Doctors predicted serious complications in all of Sue's pregnancies and they were right. But medical science could not predict the ultimate outcome of each of Sue's pregnancies. Sue had heavenly assurance that she was supposed to have these children, and the babies would be born healthy in spite of severe discomfort, pain, and being incapacitated for most of the nine months for all four pregnancies.

It is also interesting that a child scheduled to be born to her sister would end up in Sue's family. Supposedly Sue was to have only three children. Alice's vision confirmed this. But when her sister committed suicide, Sue "inherited" a fourth child whose appearance resembled that of the mother she was originally intended to have. This raises some intriguing questions as to the influence of the spiritual body on the development and appearance of the physical body.

Sometimes assurance from heaven can help parents to make correct decisions and guarantee a child the right to be born. Prior to his birth, Shawn Michael appeared to his future father to announce his name and that he would come soon. This knowledge helped Shawn Michael's mother to deal with some major decisions she would soon have to make.

"For several days I had been having severe headaches and nausea, and went to my doctor to find out why. Tests revealed that I had a walnut-sized brain tumor. I was immediately referred to the regional cancer center where they engaged in very aggressive procedures to treat the tumor--radiation, chemotherapy, and many x-rays. Almost everything they did was extremely toxic but I was told I would die without them. Of the innumerable tests I endured, none was for pregnancy, Pregnancy had not occurred to me because, after thirteen miscarriages, I had been informed that my childbearing years were over.

"The day I was scheduled to have brain surgery, friends and relatives from all over the city and country joined in prayer for me. No matter where they lived, they all synchronized their watches so that they would be praying at the same time.

"Just before my surgery, my surgeon requested an x-ray to help him pinpoint the precise location of the brain tumor including all its major blood vessels. The radiologist injected radioactive dye and took an x-ray which clearly displayed the big ugly tumor and all its associated blood vessels. As they were about to wheel me into the operating room my surgeon decided that he needed one last x-ray. The x-ray was taken and the technician had an absolutely astounded look on her face as she brought the film in to the surgeon.

"The tumor was nowhere to be seen! The blood vessels and segments of the brain were clearly visible but the tumor was gone. For no known medical reason it had simply disappeared. The surgeon was dumfounded! More experts were brought in and additional x-rays made. The tumor was completely gone. My doctor said it was a medical mystery, but I knew it was a miracle.

"There is a parallel story. Just prior to my scheduled surgery, for some reason that is not clear to me now, I insisted on a pregnancy test. After all that I had gone through they must have thought I was losing it, but they humored me. To everyone's surprise, the test was positive. I was two weeks pregnant. During those two weeks I had received massive amounts of radiation and toxic chemicals to combat the tumor. The doctors were absolutely sure that the fetus I was carrying had been severely damaged so they sent me to a specialist.

"The specialist began by declaring. 'If the tests verify serious problems with your fetus, I will abort it. Even before I run these tests I know what I will find. The fetus will be damaged, cannot help but be damaged because of the massive amounts of chemicals, radiation, and x-rays you have received. The fetus will be grossly deformed and its brain severely impacted. Even if it were to survive birth, which I doubt, it will not live long.'

"What a bedside manner! And all the time I was there he never once referred to my baby as a person, only as an it, a thing, a fetus. He continued, 'If for some unknown and totally unexpected reason the fetus survives, it would be so damaged that neither you nor husband could care for it. You would have to place it in an institution which would be prohibitively expensive and not fair to it, you, your husband, or society.'

"But as he spoke, I recalled my husband's dream. I knew that this baby was not an 'it'! He was a little boy named Shawn Michael, who had appeared to his father, declared his name, and announced he wanted to come to us.

"The doctor interrupted my thoughts handing me papers to sign authorizing the abortion. Somewhat dazed I slowly shook my head and told him in no uncertain tone of voice, 'No!'

"He pressed, 'If you will not sign, I will not run the tests.'

"His attitude aroused my motherly instincts. I arose, staring defiantly into his eyes and said firmly. 'I will not sign papers for you to abort my child. And because of your arrogance I refuse to pay for this demeaning, manipulative session!'

"And that was that. I walked out knowing that the baby I was carrying, my Shawn Michael, would be okay.

"The day Shawn Michael was to be delivered, my doctor arranged for me to be taken to the largest delivery room in the hospital. In anticipation of a severely damaged baby, special staff had been assembled along with an impressive array of machines. To the surprise of all the medical personal present, and contrary to all medical prognoses, I delivered a normal healthy baby boy. I had always known that Shawn Michael would be okay and now the medical experts knew it, too.

"There is a scale, the APGAR, which many hospitals use for evaluating the status of newborns. The scale runs from 1 to 10, ten being perfect. In this hospital, healthy babies rarely ranked over 8. Shawn was a 9! If I had listened to the doctors instead of to his spirit, Shawn would have been aborted and what a terrible waste that would have been."

It is true that some parents' desires do not reflect medical realities, but in this case and others explored in this chapter, the assurances that all is well comes from a higher power. Shawn Michael had appeared to his father to assure him that in spite of all his wife's miscarriages, he would be a father. This experience totally convinced the couple that there was no need to terminate the pregnancy.

The year was 1909. Jane Atwood was expecting her seventh child. She had already had six sons and was hoping and praying that this child would be a girl. She was an excellent seamstress and had made pretty little dresses over the years which she had never been able to use. She had dreams of teaching daughters how to sew and cook, of dressing them in pretty frilly dresses and of fixing their hair. A little girl would be a delightful respite from her rough and tumble sons. When her baby turned out to be a girl, she was ecstatic. But her joy was shattered when the baby lived only a few hours. She was almost consumed by her grief. Lying in bed, tears streaming down her cheeks, she fell into a deep sleep. She had a most vivid dream, unlike anything she had ever before experienced. She saw herself combing the hair of a little girl and standing behind the little girl was a smaller girl watching her, sort of waiting to have her hair brushed. The girl, whose hair she was brushing, had straw-colored hair and deep blue eyes. They were chatting as she brushed and braided her hair. Then she saw herself brushing and braiding the hair of the smaller girl who had brown hair and sparkling brown eyes. It was the most amazing experience. Jane was both an observer and an active participant in the dream. But what was extremely exciting was that she knew these two little girls were hers. She might have lost her baby, but this gave her assurance that she would yet have two daughters and that they would live.

Several years later, she gave birth to a little blue-eyed girl followed two years later by a beautiful brown-eyed girl with brown hair. A number of years later, as she was brushing the hair of the blond-haired daughter with her little sister standing behind watching, remembrance of her dream came flooding back to Jane.

The woman in this account was my grandmother, and the little blonde girl was my mother.

I heard this story for the first time while visiting my aunt, Verona Carroll, who was eighty-three years of age at the time and who was the little brown-haired girl in the account. I had been discussing my interest about near-death experiences when my aunt said, "Harold, I feel that I must share something your grandmother shared with me," and pulled out her journal and read the experience. A bit later she said, "Harold, now that I have told you about my mother's experience, I feel impressed to share a beautiful experience I had after I lost a baby because of Rh incompatability of the blood."

When parents lose a much-loved and desired child, they often fear to have additional children, especially if there is a probability that the same problem can affect the new baby. Rh incompatibility is one such problem. Rh incompatibility arises when a woman's blood is Rh negative and her baby's blood is Rh positive. There are usually no problems during a woman's first pregnancy with a baby whose blood is Rh positive. However, the baby may sensitize the woman to Rh-positive blood and this mismatch between the blood of a pregnant woman and that of future babies can lead to hemolytic disease of the newborn. There is a treatment for this problem now, but in the past hemolytic disease was a common cause of stillbirth or death shortly after birth of babies who were born with this problem.

After bearing three healthy boys, Verona's newborn daughter died. She learned it was because she was Rh negative and her baby was Rh positive. She had so wanted a daughter but in the 1950s there was no medical remedy for this problem.

"When my baby was delivered I knew that I had just had a baby girl and I was ecstatic because I already had three sons. But my doctors would not talk to me about my baby. When I insisted that I be permitted to see my baby, they brought her in, held her up so I could see that she was indeed a girl, and then rushed her out of the room. Unbeknownst to me, I was Rh negative and my Rh positive baby was seriously affected. She lived only nineteen hours. At that time, the early 1950s, they did not encourage mothers to see, let alone hold, dead babies. So all I ever had was a very brief glimpse of my tiny daughter.

"I was grieving beyond belief. My husband was very supportive, but his work took him out of town for extended periods. About a month after Kathy died, I was lying on my bed at home trying to read when something caught my attention and I looked up. I saw a nurse holding a baby. The nurse asked, 'Do you want to hold her?'

"I immediately said, 'Yes!' and she handed me the baby. I felt a great surge of love emanating from the infant I was holding. I knew without doubt this baby was not Kathy, but a little girl I was someday going to have. She was beautiful, and when our eyes locked, I knew she would be okay.

"Then the scene changed and I found myself in a room chatting with a number of women. As we were visiting, a young woman of about sixteen years of age came into the room and stood by me. I put my arm around her and said to those in the room, 'I would like you to meet my daughter.' As soon as the word daughter was out of my mouth, the scene disappeared. I was fully awake when this happened. It was not a dream. For the first time since Kathy's death I had something to be happy about.

"About five years later, I gave birth to a beautiful healthy little girl we named Linda. Sixteen years after Linda's birth I was at a meeting with a number of women when my daughter walked into the room. I put my arm around her and said, 'I would like you to meet my daughter.' As I said those words, I suddenly remembered the vision I had over twenty-one years earlier. It was then that I realized that I had been privileged to see the baby I was yet to have and be assured she would live and become a lovely young woman."

Aunt Verona continued, "I've never told anyone about this beautiful experience I had years ago, but I feel I must share it with you now." After the telling, she granted permission to include it in this book. Her pre-birth experience is special in that she was comforted by seeing her future daughter at not just one, but two developmental stages—as an infant and as a teenager.

In the next situation, a young woman had just given birth to her first child and was heartbroken when her physician discovered that her infant daughter had a serious congenital heart problem. Her physician visited with her and her husband and told them:

"'This type of medical problem is genetic, and any other children you might have would have a very high probability of having the same disorder. I strongly advise you not to have any more children. Children with this type of disability demand lots of attention and, as she grows, her demands on your time and energy will only increase. It would not be fair to you or your husband to risk having another child with the same disability.'

"This news was devastating since we wanted to have more children but were now afraid to.

"One evening just prior to falling asleep I beheld, in a seeming split-second, a baby. It sat upright, smiling, and appeared very robust and healthy. Our handicapped daughter is quite thin by comparison. I was filled with a spirit of peace as I prayed about this very brief vision and I was informed that the baby was indeed mine and would be just fine.

"Our second daughter was born nine months and two days following this special preview. She was indeed born 'healthy' and was a joy from day one.

"Fourteen months later, I had a dream in which I was shopping at a department store. I saw a circular rack of beautiful clothing. I was with my sister and she pointed out the most delicate and precious maternity smock I had ever seen. I held it in my hands admiring it. A second woman arrived and said, 'If you are not interested, I would like to purchase this smock.'

"My sister then added, 'You have not seen the design on the back.' She then showed me a delicately embroidered scene of a girl and boy kissing. I awoke from that dream with a strong impression that there was yet another child who needed to come to earth, and now! Its time was at hand, but the choice was mine. Again we were blessed with a beautiful and healthy baby girl.

"Later on I had another dream in which I visited my obstetrician. His nurse informed me 'the doctor would have time for me.' I awoke and thought what a curious dream that was. I wasn't pregnant at the time and had no plans to have another child. However, a number of months later my little daughter announced that she would soon have a baby brother. Remembering the smock with the two kissing figures, I immediately called my obstetrician for an appointment. The nurse informed me that my doctor was retiring just weeks before my due date and would not be able to care for me. This made me even more puzzled about my dream. Two weeks later, I called the nurse and asked her who she would recommend I see as my obstetrician. She said, 'Hold on just a second.' She returned a minute later and told me that the doctor had decided to make an exception—'He will have time for you.' During our first visit he told me that my baby would probably be the last one he would ever deliver."[1]

Medically-speaking, the risks were indeed high that any babies this woman had would have serious medical problems. But the mother's dreams clearly informed her that this would not be the case, and each of her subsequent babies was perfectly healthy.

In some situations, problems carrying babies to full term have no identifiable medical cause. Such was the case with Cathy. At the time she was interviewed, she had experienced numerous miscarriages but she kept on trying because of her very strong desire for children, and because she had a feeling that there were some children who would eventually be hers.

"I have always wanted to have a lot of kids. When I married I conceived easily but each time I got pregnant I would lose the child through miscarriage. In spite of my desire for more children and the feeling that more were assigned to me, I was successful in carrying only one little girl to full term.

"Not far into yet another pregnancy, the same old complications returned. I rushed to my obstetrician's office and started to miscarry right there in the waiting room. I had taken fertility pills to achieve this pregnancy and now panicked with the foreboding that I was losing the last opportunity to ever have another baby. I became so upset that I guess I frightened the other women in the waiting room. A nurse took me into the privacy of an examining room where I fought mightily to keep my baby. In spite of all I could do, I felt its little body slipping from me. I saw a nurse pick up the baby and place it in a small tray. Ignoring my pain, I insisted she give me the tray. It was a tiny boy. I had lost another son. I had failed to give him his chance to come to earth, to join our family. I was now sobbing uncontrollably and inconsolably. The doctor was unable to stop my hemorrhaging, so they rushed me to the hospital.

"For a few moments they left me in the operating room, but I was not alone. I heard a male voice say, 'Mom, it's okay.' I turned my head to see who was speaking, but saw no one. But I knew that it was the spirit of a young man and I could sense that he was standing beside me. In spite of his presence I was heartbroken. I had failed once again in what was probably my last chance to have a baby.

"I had clung to the little basin with the body of my son all the way to the hospital. Even now I refused to let them take it. They literally had to pry my fingers from the basin so they could work on me.

"I awoke in the recovery room. When I remembered what had happened, I wept again. That's when I heard the same voice, 'It's okay, Mom. I'm here!' I could not see him but I could feel his presence. He continued, 'It's all right, Mom. I'll be back.' Then he left. I didn't want him to go. I wanted him so much, and I wanted him NOW!

"Reassured that my son would return, I regained confidence in my ability to conceive. I succeeded several times to get pregnant only to suffer more miscarriages. After my last miscarriage the doctor informed me that my body was menopausal, and I was now too old to have children. I closed my mind in defeat. It was over and I had failed.

"My husband—a good, wise, loving man—told me that about the time the doctor was counseling me my childbearing was over, he'd had a spiritual experience wherein he was informed I had children waiting for me. He did not say a child but children. He was told they had gone to our Heavenly Father and asked to come to me, insisting, 'This is the mother we want. No matter what problems we may confront, she is the one we want!'

"About the same time, our three-year-old daughter, to whom we'd said nothing about the above, began praying for a little sister. I did not dissuade her, but I feared it would damage her faith if her prayers went unanswered. Frequently she repeated that we were going to have a little baby sister.

"Due to the health problems that contributed to my inability to carry a baby full term, I had to be careful to maintain my diet and exercise. Following a few days when I had slipped, a voice came to me one night. 'These children need to come to earth now. If you do not get your act together, you will lose your opportunity to have them, and they will have to go to someone else.' This frightened me so that I shaped up and watched my diet with extreme care.

"Later I went to my physician for a medical check up and my condition greatly puzzled him. He was so perplexed that he sent me to several specialists, and they also were astounded. To the surprise of all, my menopausal body had reversed itself and not only was I pregnant, but the doctors could hear three distinct heartbeats.

"I knew that one was the little boy who had spoken to me when I was hemorrhaging in the hospital, and that one was the baby girl for whom my daughter was praying. I had no idea who the third child was, but I would accept it gladly.

"At four-and-one-half months I miscarried one of the triplets. For reasons unknown to medical science, its little body maneuvered around the other two and slipped out. Had the miscarriage gone naturally, because of being the farthest in, this child would have dislodged the other two and I would have lost all three. I feel that he valiantly volunteered to leave so that the other two could survive. I am impressed he will yet be mine, but through adoption rather than birth. I increasingly feel he is out there somewhere, waiting for us to find and adopt him.

"The remaining two, now twins, were born with no complications. Though fraternal, they look almost identical. During the pregnancy we knew their sex and selected their names. But before birth, these determined children who fought so hard to come, vetoed our selections clearly informing us as to their correct names.

"One day when I was feeling a bit low, my son, then about three, came to me, put his little arms around my neck and said, 'It's all right, Mom.' I recognized that voice. It was the same voice that spoke by my bed in the hospital over five years ago—the same loving, comforting, reassuring voice."

Cathy's strong desire for children caused her frustration, anguish, and disappointment as she continued to miscarry time after time after time. But she never gave up. At the same time, spirits in heaven were petitioning to come to her. If this were to occur, there had to be major changes in her body, changes that do not occur naturally. But a miracle occurred and her body changed. A second miracle occurred when she lost one of the triplets but not the other two. She strongly feels that she has not really lost that child, but will eventually become its mother through adoption.

It is not unusual for pregnant mothers to be very concerned about the status of the child they are carrying. On occasions, an example of which follows, the spirits of unborn children communicate with their mothers to assure them that their bodies are developing properly.

Gail was in her fourth month of pregnancy and was having serious disagreements with her sister. She was very worried that the stress she was experiencing might be impacting her baby.

"I was very concerned that my negativity and unhealthy thoughts were affecting the baby I was carrying. I tried to relax by lying on the living room floor and letting all my negative feelings out. After about five minutes the baby started communicating with me. Not in words but thoughts. The words I will use to express what was said between us are mine.

"The baby told me not to worry, that he was a strong bright light. 'Yes,' he informed me, 'there are fragile parts to my light, which make me sensitive and vulnerable but the central core of my being is strong!'

"I asked him several questions that were troubling me. He told me that he had a strong connection with me, and that my husband would teach him how to live in this world. He also said that at this time he could see his whole life before him, but that it had no meaning or importance until he actually lived it. In other words, there was no point in talking abut future events because they are only significant when they are experienced. One last thing he said was that our next child, a little girl, (what a shock for me to hear of a next child!) would have an even greater connection with my husband."[2]

Being concerned that her emotions might be affecting her unborn son, Gail made a conscious effort to relieve her stress. It was during this period of relaxation and contemplation that her unborn son was able to communicate with her. He assured her that he was okay, and that he had a sister waiting to be born. What is particularly interesting about Gail's experience is the fact that her unborn son was aware of the road his life would take.

In the next account, Ruth's experience with her unborn son let her know that her anxieties about her son's health were totally unfounded. In addition, she was excited and amazed to discover the degree to which her son was involved in the lives of all those who had preceded him to earth.

"I had a dream that was so vivid and moving that upon waking I knew that I would deliver a son and what we should name him. In my dream, I was walking down the main street of my four-block rural Mississippi town. I was carrying a newborn baby boy. The town appeared just as it does in reality, except that vintage pickup trucks lined the street, and a solid stream of old farmers filled the sidewalk for its entire length.

"As I watched these old-timers, both white and black men, most of them dressed in overalls and work clothes, I realized that they had gathered to welcome my son into this life. They had all worked side by side with my father and his father, both long deceased, and they were genuinely interested in this child.

"I was touched and honored by all this attention. I had named my son Julian, after my father, a man who sired three daughters but no sons. Without exchanging a word, I handed the baby to the first gentleman in line. He then handed my son to the next man, and on and on to the last man.

"The striking image of this dream is that of gnarled, work-worn hands reaching out to this infant, then tenderly holding him, almost reverently, silently rocking him, then passing him along to the next set of strong, brown hands. It was as if the tribal elders had gathered to initiate a new member. The atmosphere was one of quiet import and warmth.

"I awoke with a profound sense of calm and assurance. Without doubt, I knew I would have a son and that we would name him Julian.

"After this dream, I never again suffered the normal worries and anxieties about having a safe labor and a healthy child. But more importantly, I knew that my son is a noble son of God and has a direct link with those who preceded him."

Ruth's experience with her unborn son helped her to realize that every person is a part of a great legacy. Those who have gone before are concerned about those who follow them, and this concern is not limited to their own descendants. There is a larger family, the family of God, and all those old men accompanying Ruth's father and grandfather are part of this larger family.

### Summary Thoughts

Why are some individuals' medical problems resolved while others are not? Is it the faith and desire of the unborn child or its parents or the medical expertise of the child's attending physicians? In some cases it is possible that one or all may be factors. But the real answer to this haunting question seems to lie back in heaven. Some children seem to be healed because they have an important mission to perform on earth. The mission of others is not here on earth, so they die. For still others, their mission on earth includes living with severe adversities of one kind or another as discussed in earlier chapters.

Though modern medicine has made, and is continuing to make, remarkable advances, it does have limitations. Even in situations where it appears there is no hope for an infant's survival, or that if it does survive it will have little or no quality of life, some of these children do survive and are perfectly normal. Before anyone, whether medical specialist or parent, gives up on a pregnancy it would seem wise to consult with the Ultimate Physician as to what His will might be in the matter.

## Chapter Sixteen
### Parental Visits with Their Unborn Children

Throughout this book many visits from our heavenly home are recounted. Some visits are to comfort the bereaved, some to assure parents that children will be normal despite what medical experts might say, and some to protect and sustain during times of great stress and adversity. In this chapter, unborn children visit their prospective parents to prepare them for their arrival. Various messages are given to parents such as that they need to prepare for a spirit's arrival or to change their lives so they can be born. Sometimes the appearance of unborn children serves as an introduction or a confirmation to parents that they will yet have children. And in some cases, the visit is to give women experiencing complicated or difficult pregnancies assurance that everything is progressing satisfactorily, and that the baby will soon make its appearance.

In the first account, the message to a mother was that her baby was ready to come but before she *could* come, her mother would need to make major changes in her life.

"In November of 1997, I began to be aware of a little spirit presence hovering around me. At first the awareness was dim, then it became so noticeable that I actually felt it on my right shoulder. Then for a while its presence seemed to have wandered away. After the turn of the year, the spirit reappeared, this time hovering in front of my left hip. It was at this time that I gained a visual sense of a baby.

She looked to be about six months old, dark blue eyes and dark brown hair, clearly an animated little girl. I tried to have a dialogue with her from time to time. She seemed to be communicating that I should hurry, that she could not wait much longer, that I had to heal my psychological and emotional wounds in order for her to have a safe home in which to dwell. As I continued to postpone conception, the presence gradually grew smaller until it was only a dot, still hovering but no longer communicating. A week after it disappeared, I discovered that I was pregnant."[1]

This spirit knew that she could not have a safe, nurturing environment in which to live unless her mother changed her life significantly. This woman was her preferred mother, but if her preferred mother did not get her act together, she could not come. But evidently the woman did do what was required, and this spirit was able to come to earth at the appointed time.

In the next account, Renee Stock met her daughter in an unusually vivid dream.

"My husband and I weren't trying to have a baby, but if it happened it would have been all right with us. For about a year before my daughter was born I started dreaming about her. It started with a dream that seemed to last all night. In my dream, I was talking to a little girl. We were having a lovely time visiting and chatting about anything and everything. When I woke up I remembered all aspects of it, unlike other dreams I have had. All the next day I was enveloped in a feeling of euphoria.

"Over the course of the next year, I would have a dream like this at least once a month. For a while I didn't know the little girl's name or that she was the child I would give birth to. I finally asked her if she was my daughter and she said, 'Yes.' I asked her when I would get to meet her in the flesh and she said, 'Soon.' I remember asking her name. I don't remember exactly what the first name was other than it started with an M, and it so happened that our favorite names--Megan, Melissa, and Mikayla--all started with an M. I do remember that the middle name was Carole after my own mother.

The next summer there was a crisis at work, and I was working very long hours. Just as the hard push was over, I was talking to my girlfriend's oldest daughter, Rachael, who was, I believe, five at the time. All of a sudden, she said to me, 'Renee, you're pregnant!' and got so excited, but I didn't take her seriously. I had been working long hard hours and was totally worn out. Being so absorbed in my work I hadn't noticed that my dreams of the little girl had stopped. Sure enough, a week or two later, my doctor confirmed that I was pregnant! At the time Rachael told me I was pregnant, I was five weeks along."

Children often seem to be more receptive to spiritual issues than adults. In this case, the unborn spirit let five-year-old Rachel know she was on her way and Rachel in turn shared this information with Renee. Apparently her vivid dreams were designed to introduce Renee to her unborn daughter and prepared her for Rachael's message.

Accounts such as these are not limited to a specific culture. In the next case, a Navajo woman shared her experience with her unborn daughter.

"It was a chilly autumn morning. As I knelt to say my prayers something wondrous happened. I felt someone behind me, so [I] turned around and found myself standing at the end of a great hall. At the end of this hall was a light, and from this light I could hear quiet voices and soft footsteps. They were coming towards me. One was a young woman and she was beautiful, her hair falling naturally around her shoulders. She walked with a young man. They held hands while they talked happily. They stopped near me; they hugged one another. She told him it was time for her to go, that she would see him soon. They held hands until they were out of reach. As she walked toward me she began to fade but I could still feel her beside me like a soft gentle breeze. I knew at that moment I was going to give birth to that beautiful girl. I then turned my head and saw myself still kneeling. She was born nine months later. She looks the same and smiles just like when I first saw her coming through that light."[2]

This experience let this woman see the love that those in the premortal existence have for each other, and that these two did not want to be separated as evidenced by the lingering touch of their hands. But both knew that it was the young woman's time to be born and that their separation would not be for long.

In the next case, Natalie O'Donnell was caring for her dying father. Watching him slowly die was draining, both physically and emotionally. Natalie was depressed, sad, and completely exhausted. After an especially difficult day she went to her bedroom and fell into bed. She was just drifting off to sleep when she sensed someone in her room. Startled, she opened her eyes and sat up.

"I looked around and saw a small girl standing in the doorway of my bedroom. She had one hand on the doorknob. She looked to be about two years of age. Her little body was glowing, and she had blond hair and big blue eyes. She radiated a great sense of peace and love that left me feeling relaxed and peaceful. Then she disappeared.

"The next day at 5:30 my father died. On the day of his funeral, I was fixing my hair when I heard a voice say, 'Don't be sad when you greet people today because you're pregnant'

"I thought to myself, *That's crazy! I am not pregnant!*

Two months later I realized that I had missed my period and took a pregnancy test. I *was* pregnant! Seven months later I gave birth to a beautiful baby girl whom I named Derynn. One day a couple of years after her birth, Derynn came into my bedroom. When I glanced up, I was shocked. There standing in the doorway of my bedroom was the exact image of the glowing little girl I had seen before. It was then that I realized it was Derynn who had come to comfort me at one of the saddest times of my life.

"One additional thing I must add is that when Derynn was born, she had the image of my father's face on her tiny face. My husband and my mother saw it too."

Natalie had lost her father but discovered she was gaining a new life. While a baby cannot and should not replace another person, this experience gave Natalie assurance that life is eternal, and that those in heaven were keenly aware of her.

Rare is the pregnant woman who has not wondered about the baby she is carrying. Will it survive? Will it be normal? What will my baby look like? On some occasions, the mother's concerns and questions are answered when her unborn child appears and converses with her, as in the following instance.

"When I was pregnant with my second child, I spent fifteen minutes each day practicing a relaxation/guided imagery exercise. It included soft music, progressive body part relaxation, and then simply thinking about my baby. I was very curious about 'who' was inside me. One night my daughter appeared to me in a very vivid dream. She seemed to be about fifteen months old and looked just like my husband. She said to me, 'Mom, I just want you to know that I am a girl, and I am healthy, so don't worry.' I woke up and immediately told my husband. We were both thrilled. She was born on February eleventh and looks exactly like her father."

In the next account an unborn child made a request of his mother, Rosa Alexander, which she misinterpreted.

"I had propped myself up in my bed and was reading when I heard a knock on my bedroom door. I called out, 'Who is it?' and heard what I assumed to be the voice of Alice, my five-year-old daughter say, 'Mom, it's me. Can I come in?'

"I replied, 'Yes,' and waited for the door to open and Alice to come in. When this did not happen, I called out, 'Alice! I said you can come in.' Still no response. Again, but a bit louder I repeated, 'Alice, come in.' But the door did not open. A bit exasperated and irritated, I got out of bed and opened the door only to find no one there.

"I could hear the girls' voices coming from the basement, so I called out to Alice from the top of the stairs. When she came up I asked why she had knocked on my door and what it was she wanted. She replied that she had not knocked on my door, and that she and her sister (who is seven years older than Alice) had been playing in the basement since after supper. I asked her several times, even going so far as to bribe her with a chocolate bar--Alice's weakest link--if she would tell me the truth. I thought she was afraid since the children were instructed not to disturb me after I went to bed. At that time I started work at midnight and often tried to get a couple of hours sleep before going to work. But Alice stuck to what she had said.

"About two or three weeks after this incident I found out I was pregnant. Somewhere about my second month, my husband began calling my stomach Jeffery. Pretty soon both family and friends were calling my stomach Jeffery, too. Did Jeffery kick today? How is Jeffery doing in there? etc. This created a bit of stress for me since I wanted another girl.

"Two weeks before I went on maternity leave, the girls at work threw me a surprise baby shower. All the baby gifts I received were suitable for a baby boy--blue baseball shoes and cap, a playsuit with a fire engine and a little firefighter boy on the front, not to mention a blue baby T-shirt with the name "JEFFERY" boldly printed across the chest.

"Sure enough Jeffery was born and the only person who was surprised was me.

"Today Alice is eighteen and Jeffery is twelve. What is curious and interesting is that their voices are so similar that everyone confuses them. And this confusion started well before Jeffery's birth. The knock on the door and the inquiry, 'Can I come in,' was later realized to have been a petition from this unborn son to be conceived."

While the vast majority of visits of the unborn are to prospective mothers, fathers also have been visited. While his wife saw their fourth child before it was born, Will Sensiba reported seeing their third.

"One afternoon when our daughter was five I walked into the house in a hurry and saw, out of the corner of my eye, a child sitting on the couch in the living room. But when I got to the end of the hall I was surprised to discover that both of my children were in our bedroom. I turned and looked back to the couch. No one was there, but I knew beyond a shadow of a doubt I had seen a child on that couch. A few days later I found out that my wife was pregnant.

"There is a significant time gap between our second and third child because my wife had two miscarriages. At the time I had the experience with the child on the couch, we had been trying for my wife to get pregnant because we both felt that there were more spirits waiting to join our family. We had been pleading with the Lord for my wife to conceive and had also been encouraging our children to pray for a little brother or sister. One day our daughter was saying her prayers and when my wife reminded her to ask for another baby she replied quite emphatically, 'I will not pray for that anymore. You are already pregnant!' This pronouncement startled my wife, and she wondered if her daughter might be right. The next day she went to her physician and, sure enough, she *was* pregnant.

"Just before our fourth child was conceived, my wife and I were coming home from the chiropractor because I had injured my back. My wife was driving our van and I was lying in the back in considerable pain. We had left the older children with their grandparents. Ronnie, the child who I had seen sitting on the couch, was at the time six months old and in the carseat next to my wife. While my wife drove, she felt someone tap her on the shoulder from behind and thought I was playing games. She was annoyed that I wasn't able to drive, but that I could get up to tap on her shoulder. She looked over her shoulder and was surprised to see that I was still lying flat on my back. The tap came again and this time when she turned around she saw a cute pudgy little boy with piercing brown eyes, darker complexioned than our other children. He radiated beauty and purity, and gave her the distinct feeling that it was his time to come to earth.

"She shouted back to me, 'Well, I just saw our next baby.' Sure enough when she went to the doctor, he confirmed that she was pregnant.

"When this son was about three, my wife was washing dishes and heard someone come into the kitchen. She turned to look at who had come in and gasped. She later told me, 'Honey, he is the child I saw behind me in the van--the exact image of him!'"

Why children would appear sitting on a couch or riding in a van is not known. But the message their appearance sent to this couple was clear—we are on our way to you and this is what we will look like.

Parents are not the only ones who are privileged to see the spirits of the unborn. In the next case, a grandparent saw his future grandson. Lars was sitting in his easy chair when a young man appeared to him. The young man said, "Hi, Grandpa. My name is Joshua and I will be born soon!" When his daughter informed him the next day that she was expecting, Lars was delighted but not surprised.

In the next case, very specific information was given to Missy Hale concerning the birth and career of her unborn granddaughter.

"Two weeks before my granddaughter was born, she appeared to me in a dream. She appeared not as an infant, but as a young woman of about twenty. She was dressed in a long black dress or robe with a little white collar. She announced to me that she would be born soon, late on Monday. She said that she would be intelligent like her father, but unlike her father/physician, she would work with words. With this she disappeared.

"Missy immediately called her daughter-in-law and told her about her dream. Her daughter-in-law said, 'Mother, your dream is interesting but not true. My physician has told me that if anything, the baby will be born early in the day. So your dream couldn't possibly be true.'

"Well, the information given me by my unborn granddaughter was right. She was born right when she told me she would be. As she has grown into womanhood, she is looking more and more like the young woman I saw. She is in college now, majoring in religious studies which could fit well with the long black dress/robe and her statement, 'I will work with words.'"

Apparently there is an optimum time for some spirits to come to earth. When this time draws near and prospective parents are not actively preparing for their arrival, spirits may request and be given permission to visit, motivate, and encourage them to make appropriate preparations. This happened to Jannette. Jannette was in her late thirties and felt that the seven children she already had were enough.

"Having given birth to seven children ranging in age from six to eighteen, I most assuredly wasn't planning to have any more. Then one day I entered the kitchen and was startled to see a child of about three standing there in a white robe. My older children were not home and I knew that my younger children were playing in the backyard. Besides, I'm not in the habit of dressing my children in white robes. I asked haltingly, 'Who are you?'

"The child answered telepathically, 'You don't want to have me when you're forty-two.'

"My instant and somewhat callous response was, 'You're definitely right about that!'

"The child looked dejected but continued to look at me with yearning as though I were its mother. I thought, 'Okay, I have faith. I can have another child. I can do this even at my age if it's God's will.'

"Finally I said to the child, 'I didn't want to get pregnant ever again, but I will have you if everybody else up there I'm supposed to have will come at the same time.' So that's how I happened to have twins at age thirty-eight. Twin girls. Today I realize the child I saw in my kitchen was the younger of the twins. If they had not come together, I probably would have been forty-two when the youngest was born.

"The twins are very different. They were actually conceived two weeks apart and they were not easy to get here. I have a sister-in-law who was pregnant at the same time. Our babies were due a week apart, but she lost hers in the sixth month. I was alarmed, went into premature labor, and was rushed to the emergency room. While undergoing tests, I saw the twins' spirits dressed in white standing above my bed, almost fully grown. I think Julie is going to be tall like her older sister and Jenny will be shorter like me. The sonogram showed that neither of the twins' lungs were sufficiently developed for birth, although one was about two weeks further along than the other. I was confined to bed, walking no farther than the bathroom for six weeks. Their condition stabilized and they were eventually born full term."

Julie knew that her mother would not desire to be pregnant at age forty-two. She gambled on her mother being willing to have her if she actually saw her, and it worked. But Jennie also wanted to be born to Jannette. Evidently arrangements were made for them to be born as twins even though one of the babies had already been conceived. So their desires to be born to Jannette and Jannette's desire not to be pregnant in her 40s were both realized.

Wilma was also in her late thirties and was sure that her aging body and medical problems had ended her childbearing years. These conditions enabled her and her husband to relax and enjoy the freedom that had come with the growing independence of their children. She sort of felt that she should have more children but she was also very concerned about having children in her late thirties. It was while she was having these very ambivalent feelings that the following occurred.

"At the time of my experience I was thirty-six years of age. We had two children and my husband and I were seriously debating whether we should have any more. One major concern was that I might be too old to handle all the stresses associated with pregnancy plus caring for two active children. Another was the concern of the loss of freedom a new baby would entail. My youngest was at the age where we were no longer completely tied down, and we were enjoying no midnight feedings, messy diapers, teething, or walking a fussy baby. Did we really want to do that all over again? Also, I was concerned about the increased probability of birth defects in a later pregnancy.

"One day, I was thinking about all the negatives associated with having additional children when I ran into a dear friend I hadn't seen for years. She was a little older than I and had with her a brand new baby. As we visited, I watched her gazing fondly at her son. He was healthy and beautiful. Less than two weeks later I ran into a high school friend. She was three years older than I, and she was carrying a tiny baby. I don't think that these things happened by chance. I had been questioning the ability of older mothers to have strong, healthy, normal babies, when out of the blue I met these two friends. I saw firsthand that mothers older than I were happily enjoying motherhood and managing very well. This seemed to be a message to me.

"Nevertheless I continued meditating and debating whether I should take on the awesome responsibility of motherhood for the third time. One evening as I lay in bed I saw a little girl standing at my side of the bed. It wasn't my four-year-old daughter Loire, because this child was taller, her hair was longer, and she had bangs and curls along the sides of her face. She wore pink furry pajamas. In addition, her hands were at her sides and Loire always had hers up by her face. She looked somewhat like my Loire, but I knew without any doubt that she was *not* Loire. Our eyes met and there was instant recognition. I knew this child, and there was a joyous love shared between us. My first impulse was to pick her up and embrace her. We did not speak but I did ask her telepathically, 'Oh, honey, would you like to get into bed with me?'

"'Yes,' she responded and reached for me to pick her up. I lifted the covers, moved over to make space for her, and reached for her. My arms went right through her; there was nothing there. As I watched her, she slowly faded from my sight. I lay there the longest time thinking about this experience and what it might mean. The little girl was beautiful, very loving, and I knew that somehow I knew her. She also revealed to me that her name was Martha.

"As time has passed, I have begun to realize that she could be mine if I so desire. If I elect to get pregnant, I know I will have this little girl. She will be a very loving child, and she will not be defective. All I have to do is make up my mind to have her."

In spite of all that she saw, Wilma is still struggling with fears and concerns associated with a third pregnancy. Even with the visit of the child, she is torn because of the new freedoms she and her husband are experiencing and the restrictions that always accompany a small baby. Yet she also feels a strong connection between herself and the child, feeling that perhaps she made some important commitment to this spirit. At the time this was written Wilma had not yet made the decision to have Martha.

When individuals come very close to death and have near-death experiences, what they witness is so beautiful that they often do not wish to return to life. The peace and serenity they feel and the sense of unconditional love is so wonderful that they would infinitely rather stay in heaven than go back to mortality. This was the way it was for the woman in the next case.

"I was with my husband and two sons in our car when an oncoming vehicle slid over three lanes and hit us head on. The roof of our car collapsed and my head was stuck between the windshield, dash, and roof. I was unconscious to all onlookers yet something weird happened to me. I found myself in a circle of light. I looked down upon the accident scene, into my car, and saw myself trapped and unconscious. I saw several cars stop and a lady taking my children to her car until the ambulance arrived. A hand touched mine and I turned. There was Jesus Christ. He emanated an aura of peace, bliss, and serenity. I never wanted to leave Him and lose the feeling of total love and peace.

"I was led to a well and told to look inside. I leaned over the well, and He put his hand on my back as I looked in. In the well were three children calling, 'Mommie, Mommie, Mommie, we need you. Please come back to us.' There were two boys and a girl. The two boys were much older than my two sons and I didn't have a little girl. The little girl looked up at me and begged me to go back to life—and then all at once I was in the circle of light again, His hand still on my shoulder, and I could see the accident scene again. I cried that I did not ever want to leave Him, and I knew that I would have to leave Him if I went back. But then I heard myself moan and I was back in the car. I screamed for my children. I knew where they were, but I demanded that my husband tell me about the lady taking them to her car because I wanted to make sure what I saw was real. It was.

"Several years later I had a baby. It was the little girl I saw in the well."[3]

This woman saw her unborn daughter who, along with her two young sons, were instrumental in convincing her to return to life. She saw them at the age all three would be at a specific moment in time in the future. This was a remarkable experience, but just as remarkable is the fact that this woman who met and conversed with Jesus Christ was Jewish.

Many individuals dream of marrying and starting a family. For most individuals this is not a problem. Marriage occurs, children come on schedule, and lives progress more or less as planned. But for some individuals, dreams of marriage may be realized but not those of having children. For medical reasons or for no identifiable reason, the dreams some have of becoming parents is frustrated. As they pray, seek remedies, and mourn, some receive assurance that they will eventually have children, and a few are even permitted to see their future children.

Albert R. Lyman was a rancher, settler, and cattleman in southeastern Utah in the early 1920s. Albert had some amazing experiences, one of which was when he was permitted to see the spirit of his unborn daughter. He and his wife wanted children, expected that they would come, and were distressed when they didn't. Nevertheless, Albert proceeded to build a house for his wife and the children he someday hoped to have.

"We had planned our new dwelling with great care and anticipation, but what would it be to us with no little folks? It would be they who would make it a real home, their laughter, their commotion, the concern and responsibility their coming would bring. We prayed to be honored with the trust and care of a family. But who but God could bestow that splendid gift?

"I was away on a roundup where I had been for weeks, my mind occupied much of the time with the home I was building, that home which, if ever finished, might be sadly silent for want of the childish prattle which makes a house a home. And there came to me a most impressive dream.

"In my dream I had returned home, and as I opened the front door a little girl came toddling to meet me. I knew she was my own, I gathered her in my arms and held her close, feasting my lips on her velvety cheek. What a holy moment! With this treasure, ours would be the perfect home. In complete joy I talked to her, and studied her baby face. She had come from the great world of spirits, trusting her essential training to us.

"The next day, while moving a herd of cattle toward my ranch, I pondered over my dream. My reverie was broken when I saw two horsemen ride up. They had come to help drive the cattle. One of them had a letter from Lell (my wife). I eagerly tore it open and read it. It brought fantastic, wondrous news! I wanted to shout. We were about to become parents. As I looked up from the letter to the broken walls of Castle Gulch, they had never appeared so friendly and wonderful as at that moment.

"A couple of years later, as I came through the front door, I stopped in total wonderment. My little daughter was coming toward me proudly practicing walking. She *was* that little girl I had seen in my dream, and this was the exact moment I had seen her, only this time she was not a spirit."[4]

Who knows why the spirit of an unborn child appears to one parent and not the other? But perhaps one parent needs the experience most or is more receptive. Nevertheless, the experience is usually shared and both parents benefit from it. In this case the unborn spirit appeared to Albert in a dream apparently to let him know that his prayers had been answered and that a daughter was on her way.

A similar appearance occurred to Peter Wheadon, the father in the next account. He and his wife already had four children when he saw their fifth.

"When my wife Sydney and I were courting, we occasionally discussed how many children we might have. We were eventually married and settled in Southern California. The years sped by, and we had four healthy active children. We never really discussed the desirability of having more. Meanwhile, my wife had started to pray about whether or not we should have more children.

"One Monday during our family time, we were seated in a circle in our family room, each taking turns presenting part of a lesson. There was an empty space in the circle where no one was seated. Then, quietly, the space wasn't empty any longer. I saw a baby in an infant feeding chair, surrounded by a soft glow. The image remained there for several moments, then slowly faded.

"After the children were in bed, I told my wife what I had seen, and we tearfully thanked Heavenly Father for this experience. It wasn't long until Aaron joined our family, and we rejoiced at his birth.

"One day, some years later, our son Bruce stood up in a church meeting and told of a special incident he had once experienced as a young child during one of his family's home evenings. He had seen a little baby in an infant feeding chair, surrounded by a soft glow. He had never mentioned it, he said, but wanted to express his gratitude for the experience; for he knew his brother Aaron was that baby and was meant to be a part of their family."[5]

This experience was witnessed by both the father and his son. Neither knew that the other had seen the infant until years later when the young man felt impressed to share his experience in church. This type of experience where more than one individual, independent of the other, sees the same thing, is not common.

Sometimes a mother-to-be is given a glimpse of the child she is carrying. This happened to Theresa Danna.

"One night in 1994 as I was falling asleep, when I was in that half-awake/half asleep hypnotic state, there appeared before my closed eyes the close-up of a toddler boy's face. At first he was looking down as if he was shy, then he slowly raised his eyes, looked directly at me, smiled, and said in his sweet voice: 'Mommy, I'm coming.' His eyes were the same color as mine, and in general he looked a lot like I did when I was three years old.

"I looked deeply into his eyes, so deeply that I was able to see beyond them. And what I saw was breathtaking. There was a bright white light and I felt pure, unconditional love pouring into me. I sensed that I was looking at eternity."[6]

Theresa's vision of her unborn son let her experience true and unconditional love.

### Summary Thoughts

Why do the unborn visit those on earth? As can be seen from the preceding accounts, the reasons vary widely but, regardless of the circumstances, seeing an unborn child changes the future parent or parents significantly. The reasons for visitations identified in this chapter can be summed up by the following.

- •To ask permission to come to the prospective parent/s.
- •To announce that they are on their way.
- •To introduce the unborn child to its prospective parent/s.
- •To request prospective parent/s to have them.
- •To reassure prospective parents that children are definitely coming.

•To encourage prospective parent/s to heal their psycholog-ical/emotional wounds so they can be born into a healthy environment.

•To convince severely injured mothers-to-be to want to live so they can be born.

•To comfort prospective parents.

Regardless of the feelings, concerns, or problems they are facing, once parents see the child and feel its love and excitement, they are hooked. Fears and apprehensions are turned to excited anticipation. They know the child is theirs, the pregnancy is not a mistake, and that the child will be okay. For many, they see the child at some time in the future which assures them that the child is normal and will survive.

*Chapter Seventeen*
*Playful Visits From Home*

In the previous chapter, youthful visitors from heaven had specific announcements, assurances, objectives, and instructions for those on earth. The following visits seem to have a more whimsical, playful quality. Parents reported seeing delightful giggling children who they subsequently discovered were children who would become members of their family. In other cases very young children were visited by unborn spirits who for a time became their "invisible playmates."

### The Playful Giggling Child

In the first case, Leticia Alyssa was busily cleaning up her kitchen when she heard a child giggling behind her.

"This morning had been an especially hectic one. But I was looking forward to a few quiet moments as my three children were all quietly napping.

"Then I heard a giggle behind me. My first thought was that my three-year-old son had snuck out of bed to play peek-a-boo. This was a game that we both loved to play and in spite of my fatigue, I decided to play with him. I knew that as I would turn around and see him peeking around the corner, he would see me and quickly withdraw. If he weren't so delighted with himself (and so darn cute!), I would have scolded him and sent him back to bed. But that happy little giggle had me completely charmed.

"I pretended not to hear his giggle and continued cleaning countertops,. I caught a reflection of a sweet little face in a mirror that was sitting on my counter. Quickly I turned, hoping to

surprise and delight him and then chase him back to his bed
with hugs and tickles. However, I was the one to be surprised! As
my little one turned to run down the hall I could see his naked
backside—he had taken off all of his clothes! As I chased after him
half grumbling and teasing I asked, 'Son! Where are your clothes?'

"When I turned the hall corner expecting to see him running
away from me, he was nowhere to be seen. I also thought it strange
that the house was so quiet with an active child running through
it. I called after him, 'You little scamp! You're getting too good at
hiding and teasing Mommy.'

"I peeked into the hall bath, just to make sure he hadn't gone
in there to hide. But the lights were out. I stopped in front of the
door to the nursery. Thinking I would play a trick on him, I decided
I would sneak up and grab him. The burst of laughter that he would
make when I startled him, would tickle my heart.

"I plastered myself up against the wall and slowly sneaked
around the doorway. I was having difficulty suppressing my own
giggles. Just as I was ready to jump out at him, I froze in mid-step.
There lay all three of my children napping in their beds, and all
three were fully dressed!

"Standing in the doorway looking at my sleeping children I
wondered, *Just who was my little visitor? Where did he go? How did he
get into our house? And why did he choose to visit me?* As time went on,
memories of this cute, giggling child stayed with me.

"Some years later, I had just given a bath to my youngest child.
I got her out of the tub and I was about to dry her when she
slipped out of my hands, turned and ran down the hallway, giggling
with delight. She was so pleased with herself, teasing her mother.
As I exited the bathroom and turn to run down the hall, a feeling
of déjà vu swept over me. She was the one who had visited me that
morning. I realized that I had mistaken her for my little son. At last
I knew why I could not find that little, naked, giggling child. I had
been given the incredible privilege of sharing a sweet, loving

moment with this child five years before her birth."

When I was first told of this experience, I thought that it was charming and again, unique. But in chatting with other parents and reading letters and journals, I have discovered it is not unique and has included some of the more intriguing accounts below.

A woman was sleeping on her sofa. She was awakened by a cool breeze on her arm. When she opened her eyes, she was face-to-face with a little boy. She knew that he was not one of her two sons, yet she found herself saying to him, "What are you doing up? Go back to bed!" At that, the little boy giggled, ran across the room, and hid behind a chair. She got up to look for him, but he was gone. At first she thought it might have been the spirit of the child she had recently miscarried. However, the following year she got pregnant and reports that this third son looks exactly like the boy who visited her that night.[1]

Unlike the mother in the previous account, Christine Maraccni knew that her visitor was her unborn son. Evidently his visit was to help her to endure the final months of a very difficult pregnancy.

"My pregnancy was rough. I had terrible morning, noon, and night sickness. During the last couple of months of my pregnancy, I was hardly able to lie down to sleep because my son pressed on my lungs and made it difficult for me to breathe. One evening I was completely exhausted but so tired of sleeping on the chair in the living room that I tried lying down in my bed. As I lay back I was greatly relieved to discover that my son had shifted a bit inside me, easing my discomfort just enough for me to drop off to sleep.

"That night I had the most incredibly vivid dream I have ever experienced. There I was with my unborn son, who looked to be about two years old. We were sitting on the floor playing with blocks. He said, 'Mommy, I'm going to build you a castle!' And then he giggled. I will never forget that giggle. He had sandy-blond hair and bright-blue eyes. He was a stocky little guy, sort of big for his age and he was wearing blue jeans, a little red-checked flannel shirt, and brown hiking boots. My husband was sitting near us on the sofa laughing. We played for hours including going to the park, sliding down the slide and swinging next to each other. I woke up the next morning, very excited. I told my husband that I knew what our son was going to look like and I described him. Fortunately, my husband believes in my intuitive senses, so he was excited too.

"Well, my son Bruno is almost ten months old now. He has sandy-blond hair and bright blue eyes. He is stocky and is pretty big for his age. The first time I heard him giggle, I knew I had heard that sound before, months ago, when I desperately needed encouragement and a good night's sleep. Bruno is our treasure from heaven. His daddy and I thank God every day that we have each other and him."

Having a brief glimpse into the future was a great blessing to Christine. She knew that her son would be born okay and that the pain and discomfort she was experiencing would be well worth it.

In the next account Phyllis Cavallari of Cleveland, Ohio was totally fatigued and had laid down for a much-needed rest. But her rest was disrupted by two giggling children. Phyllis recalled the events leading up to their visit.

"My husband Gus and I had almost given up hope that we would have children until I had a remarkable dream.

"We were married in 1965 and two years later we were delighted to learn that I was expecting. It would be the first grandchild and both extended families were thrilled. Unfortunately, I miscarried. As soon as I came out of the anesthesia I asked if I could still have babies.

"My doctor told me that there was no reason not to hope. But the years went by and nothing happened. I prayed and tried not to become discouraged. I was still young and time was certainly on my side. But I couldn't seem to shake my concern. I knew that my husband had been saddened by my miscarriage, but I could feel that his concern was now about my well being. He hated to see me so heavy-hearted, but there was nothing he could do about it.

"One day Gus had gone to visit his mother who lived downstairs and left me alone in our apartment. After he left, the apartment seemed unusually quiet and I decided to take a nap. I felt very tired, not my usual self and yet not at all sick. Just for a moment I wondered if my queasiness might be a symptom of pregnancy. But I knew this was only wishful thinking. I crawled into bed and pulled the sheet over me.

"I had been sleeping for some time when I was awakened by the sounds of children laughing behind me. At first I thought they must be playing somewhere outside, and yet the sound was so loud, it seemed they were actually in the room with me. The giggling continued, and it irritated me. I rolled over—and was stunned.

"There, standing next to me and looking down at me, were two children, their faces wreathed in grins.

"The boy was about eight years old with black hair and black eyes and was wearing a striped knit, long-sleeved shirt. The girl was about four. She had long light-brown hair and big brown eyes.

"I looked at the children in astonishment. Who were they? How in heaven's name had they entered the house and come up to the second floor without Gus or his mother hearing them? I wondered if I should be concerned, but the youngsters seemed so relaxed and delighted by the trick they had played on me that I could see that they were no threat. They didn't say anything, but continued to giggle. 'Be quiet,' I heard myself say. I was annoyed because they were disturbing my nap. I told them that I was trying to sleep. And I then turned back over and closed my eyes.

"An hour or so later, I awoke to an empty room. Puzzled, I recalled the odd event. Why had I not thought to question the children about who they were, or how they had gotten into my bedroom? How strange, I thought, that I felt so comfortable with them. Had I dreamed the whole thing? No—there had been nothing hazy or dreamlike about their presence, and my memory was as vivid as if they were still there. I could clearly remember their laughter, recall the boy's straight black bangs, the girl's happy smile.

"All of a sudden, as if a lightning bolt had hit me, I knew who they were--they were the children I would someday have. I knew it as clearly as I have ever known anything. God had answered my prayers, and had sent me a vision to confirm it.

"After that, I no longer worried about becoming a mother. In fact, much to my husband's obvious relief, I became lighthearted, confident—and not at all surprised when I became pregnant several months later. Those were the days before all the prenatal tests were available, so I never had any. In this case I didn't need to because I knew the baby would be healthy, and that it would be a boy. I purchased a sampler, and sewed 'Louis' onto it, along with a figure of a black-haired, dark-eyed boy in blue pajamas. I had only to wait to add his birth date and his weight to the sampler.

"Louis was born November 17, 1969. He was a fine healthy baby, with straight black hair and black eyes. When Louis was a toddler, I had a miscarriage. It was very hard on Gus and me but I refused to panic. I knew that God was sending me one more child, a girl, and He always keeps His promises. After a long wait I finally became pregnant again in 1973.

"This time I embroidered a sampler with the figure of a little girl sitting on a pink rose, and added the name Christine. My baby daughter was born September 6, 1973, almost four years after Louis.

"Louis and Christine grew to look exactly like the children I had seen looking down on me that morning so long ago. And they are 'gigglers,' especially when I am trying to take a nap. Many times

I would roll over to see them standing near my bed and laughing down at me, and I would remember that wonderful day."[2]

Miscarrying a child is a sad experience for any woman, but for women who desperately want children it is devastating. During her darkest hours, the visit of two giggling children lifted this woman's spirits and assured her that she would eventually have children.

### The Invisible Playmate

Many children have what their parents describe as "invisible friends" with whom they talk and play. It is often thought that invisible playmates fulfill a need of some children for companionship and is possibly a creative device for coping with unrealistic fears and, in some cases, a neurotic propensity. These playmates are often viewed by adults as figments of children's vivid imaginations. This may be the case for some children, but for others, their invisible playmates may well be real.

Billy was observed by his babysitter busily playing with an invisible friend. The babysitter knelt down next to him and asked, "Billy, who are you playing with?"

He looked up at her, then at his invisible playmate, then back at her and said, "My baby sister. She hasn't come yet, but she will, and her name is Sarah."

She thought to herself, *Whoa! I have heard of invisible friends, but this takes the cake.*

"I thought about telling Billy's mother about this experience with her son, but didn't because Billy's mother was over forty, and even a suggestion of being pregnant might be viewed with resentment.

"Not long after this experience I learned that Billy's mother was pregnant. Needless to say, it came as a complete surprise to her. But she accepted it with good grace. In addition to the personal challenge of being over forty and pregnant, she had to endure months of stares, nurses in her doctor's office offering suggestions of more effective birth control methods, and lots of kidding. Somehow, I made no connection between Billy's invisible friend and his mother's pregnancy

"During her pregnancy I moved and no longer babysat Billy. I didn't see his mother for nearly a year. One day while shopping, I ran into her. She had with her an adorable little baby. Of course our conversation centered on the infant. As I played with the baby's tiny hands, I ask if the baby was a boy or a girl. She responded that the baby was a girl and that they had named her Sarah.

"Glancing up I asked, "How did you come up with the name Sarah?"

"'I don't know! It wasn't a family name, and it wasn't even a name that I particularly liked. Yet I felt strongly that Sarah should be her name!'

"Her words triggered the memory of my experience with Billy and his invisible playmate Sarah, his unborn sister. And here she was.

"I looked down at Sarah and then at her mother and then shared my experience with her little son. Looking down at her infant daughter she said, 'So that is where your name came from!'

This account is informative for reasons other than a small boy's invisible friend. It was who his invisible friend was--his future sister. He knew her and the name she would be known by. Had his parents listened to him, he probably would have shared with them the identity of his "invisible friend"

Kathy's son, Shawn, also had a fascinating experience with an invisible friend. At the time Kathy was amused and a bit puzzled by his antics.

"Like most parents I could hardly wait until my baby would be able to talk. But as soon as Shawn could talk he would not shut up.

"I would put him to bed and hear him chattering away for hours. I would go into his room and try to get him to go to sleep. He would shut up until I left, but as soon as I walked out I heard him going on and on.

"Finally I asked, 'Shawn, who are you talking with?'

"In a very matter-of-fact tone he responded, 'I'm talking to the little girl who comes down through the hole in the roof.'

"When I asked him 'What little girl?' he just shrugged his shoulders.

"Shawn's conversations with 'the little girl' continued until my daughter was born. With her birth, they stopped abruptly. Shawn insisted from the moment his sister was born that she was his best friend. One of the first words she ever spoke was his name. As she grew, when she needed something she called his name, not mine, and he come running. At times he even seemed to know what she needed without being told and brought it to her. For example, we could not understand why she was gaining so much weight until we caught our son in the act of bringing her a bottle of milk in the night. When questioned about what he was doing he simply said, 'She was hungry.'"

Many adults do not recognize or appreciate the closeness of heaven and earth, especially for the very young. This case probably explains why some siblings have an especially close bond..

There are a number of cases where infants, especially twins, have their own special language. They communicate with adults in one language but, between themselves, speak another. Some individuals have speculated that the unique language they are speaking may be the language of heaven. An intriguing example was reported by Linda Loveall.

"From about age one to four, my daughter Ann had invisible playmates. I would often hear her chatting in her room with someone but when I walked in, it was empty. I would ask Ann with whom she was talking and she would gesture at various areas of her room where her friends were seated or standing. She fully expected that I could see them. She would also introduce me to them and them to me. She seemed puzzled that I could not see them.

"What I found very curious was that she would speak to them in a language I could neither understand or identify. I don't think that it was an earthly language, as she would only use this language when speaking to them. She would be speaking to me in English, turn to one of her invisible friends and start speaking to them in this strange language. I listened carefully to her and the sounds she made were not gibberish or a distortion of English. It seemed to be an organized language with rhythm, pause, and meter. It sounded vaguely familiar, but no language I could identify.

"Ann conversed in this unidentifiable language to a decreasing degree until just after she turned four. Then it stopped. It was also at this same time that her invisible playmates stopped visiting."

Many children have reported talking to invisible playmates through their thoughts or in whatever language they had been taught by their parents. Often the words, thoughts, and sentence structure used are much more sophisticated than that usual with children of their age. Perhaps the child's mind was being spoken to in the language of heaven and they responded in their earthly language. In this case Ann conversed with her parents in English and then with her heavenly visitors in their language, and she never confused the two.

In the next account, Cathy shares her experience with her invisible friends who at the time she called fairies. How a small child perceives the identity of invisible friends seems dependent on his or her experiences in life. This account is a bit unusual in that Cathy is now an adult and still has clear memories of her invisible friends Most children have lost these memories before they reach the age of five.

"When I was not much more than three, I had friends visit and play with me. I could see them very plainly, but my parents could not. They were dressed in long white dresses and taught me songs that I loved to sing. I used such phrases as, 'Glory to God, hallelujah, His majesty on high,' and so forth. My mother wondered where I had heard such big sophisticated words as we were not frequent attendees at church. My family rarely spoke of angels, but they did speak often about fairies. That is how I described my little playmates—they were fairies. When I was left alone, I was never afraid because I had my friends with me. I now realize that these invisible friends were not fairies, but angelic beings who protected, guided, and comforted me. They were not figments of my imagination! I could see them. They would come when I needed them, and they would leave when my parents or other adults arrived. I could never understand why others could not see them."

Cathy's invisible friends not only provided her with companionship and a sense of safety, they also taught her songs. These were not simple songs of childhood, but songs of praise unto God! But because her parents were not active church attendees, she did not at the time recognize the significance of the songs or the angelic identity of her visitors. Instead she identified them as fairies which were part of her family's folklore. The fact that she called her invisible playmates fairies might partially help to explain why her parents did not take her seriously.

In the final account a child's invisible visitor clearly demonstrates that death does not destroy connections between family members no matter how short a time the deceased child was on earth.

Peggy was four years of age when her parents felt it important to tell her that she had a baby brother who had died before she was born. They were not sure that she really understood what death was, but she was told anyway and seemed to understand. A number of days later, her mother was enjoying watching her little daughter swinging.

"I was washing dishes, keeping an eye on my little daughter as she swung in the backyard. She was animatedly talking to herself, and her gaze seemed to be riveted on a very specific place. As the swing moved back and forth, her head shifted as if she was looking at something. I thought her actions a bit curious but then the phone rang and I went to answer it. I got so caught up in my conversation that I forgot the strange behavior of my daughter.

"When she came in, she came up to me with her hands on her hips and said, 'Mommy, you lied to me!'

"This solemn pronouncement startled me and I was about to protest when she continued, 'Mommy, you told me my brother was a little baby when he died. But he isn't! He's a big man. He came to me while I was swinging and we talked and talked. He told me that he loved me and missed his family but that he is happy and loves being in heaven. Mom, he told me to tell you that he loves you and that it was not your fault he died. He had to go back to Heavenly Father. I wish you could have seen him, Mommy. He is not a little baby. He's big, all grown, and he had on shiny white clothes. He is very nice and he loves me.'

Her sincere and emphatic insistence that she had seen her brother, not as an infant but as a grown man, startled her mother. She had felt that his death was somehow due to something she had done or failed to do. Her daughter's experience let her know that she was in no way responsible for her son's death. In addition her little daughter clearly informed her that her son still lived, considered her to be his mother, and wanted her to know that there was a purpose to his death. What is very interesting here is that the deceased child missed his family. He was a tiny infant when he died and could not, therefore, have been aware of what families are. Except that he did. Evidently he knew them, was attached to them, and this was the reason he missed them.

### Summary Thoughts

The visit of giggling, laughing spirits to their future mothers seems to be for the same purposes as any other heavenly visit—i.e. as an introduction, as comfort, and as reassurance. Experiences such as these are delightful no matter what the purpose.

Children, too, have happy contacts with the other side which for some are not broken at birth. The spiritual eyes of a significant number of children remain open and they can see and communicate with those on the other side. Communication, as documented earlier, is often mind to mind. And when it is verbal, in most cases the language is that of the parents although in a few cases, such as one cited in this chapter, the language spoken was the language of the visitor.

For some children born into harsh environments, having invisible visitors may be one way they are sustained, comforted, and protected. For others, their invisible playmates may serve as a conduit through which messages to parents and others are conveyed.

# Chapter Eighteen
## Adoption

As has been noted frequently in this book, we were all keenly aware while still in heaven that we would have to come to earth and experience mortality and fulfill a mission to be able to progress. In some cases, we made covenants with others that they would proceed us to earth and prepare the way for us. In other situations, it was we who were to come to earth first. Sometimes it was agreed that we would come to specific families. However in some cases medical problems would prevent these commitments or plans from being achieved directly. If spirits could not be born into the families they needed to come to, other means were needed to achieve the same end. Adoption is the mechanism whereby some spirits end up in the correct family at the appointed time.

Some parents who have adopted children report encounters with their unborn adopted sons or daughters which are very similar to those that occurred between biological parents and their unborn children. With adoptive parents, the encounter assures them that they *will* be successful in adopting a child and that the child in question *does* want to come to them. The well-known entertainer, John Denver, shares a beautiful experience he had with his unborn adopted son, Zak. Denver's account is taken from his autobiography, *Take Me Home*.[1]

"When we decided to adopt I remember the occasion as a time of great humility. Whenever I found a quiet moment in the day, including just before I got out of bed in the morning, I offered a prayer to this little spirit out there: 'Whoever you are, wherever you are, I don't know what you have to go through to get here and be with us, but we love you very much and can't wait to be with you.'

"With all those anticipations streaming through me, we came to New York. I had four sold-out nights at Madison Square Garden and we were staying at the Sherry-Netherland. It was May 2, 1974, and that night I dreamed that three people in white robes came and gave me a little boy. We hadn't specified either sex in our communication with the adoption agency. All we wanted was that the baby be healthy enough to live with us in the mountains. We were active people, we liked to be outside and we wanted that for the baby as well. In my dream, I could see that the baby was a boy—a dark-faced boy with round eyes and a bit of an overbite— and as I was holding him, he looked up, grabbed my thumb, and smiled. In the morning, I recounted the dream to Annie. Eleven days later, Zak was born. We didn't see him then, but we were notified about his birth, and when he was about two months old we went to Minnesota to the adoption agency to pick him up.

"I remember hearing 'Annie's Song' come on the radio as we were driving there. It had become the number one song in the country that week which struck me as an interesting coincidence. For some reason, I automatically translated that piece of information into a projected entry in Zak's baby book: *On this hot day in August, the number one song in the country is a song Dad wrote for Mom.* Anyway, we arrived at the agency where there were papers to be signed and there was a little formal procedure to go through, designed to help the adoptive parents deal with the anxiety of meeting their child.

"They had walked us through the place when we were there before. You first went down a long hallway, and then upstairs. At the end of another hall there was a little room decorated as a nursery, with a crib and a couch. This was where you were supposed to get your first glimpse of your baby. We had just been told that the young woman who was bringing Zak had been delayed and we were trying to keep from feeling disappointed, when the door at the far-end of the hall opened and a woman appeared with our child.

"Without a word, she came running down the hall and handed the baby to me. He had round eyes and this little bit of an overbite, and when I held him he smiled and grabbed my thumb. Zak was the child in my dream—exactly the same child! I recognized his face and I think he recognized mine. At least he looked at me in the most knowing way. Right there, dream and reality came together for me."

There was no doubt in the mind of John Denver that the unborn child he saw was intended to be his, wanted to be his, and would be his. Adoption is not just a mechanism to place unwanted children in homes. It is a way that eternal commitments can be realized.

A second case of a celebrity seeing a child that she would adopt is that of Marie Osmond, a singer and actress of world fame. She had three biological children and three adopted children and at age thirty-eight, felt that her family was complete . . . that is, until her dream.

"One night I had a dream about a crying baby and it would not stop. I had the same dream for several nights until one night I picked up the baby and it stopped crying. I immediately knew that that baby was to be mine. When BreAnn came along, I fell in love with her instantly. The moment I saw her wrapped in that pink blanket and with that little ribbon in her hair, I knew that she was the baby I had picked up in my dream."[2]

Betty Eadie, a Native American and best selling author, suffered a near-death experience following a hysterectomy. Her spirit left her body in the hospital and while in the spirit world she saw a beautiful little girl run up to her husband, Joe, stand on his shoes, and reach into his pocket. She was also shown a beautiful young woman to whom she felt strangely attached. The full meaning of these scenes did not become clear until years later.

During recovery, Betty suffered ups and downs as she tried to readjust to this world following her experience in heaven. One day her sister called regarding a baby that would soon be born and placed in foster care because the parents were alcoholic. The child was Native American and a Native American foster home was considered ideal. Betty's sister suggested caring for a baby might help her return to normal. Betty and Joe discussed it with their children and applied to take the baby. After all, it was only for a month or two.

They had her for over ten months when one day the phone rang with news that a permanent placement had been located for the baby. Betty's heart sank; she had become very attached to the little girl. However, they had no choice but to release her because Betty and Joe had signed papers they would not adopt. So Betty faced "the worst agony a mother can know. I was about to lose my child."

With the loss of the child, Betty's depression returned, along with nightmares. For three months she cried and prayed for the child. She could not shake the foreboding something was dreadfully wrong. Then one night she was awakened by a spiritual messenger in her bedroom.

"The messenger said that the situation with my baby was not right and that she would be returned to me. He said that I would receive a phone call in which the caller would say, 'I have good news and I have bad news.' I did not sleep the rest of the night.

"For the next two weeks I would not leave the house. Every time the phone rang I jumped for it, waiting for that special call.

"The phone rang early one morning, and I heard a voice plainly say, 'Betty, this is Ellen (the social worker). I have some good news, and I have some bad news.' I sat up in bed and screamed. The voice continued, explaining that my baby was in the hospital. 'She couldn't adjust to the new family and kept crying. You were her mother for ten months, and she's been looking for you.'

"Ellen went on to explain that as the baby cried, tempers rose, and one night in a drunken rage the parents beat her and threw her down a flight of stairs. The baby had then been taken to a hospital and abandoned, were she lay critically ill for two weeks. She was not responding to treatment and the doctors recognized that in her emotional state she might not recover. Finally Ellen said, 'Betty, our last hope is you. We know we're asking a lot, but could you please take her back for a while, at least until she gets better?'[3]

Betty was so excited at the chance to get her daughter back that she immediately booked a flight on the same flight as the social worker and flew to the city where the baby was hospitalized. When the plane landed, Betty rushed to meet the social worker from the other agency. When she was handed the baby, she was so bruised and gaunt that Betty hardly recognized her. But the baby recognized Betty and clung desperately to her during the entire return flight.

"Joe and all six children met us as that airport on our return. Their eyes lit up in excitement and filled with tears when they saw the little bundle in my arms. The baby saw them and willingly went to each one of them as they reached to hold her. But she stayed with each only briefly, needing to return to me between hugs. She clung to me like her life depended on my existence."[4]

It was several months before the baby would speak or sleep alone in her crib. Part of each day Betty tied her on her back "papoose style" to keep her close and comforted. A doctor's visit revealed a broken arm, dehydration, malnourishment and scalp sores where clumps of her hair had been ripped out, in addition to numerous cuts and bruises.

"An attorney was hired, the evidence reviewed, and the court granted Betty and Joe the right to adopt the child. The family, observing the extraordinary bond between Betty and the baby, insisted the child be officially named, "Betty Jean" after her new legal mother.

"By the time little Betty was two and a half, she had fully recovered both physically and emotionally. One afternoon she ran over to Joe. As an impish smile came on her face, she stood up on the toe of his shoe, threw her other foot up behind her, and balancing like a ballerina reached up to dig into the pocket of his slacks. A chill ran through me as memories flooded back. Little Betty laughed, and I heard the voice of a little girl years before, a little girl who had kept us company in a hospital room when heaven and earth seemed one. Then I saw and understood more. A vision of a young woman came back to me, a memory of a beautiful and energetic spirit who had once been waiting to come to earth. I remembered her as the young spirit with whom I shared a bond in a previous time, the one in the spirit world whose loveliness and energy captivated me. I wanted to cry as everything about this precious angel came together. I had been allowed to see her as a child in the spirit. Now I knew why I had been shown her as an adult spirit ready to come to earth. I knew also that while she could not be born to me because of my hysterectomy, she had found another way to become a part of my life. And I now knew why I had been compelled to take her as a baby. We were the closest of friends forever, eternities of experiences behind us, and eternity's ahead."[5]

To some individuals, accounts of famous people seem to carry more weight or validity. But any and all reports of this type are exciting, interesting and informative as is the situation of the two ordinary people in the next case.

Mike Hansen, a Chippewa from Minnesota, is a very successful man in his early fifties. He and his wife had been married for thirty years and had just finished building their dream house when Mike had a series of strange but delightful dreams:

"We were settling down to enjoy the good life when I started having a strange, recurring dream. During these dreams I saw a little girl with curly red hair, an infectious grin, a cute giggle, and big blue eyes. She seemed to be sitting in or on a cloud that would scoot about. This child was by far the cutest little girl I had ever seen. I was so enthralled by her antics, I would wake up laughing.

"About this time we got a call from my son-in-law, Bob. He told us that he needed to go to the hospital and asked us to take care of his baby until he could return home. Our daughter, Bob's wife, had been deep into drugs and was confined in a psychiatric facility, so someone was needed to watch their daughter. My first thought was, 'Why us? Why didn't he call his parents? Or brother? Or sisters?' However I kept my thoughts to myself and reluctantly agreed to take the child, assuming it would not be for very long.

"Since I had to pick up some wheels for my truck, my wife went for the baby. At the tire store a Michelin ad caught my attention. It portrayed a cute little baby sitting in a tire. It reminded me of my dream, only the baby in the ad was bald and my baby had curly red hair. Still, the image in the ad stuck in my mind as I picked up the wheels and headed home.

"When I walked into the house I was shocked--there was the baby of my dreams! She was in a round white walker, scooting across the floor, giggling. I stood transfixed and said to my wife, 'I have seen this baby. She is the one I've been dreaming about for weeks.' She came scooting up to me and looked up with those big blue eyes. I was hooked.

"My wife interrupted with the news that our son-in-law was very sick and had been admitted into the County Hospital. Our oldest son had gone over to check on his condition and called urgently to inform us that Bob was dying. 'Please come quickly'" It seems that Bob had been bitten by a brown recluse spider directly on an artery and his body was shutting down. He had only hours to live.

"We rushed over to the hospital and Bob was very relieved to see us. He knew he was dying and his final request was that we take his daughter, Robin. Not his parents. Not his siblings. Us!

"He was very insistent and had already signed papers to that effect. Shortly after our arrival he went into a coma and was not responsive for hours. We prayed for him continually, but there was no response. Finally my wife leaned over and spoke in his ear, 'Bob, don't worry about the baby. She is with us, and we will care for her. We will make sure she knows what a wonderful daddy you were.'

"We know that he heard her because we saw a tear form in Bob's left eye and roll down his cheek. Moments later he died. Apparently he had been hanging on until he knew for sure we would care for his daughter.

"I now know that my dreams were a confirmation that we were supposed to raise this little girl. She was so beautiful, so full of life, so innocent and happy. For some reason she gravitated to me. She followed me everywhere and would fuss until I picked her up. I never felt so much love for a child even with my own kids.

"This confirmation was reinforced one day when I walked into Robin's room and was surprised to see my deceased mother standing by her crib looking at her. She turned to me and tele-pathically told me, 'Robin is a special spirit, a beloved child of God. You are privileged to have her in your family.'

"It isn't easy becoming a parent in your fifties, but my dream and the appearance of my mother clearly informed me that it was meant to be. As Mom said, it has been a privilege."

Mike and his wife were enjoying the freedom that comes when all your children have left home. The last thing on their minds was adopting a young child. But his recurring dream of a little redheaded girl prepared him for her arrival. Mike told me that he had not thought it fair that he and his wife should have to drastically alter their retirement plans but now that she is in their home, there is no way he would give her up.

Are adoptions random? Certainly not all, as demonstrated above and below. In the following case an adoption was initiated in heaven and formalized later on earth.

Dorothy and Jerry L. had been trying unsuccessfully to have children for ten years. It finally came to them that if they were to have a family, they would have to adopt.

"One night shortly after we realized this, I had a nightmare. Suddenly in my dream there was a light and a peaceful feeling. In the light I saw a beautiful baby with big dark eyes. Peace came over me. He said, 'I have been waiting a long time, and I have your name on me.' He spoke these words as one adult speaks to another, but I saw a baby's face. I did not know if the baby was a boy or girl.

"Shortly, we made plans to adopt a child. It seemed to be the right thing to do, and we were excited. Within a year, we finally received our phone call. Our baby had been born.

"We had to wait seventy-two hours before we could pick up our son, Tyler. Two days after his birth, we were told the birth mother wanted to see him. This was not a good sign. In about ninety percent of cases like this, the mother keeps the baby. I sat in my office praying. Suddenly I felt the presence of my stepfather, who had passed away many years previously. He assured me that all was well. I realized that it was the anniversary of my stepfather's death.

"The adoption went fine—without complications. In fact, we were later told that when the birth mother held Tyler, she had the distinct impression come to her mind that it really was God's will that Tyler be raised by the adoptive family. We were grateful.

"Three years later my sister had an experience in which my stepfather (her father) appeared to her in a dream. He told her: 'Tyler is a great spirit and was my good friend in the spirit world. When he found out his birth mother wanted to give him up for adoption, I asked him if he would like to come to our family. Tyler agreed.'"[6]

Obviously the actions and desires of those on earth are known to those in the pre-earthly realm. A birth mother's decision not to keep her baby is not a secret to the affected spirit. This knowledge may stimulate activity in heaven that sets in motion specific actions on earth which results in that spirit being placed in a different family. Evidently the individual's transference to a new family is recognized and condoned by the individual and by other concerned individuals in the premortal sphere. This case also demonstrates that friendships that develop premortally are deep and eternal.

Sally is a young woman who strongly believes that, although she was adopted, her adoptive family is the one she selected before she was born. Sally initiated the discussion.

"My mother, Helen, is a vigorous, active, healthy woman. She had no major medical problems until it came time for her to have children. She managed to give birth to one daughter, but severe complications prevented any further pregnancies. Mom did not give up and petitioned God repeatedly to give her additional children. Over a ten year period she had a number of dreams that she would be given a dark-haired girl. But the little girl did not come.

"For several years, Mom continued to received assurances this daughter was still coming, but that she had to be patient. In the meantime, realizing my mother could no longer bear children, she and my father applied to adopt. They adopted a son and again applied. My mother knew there was a little dark haired girl waiting to come to her."

Helen explains what happened next.

"My lawyer called, 'Helen, a young woman has just given birth to a healthy baby boy. If you want, I will start processing the necessary paper work.'

"I was hesitant. In my dreams, I had been clearly informed that I was to receive a girl. I said to my lawyer, 'As much as I want more children, I do not want to take a child that is intended for someone else.'

"'Helen,' he continued, 'I believe this child is to be yours. Why don't you think about it and give me a call in the morning?'

"That night, I had a dream in which a little boy who looked about three or four, came to me and said, 'Mom, I'm yours. Don't you want me? Your little girl will come, but it's my turn now!'

"Almost before he faded from view, I flipped on the light, reached for the phone, and called my lawyer. Even though it was two in the morning, he answered immediately. He barely finished saying hello when I said, 'I apologize for calling at such an unusual hour, but I want the baby boy!'

"When my son was three years old, he began asking for a little sister. He had been out with his father watching the horses foaling and I thought this might have stimulated his desire for a little sister. He told me to have his father go out into the fields and bring back a little sister. I explained, 'Son, that is not the way we get little sisters.'

"He thought for a moment, then said, 'Well how do we get them?'

"At age three, I did not think he was ready for a complex discussion of human reproduction or medical complications that made conception impossible. So I answered, 'If you want a little sister, you should ask God.'

"He said, 'Okay, let's pray for one.'

"More serious now, I turned to the faith of a child; 'Sam, if you feel you need a baby sister, then I want you to say the prayer. Heavenly Father listens to children's prayers and, if it's right, he will send you a sister.'

"We then knelt in prayer, and in child-like faith he requested God to give him a baby sister. When finished, he looked and said. 'She's coming soon.'

"I was a bit concerned that if we did not get the baby Sam wanted, he would lose faith in God. However, within a week my lawyer called and said, 'Helen, there is a waiting list of about twenty couples ahead of you, but there is a woman who's going to have a baby very soon. We don't know if it's a boy or a girl, but I have the distinct feeling that God wants this child to be yours.' I told them to proceed immediately with the paperwork.

"The day the baby was born, we rushed to the hospital. It was a girl, a beautiful little girl, but she had light-colored hair.

"My husband mused, "Honey, she's beautiful, but she is not the dark-headed girl you have been telling me about all these years.'

"I looked at the tiny infant in my arms and said, 'Yes. Yes. She's the one. There is no mistake. I know she is the one.' And when we returned the next day, I was not a bit surprised to see that her full head of hair had turned dark brown.

When Helen quit speaking, Sally spoke up in a voice shaking with emotion.

"I was that baby, and I believe with all my heart that Helen is my real mother. Since she could not give birth to me, I had to come to her a different way. I was named after my maternal grandmother who passed away a number of years before I was born. When you compare our baby pictures, I look just like her. I have been stopped in grocery stores by people who knew my grandmother saying, 'You must be related to Sarah B. You look just like her!'

"I have met my birth mother, and other than the fact that we are both women, there is no other resemblance. Where she is very fair, I am not. I know that my real mother is Helen. My mother knew me years before I was born. My brother testified to her that I was hers, and I feel that the bond we have extends beyond this mortal world."

What is intriguing about this case is that the adopted child took on the appearance of her adoptive parents, not her biological mother. It was as if her biological mother was a surrogate host for her real parents. This account, and others cited, raises interesting questions about the relationship between the appearance of the spirit body and that of the physical body. Normally children tend to take on the appearance of the family they are born into. But apparently some children take on the appearance of the families they were intended to become part *of* through adoption. This woman's account would certainly support this possibility.

Vickie Carter always wanted to be a mother. She assumed that with marriage, children would naturally follow, but they didn't. After considerable soul-searching and consulting with physicians, it was determined that conception was highly improbable.

"My husband and I decided that if we wanted to be parents we would have to adopt. We submitted all the necessary paperwork and were told we would not be considered until our year's study time was up. So we tried to put all thoughts of babies out of our minds.

"In early February, I had a vivid dream. I am not normally a person who remembers dreams in detail, but I will never forget this one. I was standing in my place of employment holding a blond-haired baby boy. (I thought later that the blond hair was unusual since my husband and I both have brown hair.) A lady came up to me and asked me what my baby's name was. 'Adam,' I responded.

"The next morning I shared the dream with my husband. There were a few things that I didn't understand, such as the blond hair, but especially the name. We had decided if given a boy we would name him John David. Still, the dream made a big impression on both my husband and I. We tried not to get our hopes up as the adoption agency had explained we would not be considered for a baby until May and it would probably be late fall at the earliest before they could tell us anything.

"So you can imagine how surprised and excited we were to hear from our social worker in mid-May that she had a baby for us. He had been born in mid-February and was almost three months old. The moment I saw him, I knew that he was the baby I had seen and that his name was Adam.

"Adam is now nine years of age and Vickie reported that his blond hair has turned brown, the same shade as hers as a child. Everyone they meet assumes he is her biological child."

Some individuals report a very strong link between themselves and their unborn adopted children. Such was the situation of the woman in the following case.

"I had a very vivid dream in which I was sitting in a rocking chair. Above my head floated two cherubs, one on each side, and I felt completely at peace in their presence. Several years later my husband and I adopted a baby boy. When he was two, the adoption agency called and asked if we would like to adopt a two-year-old boy as well. We were thrilled!

"One day as I was rocking my sons with one in my left arm and the other in my right, I was suddenly overwhelmed with a feeling of peace. I recalled my unusual dream about the cherubs and knew that those baby angels I saw were actually the spirits of my sons-to-come."[8]

Two spirits, hovering about her, assured her that she would eventually have children. She did, but through adoption, not birth. What is interesting here is the fact they were both two years old when the second child came to her. They had appeared together as spirits and ended up together as same age brothers.

**Summary Thoughts**

I have chosen the cases reported in this chapter for a number of reasons. First, they document the fact that some spirits have definite preferences as to whom they desire for parents. They may be intended for a particular family but when they cannot come the usual way, they may still come through adoption. Second, unborn spirits seem to be very familiar with what is going on in the lives of their biological and adoptive parents. Third, they love their prospective parents before they are even born and greatly appreciate the sacrifices being made by their biological mothers to bring them into mortality. Fourth, on certain occasions they can manifest their presence to their adoptive parents. And fifth, adoption is promoted by those in the heavenly realm while abortion is not.

# Chapter Nineteen
## Abortion

Those who have had the opportunity to see into or visit the premortal world learned that unborn spirits are intelligent beings who are anxiously anticipating the moment when they can come to earth. They know that they must leave their premortal home in order to progress, that they have an important mission which they must accomplish on earth, and that there is a definite time when they are to begin their sojourn on earth.

When they discover that their prospective parents are contemplating aborting their body, these beings are distraught, disappointed, and frustrated. If their prospective mothers have the abortion, it will not destroy them or negate their missions because in one way or another they will eventually come to earth. But it does cause deep emotional distress and feelings of rejection. They are acutely aware that certain parents can better facilitate their successfully completing their missions than others.

The individuals whose experiences are reported in this chapter shared them only after intensive soul-searching. Each individual's experience was extremely personal and it totally changed their perceptions of themselves and the unborn. Retelling these experiences was emotionally draining, even painful, but often spiritually uplifting.

This chapter will examine the impact that abortion can and does have on those spirits whose bodies are aborted. The first account clearly illustrates the distress experienced by unborn spirits when their prospective mothers aborted their developing bodies.

Cherie Logan, introduced in Chapter 5, was privileged to see all of her future children long before she married. Her firstborn, a boy named Marshall, died shortly after his birth. When Cherie was expecting her seventh child Marshall appeared to her accompanied by a child.

"My son Marshall came and stood before me and in the room were the children I had seen but had not yet given birth to. Then Marshall stepped aside and there was standing in front of me a child I had never seen.

"This child said, 'I beg entry into your family.' I agreed instantly as we were always willing to have more children.

"As if I had never spoken, he again said, 'I beg entry into your family.' I agreed again, beginning to wonder why the repetition.

"Again, a third time he spoke, 'I beg entry into your family.' This time I spoke in detail that we would be happy to have him, that we want as many children as the Lord would be willing to send us.

"As I spoke these words, the heavens opened to me and I saw Jesus Christ standing by a beautiful tree full of white and wonderful fruit. He cupped in his hand one fruit that was still hanging from the tree and said, 'This is my best fruit from my best tree. The sad part is that many do not choose the best fruit.'

"Then he took me to this field that was full of white cradles. Inside the cradles were babies, many, many, many, babies. Some, but not all, of the babies held a piece of paper clutched in their hands.

"He said, 'These are the Cast-off Ones,' meaning those who had been purposely aborted. 'My presence is all that keeps their grief from overwhelming them.' Then he looked right at me and I can say I have never been so grateful for anything as I was at that moment, that I have never been involved with abortion. He said, 'Their blood cries to me from the earth.'

"Then as I looked at the babies and the paper some held in their hands, He said to me, 'That paper represents The Willingness of Mothers.' It was said as a title. It meant the willingness of any woman to have children, even the ones who could not have children because of illness or age or because the spirit says, 'No More,' but who, in their hearts, would have children if they could. Then He said, 'It is the willingness of mothers to someday have them that gives them hope.'

"Suddenly the vision closed, and I again saw the boy in front of me. He said this time, 'I am a Cast-off One, and I beg entry into your family.'

"I said, 'Yes.' Instantly there appeared in his hand that white paper.

"Then he looked at me and said, "My name is Joshua and I bring with me an extension of your life.'

"I asked him if I could change his name to Jonathan which I thought would be a good name for an extra son. He said, 'No, my name is Joshua.'

"Then Joshua vanished from my sight, but it did not end with that. When I became pregnant with my seventh child (Ryan), I would frequently see Joshua. Often standing with him was a young woman. One time she informed me that because I was going to be Joshua's mother, she wanted to come to my family. She said that where they were she had been caring for Joshua and she wanted to be in the same family as he so she could continue caring for him."[1]

The meaning of Joshua's promise—"I bring you an extension of your life."—is not completely clear. Perhaps it is a promise of longevity for being a "Willing Mother," similar to that implied for keeping the Biblical commandment, "Honor thy father and thy mother: that thy days may be long upon the land which the Lord thy God giveth thee."[2]

But what is apparent from this account is the fact that some spirits whose bodies are aborted can request to be born into a specific family, and these alternate families will be greatly blessed if they elect to have them.

The following account was related by an expectant mother who, in spite of her own personal feelings, went with her sister-in-law when she had an abortion.

"Three weeks before I conceived, my sister-in-law had to have an abortion and asked me to come along for support. This was very difficult for me, since my personal belief is that when a little soul chooses your womb, it was meant to be.

"But anyway, during the whole process of the abortion I felt such a strong connection to that little baby and was so grief-stricken that it had to leave. The next possible time I could conceive, I did. It was a terribly inconvenient time but I knew that this little soul, who had had to leave my sister-in-law's body, needed to find another receptive womb. This realization feels true, although I have nothing to prove it, but intuitively this explanation fits. My husband agrees and we both feel very accepting and loving toward this little being who had such a rough start."[3]

Although there is no evidence that the spirit of the baby she is carrying is the one her sister-in-law aborted, this mother obviously believes that it is.

Not all decisions to abort reflect personal convenience or desire. Just prior to the birth of her son, Christina Williams was permitted to look into the mind of a woman who was tormented by the medical necessity of having an abortion.

"I have had many precognitive dreams, but I don't always recognize them as such. Years after my son Benjamin was born, I was reviewing a folder of my dreams that I'd written down the year or two before I became pregnant with him. I was struck by one dream in particular. In it there was a woman agonizing over whether or not to have an abortion. Although I couldn't bear the thought of having an abortion myself, I cannot say what it would be like to face this woman's dilemma. I felt so much compassion for her. She sorrowfully and reluctantly decided to go ahead with the procedure. This was extremely difficult for her since she really loved this unborn child. However, she felt that under the circumstances it would be best to abort him. Medical tests had revealed that the baby would either be born dead or die a difficult death shortly after birth. The mother's decision to abort was, iron- ically, made out of love. She went ahead with the procedure while mourning the loss of this child whom she had named Benjamin.

"I do not know for certain if the Benjamin in the dream is actually my son Benjamin. But both the time frame and the same name seem highly 'coincidental.' Further, I know that my son is an extremely compassionate person and seems about as glad as anyone I know to be here on this planet. From the time he was small, complete strangers have commented on how wise he is or what an 'old soul' he is."

Possibly this really was the same Benjamin for whom other arrangements for earthly parents had to be made. Whether or not, her belief that he was Benjamin created a special bond between the two of them.

Wendy learned during her near-death experience that if a woman is pregnant and terminates the pregnancy for selfish reasons, there is great sadness in the world of the unborn. The spirit who is waiting for the opportunity to come to earth may understand the thoughts and emotions of the intended mother, but is still unhappy and depressed. Although alternative arrangements can be made, the mission of that spirit will be altered in significant ways.

Are there negative implications of being born into a family other than the one originally assigned? The answer in some cases is yes. For example, Wendy had recurring sensations of being born into the wrong family. She did not feel rejected or that her parents did not love her, only that she did not belong there.

"My mother worked and on the days I spent at home alone I felt tormented by fears of rejection and abandonment. Even my name seemed wrong to me. I never could understand why I felt this way and was deeply troubled.

"My sense of misplacement was a constant source of stress that took its toll on my health. By my mid-forties, I had spent many years bedridden by illness. Even on those occasions when I was strong enough to arise from my sickbed, I still suffered from poor health. In desperation, I prayed for answers as to why so much of my life was plagued with emotional and physical afflictions. Within a couple of weeks of almost constant prayer, I received an answer to my prayers, an answer that surprised me exceedingly.

"My sister, unaware of my prayers regarding my life-long sense of misplacement, came to see me one day. In the course of our conversation she happened to share something our divorced father had once told her. He related that when he was about four years old he had a very strong impression that a lit-tle sister would be joining their family soon. He ran to tell his mother the exciting news. However, he discovered this 'news' was not at all exciting to his mother. She was struggling to care for her three children and could not face another pregnancy. Her father did not know what happened to his sister. He knew she was on her way to his family but had never arrived. He had always wondered what happened to her.

"Later that same week my mother also came to me and said she had something that she needed to share. 'One day, your father's mother confided in me that years ago she had discovered she was pregnant. At that time she was at her wits end and could not cope with another child. So she had traveled to a nearby city and had an abortion. She had never told anyone, not even her husband.'

"I listened with rapt attention. Everything was at last beginning to make sense to me. I knew that I was the sister that my father, at age four, was expecting. But his mother's inability to manage the complications associated with this pregnancy resulted in her having to wait until the next generation to be born.

"I went into deep mourning for my death some fifty years earlier. I grieved for myself and for my grandmother who should have been my mother. I loved my mother, but my affection for my grandmother was especially deep and pervasive. My grieving continued for about a year and was finally disrupted by a spiritual experience wherein I was transported back to my pre-earth life. There I saw myself watching as my mother had my body aborted. I saw myself screaming, 'Stop, stop! You have no idea what you are doing. Please stop, you can't do this,' but I could not make my mother hear my cries. In shocked disbelief I watched my perfectly formed little body aborted, then discarded. I thought, 'How could this person, my mother who had carried me inside her, do this thing?'

"Although learning this truth was hard, it also brought relief. At last I understood why all my life I had felt out of place and feared rejection."

Wendy forgave her grandmother and this forgiveness cancelled all her fears. With her fears gone her health improved. She died four years later with an inner peace she had lacked most of her life.

After Wendy's death, a brother who knew nothing of the abortion handed his living sister a note about a dream/vision he had had.

"I saw Wendy standing in heaven with her paternal grandmother. They were both radiant, and Wendy and Grandmother looked just alike—like sisters."

The impact of an abortion has far-reaching implications. For some, as in Wendy's grandmother's case, it was an act of desperation. Nevertheless, the desire of this unborn child to be a part of a particular family was so strong, that she waited two generations.

Abandoned by her second husband with four small children (two hers, two his), Pat was also devastated to discover she was pregnant. Depression set in. There was no way she could care for a fifth child. She concluded that abortion was her only solution.

"After my first husband left me, I struggled along for a number of years until I met Jim. He seemed to be an answer to prayer, but my judgment may have been clouded by loneliness, along with a desperate need for someone to help me care for my son and daughter.

"Jim brought two young children of his own to the marriage. His business required extensive travel, so I went from raising two children alone to raising four. On top of that, Jim's pay did not cover our bills, so I was forced to go to work. Soon the requirements of four active children, plus working full-time, taxed my physical and emotional resources to the breaking point.

"During this time I had a very unusual experience. While fixing spaghetti for dinner I distinctly heard a voice telling me that I was going to have another baby. At first I just brushed it off. Then for a second time I heard the voice say, 'You're going to have another baby.'

"I said to this unseen voice, 'No way. My husband is never around, we can't afford it, and I cannot handle any more children.'

"No matter how hard I tried I could not shake the feeling that I just might be pregnant. Then Jim abandoned me, leaving his two children behind. I purchased a pregnancy kit which confirmed that I was pregnant! I collapsed! I just lay there, totally exhausted and physically unable to move. How could I survive? I sobbed uncontrollably. Raising my hands to heaven I asked, "God, how could you do this to me. I am doing all I can to raise four children! I just cannot handle another!"

"I slipped into a deep depression, barely getting out of bed for nearly a week. I wanted to see or talk to no one. My other pregnancies had been fraught with complications, so I could anticipate that this one would be the same. Facing this possibility and without the help and support of a husband, left me feeling totally overwhelmed and betrayed.. I had always been adamantly opposed to abortion. To me, children have a right to life and abortion denies that right. However I could see no way to have another baby and survive. So I made an appointment with Planned Parenthood.

"The very next day a close friend called and said, 'Pat, I don't know what you're planning to do, but I need to come and talk with you.' I was startled because I had not seen this woman for some time, nor had I told anyone what I had in mind. My friend came right over and said without hesitation, 'I don't know exactly what you're contemplating. All I know is that I was told to get over here as quickly as possible.'

"Reluctantly I told her my story and concluded, 'Don't try and talk me out of this because I cannot deal with a fifth child; there is nothing else I can do.'

"When I was finished she pleaded, 'Please do not do anything right now. You will be given all the information you need. Please, please do nothing until that time.' She held me very close, and with tears streaming down her face, she left.

"Pondering her message, I was still resolved to have the abortion. But it could wait a little longer. As I lay in bed that night, I became aware of the joyous laughter of a young girl. I tried to shut it out, but couldn't. Then I heard her voice, 'You are so sad to have me, but I'm Caitlin and I'm your baby.' She pleaded, 'Please don't do this thing! Everything is going to be okay. All you have to do is ask Father in Heaven for what you need, and help will be there for you. I want to be in your life and I need to come now.'

"This made me mad. I had no way of providing for an additional child. What with the medical expenses, the other four children, and my health, I was completely overwhelmed. Now more pressure was being put on me. It was just not fair!

"Despite my efforts to resist, I began to connect with Caitlin. Frequently I felt her presence, her exuberance for life, and her excitement about coming to earth and being my child. And in spite of all my misgivings I fell deeply in love with her. Over the next few days I felt her presence become stronger and stronger, until I knew that I couldn't abort her. But before conceding all the way, I made an agreement with her! 'Caitlin, I will have you but I will need lots of help.'

"I called Planned Parenthood and canceled my appointment.

"As my pregnancy progressed, my unborn daughter guided me to changes I needed to make in my life. She promised if I made these changes, all the help I requested would be forthcoming. As we communicated, I was aware that other spiritual beings accompanied her in support of both of us. Caitlin and her spirit friends were joyous and very excited about my decision to have her. I could hear her laughter intermingled with theirs. It was obvious to me that my decision was very important to her and that her unseen friends shared her happiness.

"When Caitlin was born and they handed her to me, I knew her. I knew all her characteristics, what she would look like, her whole being. Before she was born I had been shown key episodes in her life, and though she is yet a small child, everything has turned out exactly as I was shown. Caitlin is a very effervescent child. She has an ability to read the feelings of others and to understand what they are thinking. She is joyous, and whenever she giggles, it is that same giggle I heard as I was struggling with the idea of aborting her.

"Everything that was promised was fulfilled. I've faced major challenges and still do. Things are not easy, and life is a struggle, but when I really need help, it is always there. I am enjoying life, grateful I listened to a loving friend and the pleadings of my unborn daughter not to abort her. She is a joy in my life, and that infectious giggle always buoys me up.

I now know more than ever that all life is sacred, that children need to come to earth and be born into loving families. Abortion is never the answer. It is usually an act of desperation, but with consequences that extend far beyond this earth. For those women struggling with the question of whether they should terminate a pregnancy, I would strongly recommend that they not do so. There is a child involved, a child who desperately wants you to be his or her mother. If you do not abort your child, unseen spirits will be there to help you. I know, because they have lifted me up when I asked. They have guided me and blessed my life because I chose to give life. But to receive this help I had to make major changes in my life and I did."

A young Japanese woman was another person who was visited by her unborn child as she contemplated having an abortion.

"My fiancé and I had just discovered that I was pregnant. Japan is still very traditional and my family would be put to shame by my being pregnant before marriage. I had just been offered a very good job that I could not accept in my condition. Furthermore, my fiancée was unemployed. For these reasons I was seriously considering an abortion. In the meantime we got married.

"I must have spent weeks crying, unable to make up my mind definitely. We weighed and analyzed having an abortion versus having the baby. I got all the medical information on abortion and even made an appointment at a clinic to terminate my pregnancy.

"But one night my son came to me in my dreams in the form of a boy four or five years old and begged me to keep him. His exact words were, 'Mommy, I'll be a good boy. Please keep me. I won't cause you any trouble.'

"Still not convinced, I went with my husband to the clinic on the appointed morning, with my eyes all red from crying. As I stood in front of the receptionist, cold and numb and trying to hold back my tears, she turned to me and said, 'Take this money back and go see our counselor. You're not fully sure about this and I don't want you to go through with it until you are.'

"That was the turning point. We never did go back. A week later my husband woke up one morning and told me about an unusual dream he had had. (At this point I had not told him of my dream.) In his dream he had seen a little boy and described what he was wearing. It was the same child I had seen wearing the exact same outfit as he had when I saw him—like an aristocratic English boy of Victorian days! And in my husband's dream the little boy was pointing at me saying, 'My Mommy.'[4]

In the next account Ned Dougherty, a self-professed hedonist, learned during his near-death experience that life is sacred and that abortion destroys life. Ned is a college-educated real estate broker and businessman.

"I was neither agnostic nor atheistic—I was too busy being a hedonistic and materialistic nightclub owner to be bothered with such things. All that changed on a hot July second in 1984. In a moment of rage, I attacked and tried to strangle a business associate. All of a sudden I was the one who could not breathe! I felt my lungs collapse and my heart stop beating, and fell into a state of unconsciousness. The next thing I knew I was in an ambulance hearing a paramedic say, 'I have no vitals; we are losing him!'

"I floated out of my human body and out of the ambulance. I hovered over a roadway watching as the ambulance disappeared, and I felt myself rising into the star-filled sky. I thought, 'I'm going home!'

"At that moment—free of my earthly bondage—I remembered! I had been in the world of spirits before—before I was born.

With this realization I found myself in the presence of a beautiful, radiant, and angelic being. She became known to me as the Lady of Light. At one point during my near-death experience, the Lady of Light showed me a small group of toddler-aged children who were playing in a heavenly garden.

"I particularly noticed two of the children who were to the right of the group. They drew my attention because they had turned and were looking at me. Although I perceived that one was a boy and the other a girl, I was more observant of their identical appearances. Later on, I would understand that they were twins.

"There were several more toddlers playing in the group. As I focused my attention on each of them, they looked directly and longingly toward me, as if they were seeking some acknowledgment or understanding from me. I perceived that I should know these children, but I was confused by the scene. I conveyed to the Lady of Light my need to understand what I should know about the scene before me. The Lady of Light responded by introducing me to another scene.

"In this scene I was standing with a group of people who I did not immediately recognize—except for a handsome young man dressed in a cap and gown. The scene was on an academic campus, and it was a sunny and glorious day. I was filled with love, joy, and pride for the young man, who was celebrating his graduation.

"Then I was quickly back in the heavenly garden and filled with even more questions. I told the Lady of Light that I wanted to know the meaning of these visions. I did not have any children, nor did I plan to have children. Up to that moment in my life I had thought of children only as an inconvenience.

"I was perplexed by my reaction to the young man at his graduation. During that moment, I experienced emotions that I had never known before, emotions that only a father could know!

"But I was not a father and the prospect of such a long-term commitment was actually frightening to me! As I meditated over what I was seeing the group of children slowly vanished, disappearing before my eyes. I immediately felt an excruciating loss, a terrible, heart-wrenching, and aching pain. The pain I was feeling was the loss of these children.

"I then realized who the children were. During my earthly life, the opportunities to have children had been presented to me on several occasions but I had chosen not to have them. In fact, I had insisted that the women in my life *not* bring children into the world and that they have abortions when they became pregnant.

"I could now clearly see that these children were not 'choices!' I realized that they were the spirits of children who were intended to be my children during my earthlife. They were the opportunities that I had decided were inconveniences!

"I pondered the scene before me, now absent of the children, for what seemed like a long period of time. Then a small boy appeared in the garden from the direction of the Lady of Light. The little boy was very strong and full of life. He had blond hair and big blue eyes.

"I turned to the Lady of Light and conveyed to her that I wanted to know who this little boy was, and what the significance was of the scene before me. I didn't have children, and I didn't anticipate having children. Was this little boy to be my son?

"The Lady of Light responded, 'Truly, he is a son of God!'

"I found myself being sent back to my body. I didn't want to be here but God didn't want me up there either, and it was His decision, not mine!

"As I came back from death, I was told that I was coming back with a mission in life. I didn't know what that mission was at first, but I now find that each and every day it is being defined for me a little more clearly. I know that I have a destiny!

"On April 7, 1991, I became a father. My son's name is Michael Christopher. He is named after his grandpa and also after the Archangel Michael. He is the luckiest little boy in the world, because I am a great daddy!

"I was present in the delivery room when Michael came into

this world. What an experience it was! What a miracle! The miracle of life! As I watched Michael being born, and his strong little body struggle to stay alive as his body breathed its first breath, I felt a life force of energy fill that delivery room. I felt a rush of wind roll by my ears carrying a message. It was a message I remembered hearing from the Lady of Light, 'Truly, he is a son of God!'

"Michael had blond hair that was almost golden and the biggest blue eyes I have ever seen on a little boy. I listened as the nurses marveled and commented on how strong and well developed his body was!"

This totally self-indulgent man learned a very important lesson. He had to die to learn it, but learn it he did. He learned that life is sacred, and that earthly choices have heavenly implications. These implications impact both those on earth and those in heaven. He was able to see how his actions had affected those in heaven, what opportunities he had lost, and what else he would lose if he did not turn his life around. He also discovered that the abortions he had insisted on had involved spirit beings who had been denied the chance to come to earth at their appointed time because of his choices. But he, too, had lost something—the opportunity to be a part of *their* lives. Ned teared up while remembering the children who could have been his but were forced back to heaven by the abortions he insisted his companions have. He said that losing those children was the greatest mistake of his life. How grateful he is that he learned the truth before rejecting his son, Michael Christopher, who is the greatest thing that has ever happened to him. Ned Dougherty subsequently wrote the book, *Fast Lane to Heaven*, which includes this encounter with his son and an in-depth description of his near-death experience.[5]

Following are additional accounts documenting the fact that the spirits of the unborn are acutely aware of the intentions of those to whom they are supposed to come on earth. In the first case, the unborn spirit manifested itself and its frustrations to Ann, a very close friend of its intended mother.

"One evening I went to bed and had the most vivid dream I had ever had. It was about my friend Kris and it left me terribly troubled. Normally Kris and I are very close but, because of the demands of family and work, we had not seen much of each other for a while.

"Kris was twenty-three, pregnant, and unmarried. In my dream/vision, we were in this space and she was delivering a baby. Although the delivery was difficult, I had the distinct impression that it was not the delivery she was agonizing over but the pregnancy.

"Finally, I knew the baby had been born. I didn't see its body but distinctly heard its cry. It was a cry like no other I had ever heard. It pierced my heart. The wailing continued, but there was no baby. I became increasingly distraught by the cries. I searched and searched for the baby, but to no avail. I was absolutely desperate to find and comfort that infant but as hard as I searched, I could not find the baby. It was a terribly intense and upsetting dream and made for one of the most disturbing nights I have ever experienced.

"The next day I called Kris and told her that I had to meet her and share something with her face-to-face. Two days later, she came over for lunch. As I told her about my dream, the feelings returned with such intensity that I broke into tears. Eventually I recovered sufficiently to describe seeing her give birth, hearing the baby's cries, and my frantic efforts to find the baby. I concluded that I was terribly distressed and needed to know what it meant.

"Kris's face turned white and she started sobbing. It took a while for her to speak. At last she disclosed that on the day of my dream, she'd had an abortion. She had struggled long with the decision and had not told a soul. We spent the next hour crying and comforting each other.

"Although my dream had lasted but moments, it had seemed

an eternity. Unlike other dreams, I had felt as if I was actually witnessing Kris's suffering and hearing the cries of a baby in agony. After Kris's confession it made sense—I had witnessed the grief of a soul being denied its right to come to earth to its intended body. I now know with an absolute certainty that life is sacred and has a purpose and timing we must respect."

This account is enlightening in that the emotional turmoil a spirit experienced when its body was aborted was both heard and felt by a person other than its mother.

Holly Draper, a professional counselor with unique gifts, was asked to counsel a pregnant teenager who was determined to have an abortion.

"Several years ago, I had a near-death experience that awakened within me spiritual sensitivities that I now use to help others as a counselor. One day I received an urgent call from a mother who had been referred to me by a former client. An appointment was arranged for the following day.

"A very anxious mother arrived with her husband and sixteen-year-old daughter. When the door was closed and we were all seated, the mother began, 'Our daughter is with child.' She became choked up and for moments could not speak. When she regained her composure she continued, 'We love our daughter and we love her baby. It is our hope to help raise this child, but our daughter wants an abortion. Please help us find a way to resolve this dilemma fairly for everyone.'

"The echo of her words had not ceased when there suddenly appeared to me in a heavenly light an adorable girl about age six. The scene was so vivid that I still recall it in detail. She stood above and behind her intended mother. The little girl was blonde with brown eyes. She wore a beautiful frilly dress with lace at the collar, the sleeves, and the bottom of the skirt. Even her white ankle socks had lace at the top. And her smile! The child expressed telepathic joy that it was her time to come to earth after an eternal wait. She radiated a profound love, a heavenly love, for the three individuals seated before me.

"My blissful vision was sharply interrupted by the sixteen-year-old who insisted, 'I am too young to be a mother. I *will* have an abortion!'

"The chilling words cut into the hearts of the anxious grandparents who were obviously eager to raise and love this child whether their daughter wanted her or not. I looked back at the little girl, the spirit of the infant growing within the sixteen-year-old. She did not move, hovering in the air above her chosen earth family, but her countenance changed to disbelief and sorrow as she implored, 'Please help me! Tell my mother I'm here and she promised. This may be my only chance to come to her.' It was an anguished plea to me. And then she was gone.

"Somewhat shaken, I attempted to convey the message. But how do you tell an angry, scared-sixteen-year old you've just seen the spirit of her daughter? Cautiously I explained, 'I nearly died once and my spirit went to heaven. Since returning I sometimes see spirits. The child within you is an adorable little girl. I know because I just saw her in this room hovering above you. She wants you to know how much she loves you. She has waited a long time to come and you promised her when you were friends in heaven that she could come to your family. Bringing her to earth will be a great blessing to you.'

"'Being pregnant is not a blessing!' she retorted.

"It was apparent her mind was made up. I made a final attempt to reach her on behalf of her unborn child. I asked that she go home and pray about the message I had relayed to her from her unborn daughter.

"She looked at me and said, 'I want to know one thing. Will I be damned forever if I have an abortion?'

"I responded, 'That is between you and God. But this much I

*can* tell you. If you go through with this decision you will never forget this lost opportunity.' As I hugged her I said, 'Heavenly Father will continue to love you no matter what, but you will lose the blessings your daughter would bring you. This child will never be a burden. There are many people who will want to adopt her and love her, including your own parents.'

"For over two hours, I tried to help the teenager appreciate the plea from her unborn daughter, but to no avail. She left firmly resolved to abort the baby. Through a mutual friend I later learned that she had had the abortion. It was a sad conclusion. I knew there would be regrets. There always are."

Holly had the opportunity of seeing what the impact was on an unborn spirit of knowing that she was going to lose her chance at mortality with a specific mother. This spirit's excitement turned to disbelief, then to anguish as she comprehended that her developing body was about to be destroyed. Evidently, commitments had been made and plans laid in premortality, and the abortion negated them all.

Chapter Nine discusses how some children retain memories of their premortal home for a while. Such was the case of a six-year-old boy. One day as he was playing, he casually mentioned to his mother, "Mommy, God sent me to you twice. The first time my body ended up in a jar!" His mother held him close recalling the abortion he was referring to. Evidently in a some cases the unborn soul can come back to its preferred mother at a later time.

A second example of this possibility was reported by a young mother. One day she was chatting with her four-year-old daughter, Dorothy. Dorothy got a faraway look in her eyes and startled her mother when she said:

"When I was four inches long and in your tummy, Daddy wasn't ready to marry you yet, so I went away. But then I came back." Her eyes lost that faraway look, and she was chatting again about four-year-old matters.

Her mother was silent. No one but she and her husband and the doctor knew that she had become pregnant about two years before she and her husband were ready for children, and that she had had an abortion. She had been ready to have the child, but her husband-to-be was not ready.[6]

What is informative in this account is the fact that there was no apparent recrimination or resentment by the child as witnessed in earlier accounts. Perhaps it was due to her foreknowledge that it was not her last chance to come to her chosen mother.

No one knows exactly when the physical body is developed enough to function as the home for a spirit, and perhaps it even varies from pregnancy to pregnancy. Possibly, however, a spirit can inhabit its developing body early in a pregnancy, if only briefly. And this very brief experience is all some spirits need. Such was the case of Jimmy's older brother.

Jimmy at age four, fell into the family swimming pool and, when discovered, had been under the water for at least five minutes. Emergency personnel worked on him for fifteen minutes before reviving him.

When the emergency staff had finished stabilizing him, he looked up at his mother and said, "Mommy, I met my little brother. He's over there where I was before I came to be with you. He told me all about him being pulled out of your tummy when you were thirteen." The little boy went on to describe in detail his mother's abortion, an event she had never discussed with anyone and had almost forgotten.

Jimmy was absolutely elated to discover he had a brother. Their reunion was joyous and both vowed to stay in contact now that they had met.

The message of four-year-old Jimmy to his mother would certainly seem to indicate that abortions involve intelligent beings, and that an abortion does not necessarily destroy the familial bond. This spirit still considered himself to be part of that particular family and had been there to greet his brother and send him back. Jimmy was given assurances by his deceased brother that he would watch over and protect him. These two brothers have a bond which extends between worlds.

Mary was grateful for the love and companionship given her by her elderly friend George Heath. During their weekly visits he shared with her his wisdom and love as would a kindly grandfather. Little did she know the extent to which his love and teachings would help her to survive one of the most horrendous things that can happen to a woman:

"I regularly visited a dear and very elderly friend. During one of these visits he reached out his hand and took hold of one of mine. He looked into my eyes and said, 'Mary, in one year you will receive a rose beyond the thorns and it will take your pain away. Mary, that rose will love you unconditionally, the same way that I do.'

"I had no idea what George was talking about. Pain? Thorns? Roses? His words made no sense to me. I was deeply saddened when this old man passed away shortly after our conversation.

"A couple of months later, I was raped and impregnated by a security guard. It left me severely traumatized. I felt violated, extremely vulnerable, and afraid. I was strongly encouraged—actually pressured—by my family and friends to abort the baby, but I refused. In my opinion, two wrongs do not make a right, and I could not abort an innocent baby regardless of how it was conceived. I was both surprised and dismayed at the criticism and resentment I received because I would not terminate my pregnancy. I was subjected to vicious slander, rumor, and abandonment. Some even speculated that I had made up the rape story to cover up the real reason why I was pregnant. This was an incredibly difficult time in my life, almost as severe as the rape itself.

"Before my baby's birth and while I was in the midst of a lot of gossip and speculation, I went to visit my great-grandmother.

While visiting she said to me, 'I know you didn't cause this, dear. He knows (pointing up toward heaven) your heart and that is all that matters.' She also said, 'I believe you and I believe *in* you.'"

"Her counsel was the same as George had given me before he died. Without the love and unfailing support of George and my great-grandmother, I don't think I could have endured that terrible year and continued to believe in myself.

"It was not until nine months after the rape, and one year after the conversation with George, that I finally understood what he meant by thorns. Somehow he had known that I would face a very difficult and 'thorny' time, but that out of this pain would come a beautiful 'rose.' The thorns symbolized the rape and unkind accusations. The rose was the most beautiful baby girl I have ever had the privilege to lay my eyes on. I named her Valerie after my great- grandmother Valerie Ann Brown.

"My daughter, Val has no idea of the circumstances under which she was conceived and I never plan to tell her. But strangely, she has some level of awareness. You see, at age seven Val brought me a beautiful picture she had drawn of herself and a rose. She had written under it, 'Rose beyond the thorns.'

"Being surprised I asked, 'Why did you write that?'

"'George told me to. I have always known it!' was her reply.

"I was stunned. I did not know what to say but went to my files to get some pictures I had of George and myself. I put them on the table but before I could say anything she pointed to a picture and said, 'That's him, that's my George.'

"They had never met in this life and I had never shown her George's picture, yet she recognized him—knew and loved him the same as I. He had taught her about trials (the thorns of life) and unconditional love (roses) before she came to me."

This account is a beautiful conclusion to this chapter. It demonstrates that deep love can exist between generations with an old man and old woman reaching out to a young woman and showing her complete and unconditional love. Mary was able to withstand social pressures and ostracism when she refused to abort the baby because of their love. The rape that produced the baby was horrible and evil, but out of this evil came a beautiful and innocent child who, seven years later, revealed the truth of what an old man had told her mother. Valerie and George were evidently very close in premortality, and it seems to have been George who helped Valerie prepare to come to Mary. Just think what Mary would have lost if she had had an abortion! This little girl confirmed that love extends beyond the grave, that death does not destroy relationships, and that life, regardless of the circumstances under which it begins, is sacred and wonderful.

### Summary Thoughts

Lawyers, politicians, geneticists, and many others may argue that a fetus is nothing more than the potential for becoming human. But they are wrong. The essence of an individual starts in a heavenly realm long before conception. In that realm spirits are created, develop, and as noted in earlier chapters, are assigned specific missions. When the possibility of abortion arises, those spirits potentially affected become extremely alarmed, and often go to incredible lengths to try to prevent the abortion. They may try to remind their mother of premortal commitments, or to assure her that she will receive the help she needs to raise them, or that no matter what the medical experts might say about the medical status of their unborn baby, it is okay. They may try to help their prospective mothers realize that their birth is part of an eternal plan, that aborting their bodies will have significant implications for the successful completion of their earthly missions, that an abortion will negate commitments made in heaven, and that blessings will be lost that would accompany the fulfilling of those commitments.

The accounts reported here reveal that unborn infants are intelligent, self-aware beings. The spirit that is intended to inhabit a particular developing body knows of its status and the feelings, emotions, and concerns of his/her prospective parents, certainly at least of its mother. An abortion not only impacts on a specific spirit but also on how that spirit could have affected its parents, brothers and sisters, the larger family, and the community in which it would have resided. Like the ripples in a pond, an abortion has widespread effects.

Does being aborted hurt the unborn? The answer is an unqualified yes. But the pain seems to be not so much physical as emotional and spiritual. The pain largely seems to be related to spirits' feelings of disappointment and or rejection by their prospective parents and knowing that their missions must wait until new arrangements can be made.

Does having an abortion hurt the individual *having* the abortion? The answer is a qualified yes. Blessings are forfeited and covenants made in heaven are voided, as are their accompanying rewards. In many cases there might be lifelong regret, a sense of guilt, and dreams of what might have been. While I did not come across any account where a mother had to stand before God and account for her decision to have an abortion that we know, because of what people who have had near-death experiences have consistently reported about the afterlife; that we will have to have a life review, in other words, to make an accounting to Him for every choice and action we make while on earth.

## Chapter Twenty
## Returning Home

No matter how long we have been away from home, the prospects of returning ignite feelings of longing, anticipation, and excitement. We look forward to returning home but, at the same time, are reluctant to leave those to whom we have become strongly attached. So it is with our heavenly home. Our reunion with those we left behind when we came to earth will be joyous but it is with sadness that we leave loved ones behind when we return home to heaven. Even when we understand that our dying loved ones will be returning home to God, many of us are very concerned about the pain and suffering involved in dying. We wonder whether they will experience severe pain. Will they have to face death alone? What will happen to them? These questions are addressed in this chapter.

### What It Is Like To Die

Answers to these haunting questions can be provided by those who are with and/or care for those as they die. They often report observing dramatic changes in their patients just before they die. If dying persons are not so heavily medicated that they cannot speak or move, many display behavior that can only be described as euphoric. Their faces light up, the ravages of age or disease drop away, and they begin chatting with unseen beings. And these unseen beings are not the product of a drug-induced mind or a high temperature. They are actual beings who have already died, usually someone known and loved. For a parent, it is often a child who died. For adults it could well be their deceased spouse who is there. For some, it seems that there is a veritable welcoming committee assembled to greet and escort them back to their heavenly home. Evidently we are never alone on our way between heaven and earth or between earth and heaven, but are accompanied by beings who love and care for us.

For those who are privileged to witness such a joyous reunion, the sting of death is removed and replaced by a sense of peace and closure. Loved one will be sorely missed, but there is great comfort in the knowledge that this person still exists and is back home in the presence of loved ones.

Physicians Osis and Haraldsson interviewed nearly 2,000 physicians and nurses as to what their patients said or did at the moment of their deaths. Physicians and nurses are trained to be objective observers and to record their patients' physical conditions on a regular basis. These physicians and nurses were from the United States and India and so, represented completely different cultures. They had widely varied religious beliefs (or nonbeliefs) and included Christians, Muslims, Buddhists, agnostics, and atheists. Over 50% of the doctors who responded reported that their patients appeared to be seeing and experiencing something so exciting at the moment of death that it visibly transformed them. Being physicians and scientists, Osis and Haraldsson checked the patients' records for factors that potentially might be causing this phenomenon such as the medications they were receiving, elevated temperatures, or religious predispositions. None of these factors could account for the patients' behaviors.[1]

### What The Dying See

Typical of the reports made by nurses and physicians is that of a sixty-year-old woman who had suffered excruciating pain from intestinal cancer. The doctor reported:

"All of a sudden she opened her eyes. She called her [deceased] husband by name and said she was coming to him. She had the most peaceful, nicest smile just as if she were going to the arms of someone she thought a great deal of. She said, 'Guy, I am coming.' She didn't seem to realize I was there. It was as if she were in another world. It was as if something beautiful had opened up to her; she was experiencing something wonderful and beautiful."[2]

While Osis and Haraldsson did their research in the 1970s, Sir William Barrett collected accounts around the turn of the twentieth century. These fascinating accounts were compiled and published in 1926 in a book entitled *Death-Bed Visions*.[3] One nurse in reflecting on how her patients reacted stated, "It was as if a light bulb had been turned on inside them. Their eyes shone, and they had a very tranquil and peaceful look about them."

Some patients stare at a very specific place on the wall, usually across or above them. A look of excitement radiates in their faces, and they attempt to raise their arms as if in a greeting or an embrace. Then their arms fall back, and they are dead. They do not always say something but their actions indicate that they have seen something wonderful.

Other individuals carry on an animated conversation with deceased loved ones. In some cases, while in conversation with a family member, nurse, or friend, they suddenly stop in amazement and start chatting with someone else. Their discussion is so animated that family members often turn around to see who came into the room. The names used inform observers of the identities of the person(s) the dying patient is visiting with and their conversation is like listening to one side of a telephone conversation. It is interesting that these "hallucinations," as many medical people are apt to classify them, never include the living. Even very young children see only persons who pre-deceased them.

In some cases, the dying individuals were not even aware that the relative or friend with whom they were talking had died. Yet, there they were, a part of the welcoming committee. It is accounts like these that show the importance of the family in the eternal scheme of things. Take, for example, the case of a twelve-year-old girl whose vital signs had completely ceased but who unexpectedly revived. As soon as she could speak, she told her physician that she had been "on the other side." She excitedly told her doctor that she had been met by her older brother, whom she described in detail and in terms that made him seem like an angel. This little girl had never been told that she had a brother. He had died three months before she was born and her parents' grief had been so intense that they never spoke of him to anyone.[4]

Doris saw and conversed with her father who was accompanied by her sister, Vida. Doris was in her later years and in very precarious health. Her family was extremely concerned about her deteriorating health and when her sister unexpectedly died, they decided not to tell Doris fearing that the shock of losing her sister might prove fatal. Her nurse reports:

"I was present when Doris died. Her husband was leaning over her and speaking to her, when pushing him aside she said, "Oh, don't hide it; it's so lovely and bright." She fixed her eyes on one particular spot saying, "I can see father; he wants me." She spoke to her father saying, "I am coming." Turning at the same time to look at me she said, puzzled, "He has Vida with him."[5]

Doris's joy and excitement at seeing her father and with him her sister who was waiting for her, helped her family cope with her death and that of her sister.

It is not only immediate relatives who gather to welcome individuals home. In the next situation, Edith and Jennie were very young girls and the best of friends who both contracted diphtheria when an epidemic swept through their town. Jennie died on Wednesday and Edith's parents were notified. As Edith was a very sick little girl, they decided that it would not be wise to tell her of her little friend's death.

On Saturday Edith's condition deteriorated to the point where she was on the threshold of death. Just before she died she opened her eyes and turned to those present:

". . . She had roused and bidden her friends good-bye, and was talking of dying, and seemed to have no fear. She appeared to see one and another of her friends she knew were dead. . . But now suddenly, and with every appearance of surprise, she turned to her father, and exclaimed, 'Why, papa, I am going to take Jennie with me!' Then she added, 'Why, papa! Why, papa! You did not tell me that Jennie was here!' And immediately she reached out her arms as if in welcome, and said, 'O, Jennie, I'm so glad you are here!'"[6]

The parents of two very young sons reported that a very similar thing had happened to them. Scarlet fever was ravaging their community and they had just lost their infant son to this terrible disease and were on the verge of losing their four-year-old son. Moments before he died, he suddenly sat up in his bed, pointed to the bottom of his bed, and said distinctly, "There is little Harry calling to me." With that he fell back on to his bed and died. [7]

We are very fortunate to live in an age when the plagues that formerly took the lives of so many people have been virtually eliminated. In days past it was a rare family who did not lose one or more children in childhood. Things were different then in another way, too. Parents tended to be with their children when they died and were, therefore, more likely to be aware of what their children did or said as they died. Many learned from their children that death is a point of transition, not the end of life, and especially not the end of relationships.

A case in point occurred in the summer of 1883. Fred and Annie Giles of Nothingham England, aged seven and eight respectively, had died and been buried several weeks, when their four-year-old brother showed signs of the same disease. His father was with him the night he died and relates the following:

"...the little boy, sitting upright in bed, cried out: 'There's Fred and Annie.' 'Where, my boy?' asked the father. 'Don't you see them there—there?' said the lad, pointing to the wall. 'They're waiting for me to go to them,' and the next minute the little sufferer fell back on the pillow, dead."[8]

From reading the literature and from many personal interviews, it seems that the persons who greet and escort the dying are often persons they have been close to in life. When a child dies, a sibling will be there if there is a sibling who predeceased them. Awareness of the existence of such a sibling is not even a requisite. For example, I have come across a number of cases where stillborn or miscarried children were there to greet a brother or sister at death. In addition, there are accounts of children being met by a parent they had never known.

"She was having another bad episode with her heart, and said that she saw her mother in a pretty white dress, and that her mother had one just like it for her [the patient]. She was very happy and smiling, and told me to let her get up and go over there—her mother was ready to take her on a trip.

"The vision lasted for a half an hour. It left the girl serene and peaceful until her death, four hours later. The unusual part of this case is that the girl never knew her mother, who had died when giving birth to her."[9]

This eleven-year-old girl never had the chance, in this life, to grow close to her mother. Yet, during her last hour on earth, her mother was there.

I have identified the following individuals serving as escorts for those who died and, of course, there may well be others:

Family

| | |
|---|---|
| Husband | Wife |
| Maternal Aunt | Fraternal Aunt |
| Mother | Father |
| Great-Grandmother | Great Grandfather |
| Uncle | Cousin(s) |
| Mother-in-law | Father-in-law |
| Brother(s) | Sister |
| Stillborn Children | Miscarried Children |
| Son | Daughter |
| Grandfather | Grandmother |
| Daughter | Son |
| Sister-in-law | Grandchildren |

Other People

| | |
|---|---|
| Spirit Beings | Nice Old Man |
| Friends | Angels |
| Jesus | |
| People Dressed in White | |
| Blonde Woman In White | |

A few individuals present at a death have actually seen the dying person's escort. One example is that of a young Italian girl, three-year-old Hippolyte Nortari, who was present at the death of her baby brother. The following occurred about fifteen minutes before the death of the baby:

". . . little Hippolyte Nortari stretched out her arms saying, 'Look, mother, Aunt Olga.' The parents asked, 'Where do you see Aunt Olga?' The child said, 'There, there!' and tried insistently to get out of bed to go to her aunt. They let her get up. She ran to an empty chair and was much discountenanced because the vision had moved to another part of the room. The child turned round and said, pointing to a corner, 'Aunt Olga is there.' Then she became quiet and the baby died.

"Aunt Olga, a sister of the child's mother, had died a year before."[10]

Paul Savastano saw the spirit of his twelve-year-old son, Adam, as it was disengaging itself from the physical body.

"The cloud-like vapor took on human shape, clapped its hands for joy, then passed upward through the ceiling in the company of an angel."[11]

When Earl Dayley's ten-year-old son Bruce died, he saw his spirit leave his body as a luminous cloud and rise upward through the ceiling.

"On either side of my son's spirit body I saw an angel. . . Both were clothed in white and emanated a brilliant light."[12]

In the next case, a mother was sitting with her dying child. In the same room was her three-year-old son.

As the former was dying, the little brother woke up, and, pointing to the ceiling with every expression of joy, said, "Mother, look at the beautiful ladies round my brother! How lovely they are, they want to take him." The child died at that moment.[13]

Family members are not the only ones that have seen the spirit leave the body in the company of angelic beings. Dr. Marshall Oliver was visiting one of his patients who was slowly dying from complications associated with pneumonia.

"As I turned to pick up my medical bag, I saw a beautiful 'lady' dressed in white approaching the child's crib. . . I knew that I was not observing any member of that or of any other earthly family.

"The lovely being bent over the crib, and I saw a mist-like substance begin to flow from the child's mouth. The mist seemed to collect in a kind of puddle above the child until it grew more definite in shape and became an exact counterpart of the infant. The beautiful entity in white then took the spirit form of the child into its arms—and passed right through the wall of the nursery with the child cradled next to her breast.

"When at last I recovered my mental equilibrium, I examined the child and found that it had died at that moment."[14]

A man was in a hospital dying from pneumonia. He was a good man and his only regret was having to leave behind his beloved wife. She was sitting by his bed when he died. Joy Snell, a nurse who was also present reported what happened.

"...About an hour before he died he called her by name and pointing upwards, said: 'Look, L___, there is B___! He is waiting for me. And how he smiles and holds out his hands to me. Can't you see him?'

"'No, dear, I cannot see him,' she replied, 'but I know that he is there because you can see him.'

"B___ was their only child who had been taken from them about a year before, when between five and six years of age. I could plainly see the little angel with curly flaxen hair and blue eyes, and garbed in what I call a spirit robe. The face was just that of a winsome child, but etherealized and radiant as no earthly faces ever are.

"The father had been greatly weakened by the ravages of his disease and the joyful emotion occasioned by seeing his angel child seemed to exhaust what little vitality he had left. He closed his eyes and sank into a placid sleep. He remained in that state for about an hour, the angel child meanwhile, staying poised above the bed with an expression of glad expectancy on his radiant face. Occasionally he looked lovingly at his mother.

"The breathing of the dying man grew fainter and fainter until it ceased altogether. Then again I witnessed what had now become a familiar spectacle to me—the formation of the spirit body above the discarded earthly body. When it was complete, the angel child clasped the hand of the now-angel father, each gazed into the eyes of the other with an expression of the most tender affection, and with faces aglow with joy and happiness they vanished."[15]

Lance Richardson recounted this experience when he died.

"Entering into the Spirit World, or dimension where spirits reside after this life, had taken place so quickly that I hardly discerned my location before seeing my dead relatives who were present to greet me. It was such a comforting aid to my arrival. Randy [his cousin who had died nearly twenty years earlier from leukemia] assured me that everyone who dies has close relatives and friends present to greet them when they pass through the veil which separates our two worlds.

"I watched numerous people pass through that veil while I was there. It was most enjoyable. I witnessed an elderly woman whose family anticipated her arrival. They were jumping up and down excitedly, as if waiting for a loved one to come off an airplane. A slender man, who was most obviously the husband of the woman, paced back and forth nervously. The two women kept patting him on the back and excitedly hugged him as they anticipated the arrival. There was a group of nearly twenty individuals standing together.

"Another man, who acted as a leader to the group, then stepped partly through the veil so that I could not see him. He then stepped back, announced happily, 'It is time,' and turned back to the veil. He reached his arm forward and drew it back holding the hand of the elderly woman. She seemed startled, and a bit blinded at first. Then upon seeing the group, her expression turned to one of absolute splendor. The group parted for her to see the gentleman at the back of the pack; the one who appeared to be her husband. They rushed into one another's arms. The entire company encircled them and eagerly welcomed her home.

"I was deeply moved. I realized very quickly that a spirit can experience great extremes of emotions, as I was feeling at that moment.

"'Is this how it happens?' I asked Randy, choking with emotion.

"'Isn't it beautiful? I never tire of seeing it,' he answered me.

"The group began to walk away together. 'They are going to where a family celebration has been planned,' Randy explained.

"'Celebration? I guess I had never thought of the Spirit World having celebrations. What is it like?'

"'Oh, it's wonderful! Families get together when loved ones pass into our world.'"[16]

Evidently some spirits do not immediately realize what has happened to them as they step through "the veil" separating life and death. But the reactions of these beings when they recognize those assembled to greet them must be glorious to witness. The excitement of those waiting, the support that they give one another while waiting, the exquisite joy of recognition, surely puts a completely different twist on the meaning of death.

### Summary Thoughts

When we came to this earth, we did not come alone nor will we be alone when we leave it. One of the negative legacies of modern medicine is that people who are critically and/or terminally ill are often heavily medicated, surrounded by sophisticated machines and highly-specialized medical staff who are working on the body attempting to keep it alive. They are trained and conditioned to do everything they can to prolong life with every medical resource available. So rather than seeing death as a natural part of the life experience, they tend to view it as failure, the cessation not only of the functioning of the physical body but of the essence of the person as well.

Also, many working in medical fields tend to discount the existence of a soul. So behaviors of a dying person which cannot be accounted for in physical terms are often dismissed as hallucinations caused by medications, fever, oxygen deprivation, and so forth.

Further, family members are not generally encouraged to be with the patient at the moment of death. This is unfortunate because the terminally ill are extremely concerned about the amount of pain they will experience, suffocation, losing control of everything that is important to them, and of dying alone. And of the four fears, dying alone, isolated from friends and family, ranks as the greatest fear. Modern medicine can address the fears of pain and suffocation quite well but doing so often assures that the dying patient loses control of his or her life and dies away from family and familiar surroundings.

Death is a natural part of life and is not the end of an individual or of relationships. Life is to be cherished, to be lived to its fullest, and to be continued until one's mission on earth is completed. But modern medicine has blurred the point where life ends and death begins. Medical personnel often are so glued to their monitors and their computer screens, or are otherwise so busy that they do not hear or observe what happens to many of their patients at death. If their patients are not so medicated that they cannot speak or move, it is possible that many might be observed displaying the remarkable transformations described in this chapter.

Sooner or later all of us must die. It will be so much easier for those who understand that death is not the end but a beginning, a door to a joyous reunion with departed loved ones and with our Heavenly Father. Death is the way we get back home, a trip that we will not have to make alone.

# Chapter Twenty-One
## Mission Completed: Our Final Reward

A surprising number of people have visited heaven during near-death experiences (NDEs). Those who have had this remarkable opportunity report that they experienced an indescribable sense of love--total love, unconditional love, love that permeated their entire beings. When Elisabeth Kubler-Ross, the noted author and researcher on death, grief and bereavement, was told by some of her patients that during their near-death experiences they were received with overwhelming love regardless of who they were or what they had done while on earth, she was deeply troubled. Dr. Kubler-Ross had been raised in a religious tradition which taught that God loved those who lived a good life and obeyed his teachings, and hated those who did not, and that there was a heaven for the obedient and a hell for sinners. This did not agree with what her patients were telling her. They told her that God loves everyone, even the unrepentant sinner. She wondered how this could be possible until she analyzed carefully what they were telling her. She discovered that while it is true that God is all loving and all forgiving, individuals will still end up in different places in the afterlife based on the choices they made in their lives and by their desire and ability to live within the light of God.

### The Life Review

Some of Dr. Kubler-Ross's dying patients had encounters with a Being of Light during their NDEs. This Being asked them penetrating questions about what they had accomplished on earth and gave them a visual review of their lives. The patients reported seeing themselves in vivid three-dimensional detail reliving their lives, especially their interactions with others. They not only saw their own actions but felt the impact their actions had on others. They felt the pleasure and joy of those they had complimented, comforted, and helped, and the rejection, disappointment, and pain of those they had hurt. They saw the long range implications as well as the immediate impact of every action and how the feelings generated by those acts impacted on the next person and the next, like ripples on a pond. They could clearly see the consequences of what they had thought of as "small" acts.

As they reviewed their lives, these NDEers were acutely aware that the Being of Light and all others present could see everything they were seeing. Surprisingly, they realized that there was no withdrawal of love emanating from those present, including the Being of Light, no matter how bad the revelations. But they also felt pain, regret and remorse for the hurt they had caused others and for all the lost opportunities to serve. Dr. Kubler-Ross came to believe that hell was not so much a place as it was something we carry with us through eternity. She mused that selfless individuals such as Mother Teresa would feel and experience the joy and gratitude of the many thousands of sick, rejected, and dying she had helped. Hitler, on the other hand, would have to live with the pain, suffering, and agony his actions caused millions. Both Mother Teresa and Adolph Hitler are children of God and therefore loved by Him. But how they elected to live their lives, how well they treated their brothers and sisters, and how well they completed their missions on earth is what will determine their ultimate status throughout eternity.

A case in point is that of George Ritchie. During his NDE, George found himself standing before the Being of Light who asked him what he had done with his life. In the resulting life review George's attention focused on specific occasions when he had felt proud of what he had done such as when he had achieved his Eagle Scout rank. He turned to the Being of Light expecting to receive assurance that this was good. However the Being of Light was unimpressed saying, "That glorified you! What have you done to glorify me?"

Then George's attention was drawn to a scene in which he had come home late one evening. As he was walking down the hall to his room he heard his little sister crying. He entered her room and took her in his arms to comfort her. As he watched this scene, he felt her relax and a sense of peace flow over her. When he looked up, the Being of Light was looking at him. The message George received was, "Now you are beginning to see what really counts."[1]

Howard Storm, a university professor, was shown during his near-death experience a scene where he was pretending to be sympathetic to one of his students' problems, while in actuality he was impatiently waiting for him to leave so he could get on with his work.

"I could see how selfish I was and how out of touch I was with God and everything of real importance. At the time I had this experience I was an agnostic professor. But I now knew without any doubt that there was a God, that I was loved of God, and that I had let him down. I knew that I must change my life significantly, which I have.

"In the Bible is a statement of Jesus Christ which clearly illustrates what is of real significance. It came in response to the question He was asked as to which commandment was the greatest of them all.

'...Thou shalt love the Lord thy God with all thy heart, and with all thy soul, and with all thy mind. This is the first and great commandment. And the second is like unto it. Thou shalt love thy neighbor as thyself.'"[2]

When the question arose as to what was really important in this life, Christ said the following:

*When the Son of man shall come in his glory, and all the holy angels with him, then shall he sit upon the throne of his glory:*

*And before him shall be gathered all nations: and he shall separate them one from another, as a shepherd divideth his sheep from the goats:*

*And he shall set the sheep on his right hand, but the goats on the left.*

*Then shall the King say unto them on his right hand, Come, ye blessed of my Father, inherit the kingdom prepared for you from the foundation of the world:*

*For I was an hungred, and ye gave me meat: I was thirsty, and ye gave me drink: I was a stranger, and ye took me in:*

*Naked, and ye clothed me: I was sick, and ye visited me: I was in prison, and ye came unto me.*

*Then shall the righteous answer him, saying, Lord, when saw we thee an hungred, and fed thee? or thirsty, and gave thee drink? When saw we thee a stranger, and took thee in? or naked, and clothed thee?*

*Or when saw we thee sick, or in prison, and came unto thee?*

*And the King shall answer and say unto them, Verily I say unto you, Inasmuch as ye have done it unto one of the least of these my brethren, ye have done it unto me.*[3]

### What Is Important In Heaven

Like George Ritchie and Howard Storm, many individuals discovered during their life reviews that power, wealth, and the esteem of men are unimportant factors in heaven. What does seem to be crucial is our service to others. However, service that is done to impress or to gain favor or to draw attention to one's self is self-serving even if it does help others. It is the selfless service, service done out of love and compassion, which is the brick and mortar that make up the building materials of our heavenly mansions.

In this regard, Mary Hales noticed a vast difference in the size and beauty of the buildings she passed while being escorted by her brother during her brief visit to the heavenly realm.

She inquired of her brother why some buildings were spacious while others were very small and he replied, "That was what they sent up to us."

When she asked, "What do you mean?"

He responded, "That was all the good works they sent up." I took his answer to mean that the size of a house one receives in heaven is determined by our activities on earth.

"I had read in the Bible the verse that stated, 'In our father's house are many mansions.' What I saw confirmed this as apparently the quality and grandeur of the houses we will inherit is determined by the quantity and quality of the good we do while on earth.[4]

It is not enough just to believe in God or have the ability to empathize with the pain, anguish, and suffering of others. Hunger, loneliness, sickness, and depression will never be eliminated unless action is taken. Standing by and doing nothing, does not help the human condition to improve. Consider the words of James in the Bible, "Therefore to him that knoweth to do good, and doeth it not, to him it is sin."[5]

Lance Richardson learned this principle during his NDE. His cousin Randy, who had preceded him in death by twenty years, introduced him to two men dressed in white robes. As they approached, Lance instinctively recognized them.

"I felt a flood of emotions erupt within me. I cried as I wrapped my arms around them and welcomed them. These were two of my best friends but not from this mortal life. I had known them when all of us lived as spirits with God before we were born into mortality. My spirit, however remembered them completely. I loved them now as I did then.

"One of them had lived nearly two hundred years ago, and the other had lived on earth thousands of years before I had. But this did not matter. I yet knew and loved them from our associations in heaven before we were born.

"'It is so good to see you,' I said. 'How have you been?'

"Ben, who stood a bit over six feet tall and carried a powerful build, spoke first. 'We are very good. We were both so excited to hear you had been allowed to visit this world. We have been informed you will be going back soon, but we were asked to visit you and help you remember some important matters.'

"Samuel, who had lived long ago, also stood nearly six feet tall. His build was smaller than Ben's but still strong. He had very striking good looks, with black wavy hair. He spoke to me with an easy smile. 'Lance, the Lord knows and loves you. He truly knows each of us and is our Savior. Can you remember that?'

"As they spoke, my mind began to open as if a screen were before me. I suddenly remembered how each of us loved Him. We adored and worshipped Him. Only through Him was our salvation. Yes, I knew Him and loved Him.

"With that memory in place, a larger part of my mind had been opened. I remembered that each of us had promised our Lord we would do certain things with our lives. There were reasons why we were born when we were born, and it mattered. Ben and Samuel helped me remember some of the things I had promised to do with my life and that I had not accomplished them.[6]

"A great truth was then shown to me. 'The greatest principle in the creation of a society such as ours is Service,' Samuel said. 'Each person in our society is involved in service to others continually. It is the mode of heaven. It is one of the great eternal principles that creates a heaven. Each seeks for the betterment of the whole, not of themselves. Each seeks to serve God, our Father, through following His command to love one another,' Samuel continued.

"'Service is that action form of loving one another. When you truly love someone, you seek to serve them. Your concerns are for their happiness and welfare.'

"Ben then explained to me that if the people of this nation (the United States of America) would go out and begin serving— first the members of their families more fully, then their neighbors and community, and then their extended family (the brothers and sisters of the world)—it would do more to change the hearts of people than any other thing that could be done.

"'If you will go out and serve one another,' Ben continued, 'you will learn to love one another in a way you have never experienced before. If you will serve one another, you will love God and grow closer to Him. If you will serve one another, your nation will be transformed into a haven of real peace and freedom.'"[7]

It would seem very definite that our status in the heavenly home is contingent both on what we do, as well as what we fail to do on earth. It is apparent that procrastination, avoidance, and neglect are not qualities that contribute in a positive way to one's eternal heavenly status.

### Multiple Heavenly Realms

Those who have had near-death experiences or who have had the opportunity to see into the heavenly realm in some way, discover that there is more than just a heaven for the good or a hell for the wicked (contrary to the teachings of some religious traditions). As Jesus told his disciples just prior to his death, "In my Father's house are many mansions."[8]

It is apparent from this quote and the references cited above that there are multiple realms there and our assignment to one or another will depend on how well we complete our missions on earth. But it also appears that even within these heavenly realms there are different levels.

Emanuel Swedenborg, an eighteenth-century scientist and statesman was one of those who visited multiple heavenly realms during his near-death experience. He reported that heaven is divided into two kingdoms, regionally into three heavens, and locally into countless communities.[9]

He reported that people who were moved by divine truths and let them control their actions and thoughts inhabit the third (highest) heaven. Those who did not let truth into their lives, who intended to do good but did not, are those in the second heaven. Then those in the first heaven are good people who lived upright lives and believed in God but made no attempt to learn about Him and his principles.[10]

In each heaven are many communities separated from each other by the state of love exhibited by its inhabitants. Within a given community, all the individuals are distinguished from each other according to the light they exhibited. The most perfect ones are in the central region—that is, are outstanding in goodness and thus in love, wisdom, and discernment. The less outstanding ones are around the outside, at a distance proportional to lessening levels of perfection. It is arranged the way light decreases from a center toward the periphery. The people at the center are in the greatest light, those toward the fringes progressively in less of the light.[11]

Other individuals have also reported witnessing this phenomenon. One such individual was the Native American chief, White Thunder, who during his visit to the world of spirits, was shown by his spirit guides "various areas of the spirit world—some containing happy spirits and others peopled by unhappy evildoers." [12]

George Ritchie wrote a popular book, *Return from Tomorrow*, which was later republished as *Ordered to Return*, describing his remarkable near-death experience. He, too, reported seeing multiple realms in heaven. One realm consisted of individuals who were so tied to their addictions, preoccupations with worldly matters, angers, and obsessions with revenge that they were earthbound. Ritchie could see those from the heavenly realm trying to reach out and help them but being unable to do so because those in this unhappy place refused to look up to heaven.

In a second realm, the deceased had left the earth but were still impacted by what had happened to them while they were on earth.

Just as there are areas in our own cities, which are divided by ethnic and moral standards, so it is in the astral realm. There were definite areas of this dimension that I would not want to be caught in, just as there are areas in our own towns and cities in which we don't feel safe.

There were two things distinctly unique about the beings of this realm. Since hypocrisy is impossible because others know your thoughts the minute you think them, they tend to group with those who think the same way they do.[13]

George reported seeing still another realm which he defined as being hellish in character and atmosphere.

"I was taken to another place where people arrive who had committed suicide out of hatred, jealousy, resentment, bitterness and total disdain for themselves and others. These were the ones who had the same type of powerful emotions which people who have committed murder have. The only difference is they believed because of religious teachings that committing murder was a worse sin. Their motivation was, 'If I can't kill you, I shall kill myself to get even with you.'

"I am not talking about people who are what we call insane and no longer responsible for their actions. Nor am I speaking of people who are dying from a horrible long-suffering illness.

"I understood that these people are confined in a state where they are given a chance to realize two very important facts. One, you can only kill the physical body, not the soul. Two, that only love, not hate, can bring true happiness.

"I was taken to a different location in this place and we were standing on a high porch in front of a huge building. What I saw horrified me more than anything I have ever seen in life. Since you could tell what the beings of this place thought, you knew they were filled with hate, deceit, lies, self-righteousness bordering on megalomania, and lewd sexual aggressiveness.

"This was breaking the heart of the Son of God standing beside me. Even here were angels trying to get them to change their thoughts. Since they could not admit there were beings greater than themselves, they could not see or hear them. There was no fire and brimstone here; no boxed-in canyons, but something a thousand times worse from my point of view. Here was a place totally devoid of love. This was HELL."[14]

From this dark and depressing place devoid of love and light, George was taken to a place of hope, joy, and growth. He saw beings there creating glorious music, learning about things that have eternal consequences, attempting to make the earth a better place.

"As I watched these beings at their work, I suddenly realized there was no racial or color differences in any of the realms. Then Christ spoke to me. He said, 'If you come to know the Father, you will come to know me. If you come to know me, you will come to know that love includes all beings regardless of their race, creeds or color.'"[15]

From these realms which are located somewhere close to earth, George Ritchie was taken to what he called the Celestial Realm, or Heaven.

"We never actually reached the streets of the City of Light but hovered a short distance above it. We could see its inhabitants and they us. This was the first realm in which the inhabitants could see the Christ and myself. Even more amazing, they exuded light almost as brilliant as that of Christ. Two beings approached us and I could feel the love flowing from them toward us. The complete joy they showed at seeing Christ was unmistakable. There was no question whatsoever that what I was seeing was heaven, a magnificent city of light."16

Ritchie's experience is most informative. It would appear that there is no one set place for all the inhabitants of the earth to go to after they die. Those who prepare themselves through a lifetime of service, and who have sought out the light and love of God, qualify at death for immediate entrance into the City of Light. And evidently the vast multitudes that did not know God in this life can be instructed, taught, and prepared to dwell in the light. The key seems to be that they have to be willing to be taught to be receptive to the angelic beings assigned to watch over, teach, and care for them. But as was clearly pointed out in chapter three, one of the eternal principles that governs man's behavior is that of free choice. There will be a place for those who cannot stand the light and/or who prefer to live in the darkness. God, being all merciful, would not force anyone to live in a place where that person would not feel comfortable and fit in.

Many people have reported seeing cities of light in heaven. It is difficult to imagine a city where everything from the smallest flower to the most massive of buildings exudes a brilliant light. It is even more difficult to imagine multiple cities of light with differing magnitudes of light and splendor. But that is just what various individuals have reported seeing.

John Powell reported visiting three heavenly cities, each vastly different from each other.

"A personage come to me and said, 'Come!' My spirit left my body and went with my guide who took me to the next planet. Here I beheld the inhabitants. The houses were beautiful to behold. I was so amazed and delighted that I requested my guide to permit me to stay and dwell there, for all things were far superior and in advance of this world that I had come from. He answered, 'No!' and said, 'Come!'

"He then took me to the next kingdom which so exceeded the first in beauty and glory that I was again amazed and requested permission to stay. I cannot command language to describe the beauty of the inhabitants and scenery, but my guide said, 'No, come!'

"He then took me to the next kingdom which was far more beautiful in glory and order than the former two. The beautiful flowers, trees, gardens, people who were dressed in pure white, and so pure that I was overwhelmed with joy and most earnestly implored my guide to allow me to stay, but he said, 'You cannot go any further, for this is next to the throne of God.' He then said, 'Come!'

"He then brought me again to this earth. When I saw my body lying on the bed I did not want to enter it again, for I felt so happy out of it that I could not bear the thoughts of entering it again, but he said, 'Enter,' and I had to obey."[17]

Besides the cities of light, there are also realms without light. As discussed previously, we were granted our free agency when we came to earth. With our agency we make choices. Whether we choose to carry out our mission on earth, whether we choose to serve our families and fellow beings, and whether we choose to follow God seem to be the factors which determine the place where we will feel most comfortable dwelling and which will therefore decide our ultimate and eternal destiny.

### The Being of Light

Probably the most awe-inspiring aspect of any near-death experience is the encounter with a Being of Light although this does not happen to everyone. This being emanates light that is indescribably brilliant and permeates their entire being. This light comforts, calms, and radiates a sense of total unconditional love.

The terms which have been used to describe the Being of Light by those who have seen him include:

- A powerful masculine being
- A majestic man
- A being in long flowing radiant robes
- A being who is all knowing, all powerful, and all loving
- A being who knew me intimately
- A being I knew long before I came to earth
- A being whose eyes flashed with the brilliance of lightening
- A being whose hair was white as the driven snow and flowed about his face

Those who have seen this being have no doubt as to his identity. For some the recognition was immediate--he was Jesus Christ, the Son of God. For others such as George Ritchie, the being's title was announced. George was told, 'Stand up! You are in the presence of the Son of God!' Still others saw the wounds in his hands and feet and knew who he was even before they looked at his face. For some the recognition of who he is came from an awakening of premortal memories. For many, this being of light is God.

John Monsen drowned leaving a pregnant wife and four very young children. John was given permission to return from the spirit world for the express purpose of helping his wife to understand the reason for his death, and to give her some insight into the state of those in heaven.

"I had been thinking of John and how much I missed him. I was heading for the bedroom when I felt a warm sensation rise in my chest and radiate outward. I knew that John was near.

"I stopped in the doorway and felt an incredible joy flood my heart. *John, you're here*, I thought.

"In answer, my husband's warm, resonant voice, entered my mind. 'Yes, Chris,' he said, 'I want you to know something.'

"'What is it? Tell me.'

"'Chris, there is a Christ. He was there to meet me when I died.'

"These words flowed like cool water through my soul.

"'He knew me, and called me by name. He comforted me, encircled me with his love. He said, 'Thou good and faithful servant, thy work is well done.' He told me that I had completed everything Father in Heaven had assigned me on earth, and that now I was needed here.'

"'Oh, Chris!" he continued. 'He lives!'"

John then shared with his wife information that helped her to accept his death and to look forward to the birth of their son.

"'I saw all the spirits of our posterity. I was overwhelmed with joy. Our posterity is greater than you could ever imagine, Chris. Our children's children, and their children, and their children, and on and on. They will accomplish marvelous works. You should be very proud.

"'And Chris,' now his words touched my innermost feelings, and I felt his love for me, 'I went to the premortal world and met our baby's spirit. We spoke. What a strong and special spirit! This child will bring you happiness, Chris. This last child is my final gift to you from your loving husband.' And then I felt him leaving, his words and his presence slipping away. 'Lots of happiness,' he whispered and was gone."[18]

Betty Eadie has received thousands of letters from people who have read her book *Embraced by the Light* and been touched by her experience. Among the vast number of letters are those from people of many different religious traditions who shared with her their encounters with the Being of Light. One man related the following:

"My wonderful dad went to the Lord after battling liver cancer. He was Jewish in this life, a soft-spoken, generous man. I asked him to come back to me after he was gone, if he could. I never expected it would happen, but it did. It was not a dream, not a ghost. He was as three-dimensional as you and I. This Jewish man told me about the light. He also told me about Jesus Christ--imagine that--and said that he was happy. I was in awe of all this. I hugged him and he was gone as quickly as he'd come. Never have I seen his face again."[19]

A second individual, agnostic in belief, if not an atheist, wrote the following to Betty:

"In my life, much of the teaching I received about the Lord was done through fear, such as 'If you don't go to church you'll go to hell.'

"I got involved with drugs in my teens, and at seventeen ended up getting in a near-fatal auto accident. My body lay in a field for some time before it was found, and it was during this period that I had my experience.

"I found myself above the earth, suspended in the universe. I sensed a oneness with all Creation, and during this sense of awe, a kind voice spoke to me calling me by name and said, 'Are you willing to receive me?' I asked who he was, and he said, 'This is Jesus who is speaking to you.'"[20]

Jesus is not just the savior of a small group of people or of believers. He is the Savior of the world. For many, it is not until the moment of death that this fact is realized. Some individuals, such as George Ritchie witnessed the masses of humanity who were rushed into death through wars, plagues, and natural disasters. These were people who never heard of Jesus Christ while on earth. They were being escorted to places where they would have the opportunity to hear of Him and His teachings. They will have the chance to accept Him as their Savior, if they so desire. No one will be forced to accept Jesus or his teachings.

### The Being of Darkness

A large number of people have told me that it is their sincere belief that there is a God and that God is the author of all good, but that they do not believe there is a devil or Satan. In their minds there are only degrees of good. They feel that evil is manmade, the result of selfishness, narcissistic behaviors, or the inability to empathize with the plight of others.

Such was the thinking of Don Brubaker until his near-death experience. Don was rushed to the hospital with symptoms of a pending heart attack. As his doctors wheeled him into an elevator, Don's heart stopped and he found himself falling feet first in what he described as a dark, damp, musty tunnel. Even though he was on his back, he could see ahead into the depths of the horrible tunnel. He saw a large glowing red ball . . .

". . . almost like the light on the front of a train. In that instant, as the red ball rushed toward me, I knew terror like never before. As it approached, I realized that it was really a large, eerie red eye. It stopped when it got close to me, and then began traveling alongside me through the tunnel. I could hardly stand to look at it, its gaze was so piercing. It felt like it was looking right into my mind, into my very soul.

"As the red eye glowered at me, the thoughts began to arrange themselves, coalescing slowly. Suddenly, the idea was undeniable.

"I was in Hell.

"The realization swept over me like an ocean wave, unstoppable though I tried desperately to dismiss it. Hell! I didn't even believe in hell! And here I was. This was it?

"I had only the briefest moment to react to the thought when a deep, comfortable voice echoed through the tunnel.

"'Have no fear, my son,' the voice said with a certain resounding nobility, 'for I am with you. I have chosen you to write about the experience you will go through.'"

When Don wondered why he had been chosen to have this experience, the voice responded.

"'You will first experience hell to prove to you the reality of evil. You've only believed that there was goodness. You must see for yourself that hell is real. And then you can tell others about the awful reality of hell, and about the beautiful glory of heaven.'

"Don asked, 'But why me, God?'

"'Because you represent common man. You're not a noted minister or a highly-educated theologian. People will more easily relate to and accept your story.'"

After this experience with God, Don regained consciousness and tried to tell his physicians and nurses what had happened to him but they virtually ignored him believing he had suffered oxygen deprivation. He then found himself once more plunging back down the dark tunnel and into hell. He sensed the presence of a powerful being. This being informed Don that he could avoid all the pain and anguish if he would just follow him. Not only would all the pain disappear, but he could have anything his heart desired. Then his eyes were opened.

"Visions of wealth appeared before my eyes, like a three-dimensional movie. Diamonds, money, cars, gold, beautiful women, everything. I was overwhelmed by the vision. I could almost touch it. It seemed so real."

Don then realized that the tempter was Satan, who was bargaining for his soul. He struggled mightily to shake himself free of these images. He said that he could clearly hear the words "enjoy, enjoy" in one ear and "resist, resist" in the other. He felt as if he was caught in a huge tug of war and was literally being torn apart. And one party to the battle for his soul was Satan, a being he had never believed existed. But now he knew from first hand experience that Satan *did* exist.

Then Don experienced a life review, but a hellish life review.

"I heard a laugh, a sniggering laugh from somewhere in the darkness. Images appeared before my eyes, as if projected on a giant screen.

"I was seeing myself. All of those times in my life when I had done something wrong were being shown back to me. As I watched, I was embarrassed, then ashamed. When the long chronicle was over, I began to watch scenes of the things I had only wished for—worse things than I had actually done—a repulsive but exciting but disgusting but exhilarating experience. My emotions became tangled and knotted."

After the review Don was feeling abandoned and lonely. He longed for his family and to be able to tell them how much he loved them, how much God loved them. Then out of nowhere he heard the voice of God. The voice told him that his mission was to tell others that there is a God, and that they must learn to love others, to have compassion, and to forgive. Don was told that he must live his life so that others could see the influence and reality of God through him. God also informed Don:

"Your physical healing will take a long time, but you will live. Remember that. you will recall all of your experiences clearly, and you will write a book. You must tell others about me and about

Satan. You must make them understand that there are very real choices they must make. I have chosen you for this work. You will succeed. You will be safe. I am always nearby. You are never alone."

Don saw bedraggled beings shuffling along in the "dark, damp, musty cave" blindly following each other, convinced that they were trapped in their sins and could not be saved. Don knew that if they would just look up to God they could be saved from eternal enslavement, but they resisted. They had been so blinded by Satan that they could not believe that God could or would forgive them.

Don's message to the world is that heaven is real and so is God. But hell is also real and so is Satan. God is always waiting for you to turn to him. He will help you escape the clutches of Satan. Love is the essence of heaven and everything else leads away from love and God.[21]

Don was not the only individual to report having seen those trapped in hell. George Ritchie, Betty Eadie, Margot Grey, Elane Durham, Harriet Lee, and Lorenzo Dow Young are among those who have been permitted to look into this nightmarish realm, to see the condition of those dwelling there, and discover that they are prisoners of their own doubts and feelings of worthlessness. Blinded by satanic philosophies, they can not, they will not, accept the fact that it is possible to escape, that there is a loving God who wants to save them.

Karen also discovered that hell is real and was able to experience briefly its realities. Karen was going through a divorce and became so depressed that she attempted to kill herself.

"One night as I was lying in bed, asleep, I was awakened by a male voice saying: 'I'm going to get you sooner or later. I'm going to get you.' The event frightened me and I sat up, wide awake. I told my roommate, and she said it was just a dream, and not to worry about it.

"About a week later, everything seemed so hopeless that I took the bottle of tranquilizers. My full intention was to end my life. It seemed the best way to handle my problem, just to go to sleep forever. At the hospital, I found out later, they pumped my stomach and put charcoal in it. They didn't think I was going to make it. My heart had stopped, and they used defibrillator paddles to restart it.

"During this period I became aware that I was conscious. But I was enveloped in total darkness. It was pitch-black all around, yet there was a feeling of movement. My conscious self assured me that I was in the form of a spiritual body.

"A male voice spoke to me, a different voice than the one I heard a week before. This voice said, 'You have a choice. You can stay here, or you can go back. If you stay here, your punishment will be just as it is, right now. You will not have a body, you will not be able to see, touch, or have other sensations. You will only have this darkness and your thoughts, for eternity.'

"Terrified because of the experience, and because of what I had heard, I understood that this would be my private hell. There would be no contact with other life or with the sensations of life, for eternity. Yet I would remain conscious with my thoughts in total blackness.

"Frantically scared, I knew immediately that I had made a terrible mistake. Telling the voice that I had made a mistake, I asked to be permitted to return to life. The voice said, 'All right, you may return.'"[22]

Various near-death researchers have discovered that of those they interviewed who had had an NDE, at least 20% reported that part of their experience was negative/frightening on the order of Don's and Karen's. Doctor Barbara R. Rommer refers to these experiences as *Blessings in Disguise* (also the title of her book reporting on these experiences) because of how they transform the experiencer.[23] These negative experiences seemed to have been for the purpose of revealing the realities of the Being of Darkness and his minions and the state of those who follow the Being of Darkness. The hellish experience helped them to realize the power that the Being of Light has over the Being of Darkness; that no matter what they had done, they could change; that there is hope; that they are loved and are valued by God and if they will turn to Him, He will help them.

### Summary Thoughts

Each individual's NDE is unique although there are common features that run across them. Individuals struggle to find words to describe accurately what they saw and experienced but fail. They express a strong sense of frustration that they cannot begin to convey the beauty and grandeur of heaven or the frightening and depressing nature of hell. But for those who returned to life, who came back either to share their experience or to complete a mission, their NDE was an amazing and all too brief glimpse into eternity and their potential role there.

Each NDE is intensively personal, even sacred, and some aspects may well not be shared with others. However, some individuals are instructed to share part of their experience so that their families and others might know that God lives, loves them, and desires for them to return home to Him eventually. Lance Richardson learned this first hand from his escort Ben.

Quite often those who are allowed near-death experiences forget much of what they see and hear. Some of it is blocked purposely, by God. But other parts are forgotten because of the trauma through which they go in reentering the body and recovering from injuries.

"There are parts of this experience, Lance," Ben explained, "which will be purposely blocked from your memory, as well. There are other parts which are very sacred, which you should not share openly. And then there is much which we are counting on you remembering. The time will come when you will be prompted to write a book sharing some of these wonderful experiences, in order that others may be strengthened, comforted, and inspired.

Lance Richardson was impressed that he should share his experience and wrote a book that he entitled, *The Message*.[24]

These NDEs teach of the reality of a Being of Light and a Being of Darkness. The degree to which individuals pattern their lives after either Being determines their ultimate state in the hereafter. Everyone in the afterlife knows what everyone else thinks, desires, or is preoccupied with; therefore individuals will seek out those with whom they feel comfortable. The degree to which people love the light, feel at home in the light, or can tolerate the light will determine which area of the afterlife they will call their eternal home.

It would seem that every opportunity will be given after death to those who died without having the chance to accept the Light while in mortality. But as everyone has the right and gift of free will, no one will be forced to choose the Light. The apparent excitement and pleasures proffered by the extremely diabolical and unscrupulous Being of Darkness will so entrap some that they will not wish to associate with those who love the light. For some the light will be obscured by the lust for power, the esteem of men, and the love of wealth and possessions. For others it will be their feelings of low self-esteem or depression. Guilt and a strong sense of worthlessness make it difficult for some to realize that they will receive light if they ask for it and, unless they do so, they will live the rest of eternity in some degree of darkness away from the presence of God.

This does not need to be. No matter how dark life may seem on earth, no matter what acts of darkness one has committed, the Light always beckons. The severely abused Angie Fenimore discovered that she was not human garbage as she had been conditioned to believe but rather a divine daughter of God. Once she accepted this fact, she turned to the Light and her whole life changed. She, like many others, discovered that the way out of the darkness is difficult but well worth the effort. It is not easy to change one's way of acting, living and thinking but, as in Angie's case, it is possible.

If we chose the light we can live with God in the City of Light. The City of Light is our original home and every one of us can return to it if we learn to love and give service to God and His children. We chose to come to earth where we could learn, experience major challenges, and be tried. Eternal growth comes from overcoming adversity and the recognition that we have divine origins and that we are truly sons and daughters of God. The Being of Darkness will do all in his power to obstruct our growth, to divert us away from the light and into the darkness of depression, anger, greed, and selfishness. But the light of God can penetrate every corner of our lives, overwhelm the darkness and prepare us to live in His presence.

Heaven is our original home and our ultimate goal is to return there. We are not alone in our quest. Legions of angels, loving and concerned deceased relatives, and our eternal Father in Heaven, are all anxious and eager to help us.

# Epilogue

Throughout this book are many accounts of individuals seeing beautiful radiant beings in the heavenly home. Some turn out to be deceased relatives who have been permitted to come to earth to help them in times of emergency. The fact that these deceased relatives have become beings of light would seem to indicate that we, too, have the potential of achieving this state. Barbara Chapman had an experience that clearly showed her who she is or could become if she successfully accomplished her earthly mission.

"From about the third grade through the sixth grade, my teachers would allow us to draw when our work was finished. I invariably drew a picture of a young woman with her hair up in a fancy style and I always drew my pictures with pencil on white paper so that I could make it more detailed. I finally stopped drawing her when I got to junior high. I know now that this person was someone deep in my subconscious who I was remembering.

"Years went by and I never thought about her again until one night shortly after I married. I had fallen asleep and I was in that alpha or twilight state when you are unconscious but your subconscious is still awake, or so it seems. I had the most profound and moving experience which I will never forget and I will be forever grateful to God for giving it to me.

"I found myself in a place of great whiteness. I could not see anything but this beautiful, peaceful white light. I stared and stared. Finally, in the midst of this white light, I saw a personage. She was a beautiful woman. At first I saw her from behind. She had long hair past her waist and every hair on her head was made of this glorious light. It was exquisite and unlike any color I had ever seen. I can only describe it as pale, silvery, golden hair. Her hair was braided and coiled up into two hoops on the back of her head. She turned slowly as a model would but with the grace of a swan and stopped so that I could observe her side profile which was perfect. I could see that her hair was pulled back gently with lovely soft hanging curls about her face and neck. She was neither thin, muscular, nor fat. Her figure was like an hourglass. Her nose and all of her other features were in perfect proportion. She wore a shimmering floor-length white gown, simple and straight, with long sleeves. She wore plain white satin slippers and tiny gold earrings. Light radiated out a great distance from her countenance. It was at this point I realized that she was the source of this beautiful light.

"Then, with her right arm extended forward, she continued to turn until she was facing me. I was startled by her eyes. They were like flaming fire which did not detract from her beauty but enhanced it just as a lightbulb is more beautiful when it is turned on. Her eyes were so clear they were like looking into the depth of the ocean. They were an unearthly color, a beautiful deep shade of blue/green. Her complexion was perfect like that of a newborn baby and her cheeks were a peachy color. No wrinkles, blemishes or pores were visible. Her lips were full and moist--a deep ruby color like the perfection of a prize-winning rose. She was not a spirit as her body appeared to be physical in every way. Her countenance radiated every Christ-like quality: intelligence, beauty, wisdom, love, compassion, gentleness, and on and on. With her right arm extended she spoke to me with her eyes and her thoughts. Her mouth did not move. She said, 'Barbara, you cannot achieve this level of perfection in this life, but in the next life you shall achieve it.'

"Nearly two years went by and I prayed to know who this glorious woman was. She seemed so familiar to me, but I could not remember. It seemed that her name was on the tip of my tongue, but it continued to escape me. Finally, I gave up asking and thought that if God wanted me to know He would tell me, but for now I would have to be satisfied with the experience itself.

"I had been married before I met Larry and Larry and I were married in a civil ceremony. Larry wanted us to have our marriage vows solemnized in the temple but I was very reluctant because I was afraid that this marriage would also fail. We were on our way home from church one day and he began to pressure me to get married in the temple. This upset me and I jumped out of the car and ran into the house ahead of him. As I crossed the threshold of the door into the kitchen, I heard the voice of God say to me loud and clear, 'Barbara! Would you like to know who the celestial woman was that you saw in your dream?' I turned around because the voice seemed to be coming from behind me. Although I didn't see anything, I said out loud, 'Yes, Lord. Who is she?'

"The Lord said, 'She is who you will become if you do what you know you should do.' I was absolutely astonished and startled. Never did I imagine that I could be so glorious. I cried for three weeks because of this experience."

Barbara was permitted to see what a perfect celestial being looks like, what she herself might become if she would live a life of love and service.

We are all children of God and we, like Barbara, have the seeds of divinity planted within us. If we nurture these seeds, we too can become like the individual Barbara saw, perfect, glorious, and radiant.

Our Father in Heaven wants us to return home. Our elder brother Jesus made it possible for us to do so. It is up to each one of us whether or not we make those choices that will enable us to achieve that goal.

# References

## Chapter One: Our Original Home

1.Lawrence E. Tooley 1997. *I Saw Heaven*, Bountiful, Utah: Horizon Publishers, Inc., pp. 60-61.

2. Steiger, Brad & Sherry Hansen Steiger. 1999. *Touched by Heaven's Light: Inspiring Personal Glimpses Into the Afterlife*, New York: Signet.

3. Maggie Callanan & Patricia Kelly. 1992. *Final Gifts*, New York: Bantam Books

4. Raymond A. Moody, Jr. 1975. *Life After Life*, New York: Bantam Books.

5. Sarah, Hinze. 1994. *Coming from the Light*, Springville, Utah: Cedar Fort, Incorporated;

6. Sarah Hinze. 1997. *Coming From the Light*, New York: Pocket Books.

7. Elizabeth M. Carman & Neil J. Carman. 1999. *Cosmic Cradle: Souls Waiting in the Wings for Birth*, Fairfield, Iowa: Sunstar Publishing, Inc.

8. Hallett, Elisabeth. 1995. *Soul Trek: Meeting our Children on the Way to Birth*, Hamilton, Montana: Light Hearts Publishing.

9. Maggie Callanan & Patricia Kelly. 1992. *Final Gifts*, New York: Bantam Books.

10. Osis, Karlis & Erlendur Haroldsson. 1977. *At The Hour of Death*, New York: Avon Books.

11. Bill Guggenheim & Judy Guggenheim. 1995. *Hello From Heaven*, Longwood, Florida: The ADC Project.

12. LaGrand, Louis E. 1997. *After Death Communications: Final Farewells*, St. Paul, Minnesota: Llewellyn Publications.

13. LaGrand, Louis E. 1999. *Messages and Miracles*, St. Paul, Minnesota: Llewellyn Publications.

14. Craig R. Lundahl & Harold A. Widdison. 1997. *The Eternal Journey: How Near-Death Experience Illuminate Our Earthly Lives*, New York: Warner Books.

15. Frances Gomez. 1998. *An Angel in the Making*, Salt Lake City, Utah: Frances Gomez.

16. Angie Fenimore. 1995. *Beyond The Darkness*. New York: Bantam Books.

17. Houston IANDS. 1996 *When Ego Dies: A Compilation of Near-Death & Mystical Conversion Experiences*, Houston, Texas: Emerald Ink Publishing, p.21.

18. Ibid. p.77.

19. McCracken, Gloria Ekberg. 1996. NDE, Crown.Net Inc.

20. Richard Paget. 1979. *Beyond Death's Door*, Port Washington, New York: Ashley Books, pp. 81-82.

21. Wordsworth, William. 1924. "Ode: Imitations of Immortality from Recollections of Early Childhood," *The complete Poetical Works of William Wordsworth*, p. 359.

22. Elisabeth Kubler-Ross. 1969. *On Death and Dying*, New York: The Macmillan Company.

23. Melvin Morse. 1990. *Closer to the Light*, New York: Villard Books.

24. Canfield, Jack & Mark Victor Hansen. 1993, "Sachi," by Dan Millman, in *Chicken Soup for the Soul*, Deerfield Beach, Florida: Health Communications, Inc., p. 290.

25. Elisabeth Hallett. 1995. *Soul Trek*, Hamilton, Montana: Light Hearts Publishing, p. 263.

26. Lawrence Tooley, *I Saw Heaven*. p. 89.

**Chapter Two: The Appearance of Our Heavenly Home**

1. W. David Goines. 1997. *My Story*, Royal Publishing Division, Royal American Inc.
http:www.geocities.com/HotSprings/9368/li00002.html

2. Atwater, P.M.H. 1999. *Children of the New Millennium*, New York: Three Rivers Press, Pp. 61-62..

3. Joseph Heinerman. 1985. *Guardian Angels*, Salt Lake City, Utah: Joseph Lyon and Associates, P. 104..

4. Mally Cox-Chapman. 1995. *The Case For Heaven*, New York: G.P. Putnam's Sons, p. 26.

5. Lawrence Tooley, *I Saw Heaven*. 88-89.

6. Roy Mills. 1999. *The Soul's Remembrance*, Seattle, Washington: Onjinjnkta Publishing.

7. Melvin Morse, *Closer To The Light*.

8. Edward Hoffman. 1992. *Visions of Innocence*, Boston: Shambhala, p. 111.

9. Arvin S. Gibson. 1993. *Echoes From Eternity*, Bountiful, Utah: Horizon Publishers, pp. 100-105.

10. Elisabeth Kubler-Ross. 1983. *On Children and Death*, New York: Collier Books, pp. 131-134.

11. Jackie Pullinger. 1980. *Chasing the Dragon*, London: Hodder and Stoughton, Pp. 224-225.

## Chapter Three: Life in the Celestial Home

1. LeRoi.Snow. 1929. "Raised From The Dead." *Improvement Era*, (Volume 32, Number 12, October, Page 977.

2. George Ritchie. 1978. *Return From Tomorrow*, Waco, Texas: Chosen Books, p. 69.

3. Young, Lorenzo

4. Alma P. Burton. 1970. *Doctrines from the Prophets*, Salt Lake City, Utah: Bookcraft p. 423.

5. Angie Fenimore. *Beyond The Darkness*. p.131.

6. Melvin Morse. 1983. "A Near-Death Experience in a Seven-Year-Old Child," *American Journal of Diseases of Children*, Vol. 137, number 10, October 1983, pp. 959-961.

7. Roy Mills, Taped interview.

8. Cherie Logan. 1998. *Before, Now and Forever: A Christ-Created Family*, Unpublished Manuscript.

9. George Ritchie, *Return From Tomorrow*. p. 69.

10. George Ritchie. 1998. *Ordered to Return*, Charlottesville, Virginia: Hampton Roads Publishing Company, p. 43.

11. Bonnie's NDE. 2001, International Association for Near-Death Studies—Seattle Washington Chapter, Seattle IANDS, News Letter.

12. Elisabeth Hallett, *Soul Trek*, p. 150

13. Theresa M. Danna,. 1998. *Communications before Conception: A Spiritual Frontier.* Http://www.birthpsychology.com/lifebefore/conception2.html.

14. Ibid,

15. Angie Fenimore, *Beyond The Darkness*. 110–111.

16. Roy Mills, *The Soul's Remembrance*, Pp. 123–124.

17. RaNelle Wallace, from taped interview, 1999.

## Chapter Four: Preparations for Earth Life

1. Roy Mills from taped interview..

2. Elane's experience has been subsequently recorded and published in book form, *Elane Durham, I Stand All Amazed: Love and Healing From Higher Realms*, Orem, Utah: Granite Publishing, 1998.

3. Frances Gomez. *An Angel In The Making*, 64–65.

4. Arvin Gibson S. 1992. *Glimpses of Eternity*, Bountiful, Utah: Horizon Publishers, pp. 170–176.

5. Angie Fenimore, *Beyond The Darkness*, 126–127.

6. Arvin S. Gibson. 1994. *Journeys Beyond Life*, Bountiful, Utah: Horizon Publishers, Pp. 182–196.

7. RaNelle Wallace, taped interview.

8. Betty J. Eadie. 1992. *Embraced By The Light*, Placerville, California: Gold Leaf Press, p. 92.

## Chapter Five: To Leave Our Heavenly Home

1. Elisabeth Hallett, *Soul Trek*, p. 132.

2. Richard Dreyfuss, 1996. "Interview with Barbara Walters after the 1996 Oscars®".

3. Cherie Logan. 1998, *Before, Now and Forever: A Christ Centered Family*, Unpublished Manuscript..

4. Colette L. 2000. "Pre-Birth Experience of My Last Two Children. Disc.server.com/discussion.cgi?id=68996@article=70.

5. Ecclesiastes Chapter 3: versus 1–2. The *Holy Bible*, King James Version.

### Chapter 6: Leaving Home

1. Roy Mills, *The Soul's Remembrance*, Pp. 15-19.
2. Lawrence E. Tooley, *I Saw Heaven*, 129-130.
3. Arvin S. Gibson, *Echoes From Eternity*, Pp. 54-55
4. Christine Tuttle Monsen. 1994. *Guide Me To Eternity*, Salt Lake City Utah: Aspen Books, pp. 147-148.
5. Michael H. Maguire. 2001. *Before Birth Experience*, <netweb.com/board39

### Chapter 7: Being Escorted To Earth

1. Kjirstin Youngberg. 1998. *The Promised Twin*, Utah: Granite Publishing and Distribution, pp. 79-80.
2. Lammert & Friedeck, *Angelic Presence*, Pp. 81-83
3. Seattle IANDS, News Letter. 2000. *Near Birth Experience*, Volume 1, Issue 4, (August), P.1.
4. Michael H. Maguire, 2001, .

### Chapter 8: Arriving on Earth

1. Thomas Verny with John Kelly. 1981. *The Secret Life of the Unborn Child*, New York: Dell Publishing Company, pp. 12-13.
2. Ibid, Pp. 12-13
3. David B. Chamberlain. 1988. *Babies Remember Birth*, Los Angeles: Jeremy P. Tarcher, Inc. p. xiii.
4. Ibid, p. xxi
5. Ibid, p. 123.
6. Ibid, p. 124.
7. Ibid, p. 129.
8. Ibid, p. 133
9. Ibid, pp. 153-154.

### Chapter 9: Children's Memories of Their Heavenly Home

1. Joan Wester Anderson. 1996. *Where Wonders Prevail*, New York: Ballantine Books, p. 50.
2. Diane M. Komp. 1992. *A Window to Heaven: When Children See Life In Death*, Grand Rapids, Michigan: Zondervan Publishing House, p. 80.

3. Betty Clark Ruff, 1963. "My Toddler taught Me About Preexistence and Death," *Instructor*, (February), P. 61.

4. Elisabeth Hallett, *Soul Trek*, p. 158.

## Chapter 10: Unique Qualities Brought To Earth

1. Shirlee Monty. 1981. *May's Boy*, New York: Thomas Nelson Publishers.

2. George G. Ritchie. 1998. *Ordered To Return*, Charlottesville, Virginia: Hampton Roads Publishing Company, p. 42.

3. Joseph Fielding McConkie. *Truth and Courage: The Joseph F. Smith Letters*, pp. 23-25.

4. Hancock, Mosiah. Undated. *The Life Story of Mosiah Lyman Hancock*, p.71..

5. Joseph Fielding Smith. 1938, *Life of Joseph F. Smith*. Pp. 138-9.

6. Albert R. Lyman. 1996. *The Great Adventure*, Yorba Linda, California: Shumway Family History Services.

7. The *Holy Bible*, Luke 1:13

8. The *Holy Bible*, Luke 1:31

9. Elisabeth Hallett, *Soul Trek*, p. 74.

10. Ibid, p. 60.

11. Ibid, p. 71.

12. Kjirstin Youngberg, *The Promised Twin*, Pp. 102-3.

13. Elisabeth Hallett, *Soul Trek*, Pp. 42-43.

14. Ibid, p. 53.

15. Kjirstin Youngberg, *The Promised Twin*, p. 100,

16. Hancock, Mosiah, *The Life Story of Mosiah Hancock*, P. 36

## Chapter 11: Why Adversity

1. Elane Durham. 1998. Taped interview. For a more detailed discussion see her book, *I stand All Amazed*, Orem, Utah: Granite Publishing, 1998.

2. Roy Mills, 1999. Taped interview. For a more detailed description of his account see his book, *The Soul's Remembrance*, published in 1999 by Onjinjinkta Publishing, Seattle Washington..

3. Angie Fenimore, *Beyond The Darkness*, Pp. 142-143.

4. Lee Nelson & Richard Nelson. 1994. *NDE: Near-Death*

*Experiences*, Springville, Utah: Cedar Fort, Inc., pp. 82-83.

5. Ibid, pp. 37-38.

6. Michele R. Sorensen & David R. Willmore. 1988. *The Journey Beyond Life: Volume One*, Orem, Utah: Family Affair Books, pp. iii-vi.

7. Howard Storm. 1998. From a taped interview. For more details see his book, *My Decent into Death*, published in 2000 by Clairview press of London, England.

### Chapter 12: Why Disabilities and Handicaps

1. Arvin S. Gibson. *Echoes from Eternity*, op. cit., pp. 123-4.

2. Kenneth Ring & Sharon Cooper. 1999. *Mindsight: Near-Death and Out-of-body Experiences in the Blind*, Palo Alto, California: William James Center for Consciousness Studies. Vicki's account can be found on pages 22-28, 42-59, 127, 133, 139, 153.

3. Lake, Robert Adlai with Doug Mendenhall. 2001. *My Peace I Give Unto You*, Salt Lake City, Utah: Privately Printed. Pp. 94-97.

4. Ibid., Pp. 109-110.

### Chapter 13: Comfort From Home

1. Joseph Fielding Smith, *Life of Joseph F. Smith*, Pp. 456-457.

2. Joseph Fielding McConkie, *Truth and Courage*, p. 56.

3. Joseph Fielding Smith, *Life of Joseph F. Smith*, p. 463.

4. Christa M. Marsee. 1998. "Blessed for Trying," *The Ensign*, (August). Volume 28. Number 8, p. 60.

5. Richard Paget. 1979. *Beyond Death's Door*, Port Washington, New York: Ashley Books, Inc., pp. 25-30.

6. Joyce H. Brown. 1997. *Heavenly Answers for Earthly Challenges*, Pasadena, California: Jemstar Press.

7. Sandra Rogers. 1995. *Lessons From the Light*, New York: Warner Books.

8. Angie Fenimore, *Beyond The Darkness*.

9. Sandy, 1999. *A Child's NDE*, http://www.ndef.orgarchives_1998_2001(#8).

10. Brad Steiger & Sherry Hansen Steiger. 1995. *Angels Over Their Shoulders*, New York: Penguin Putnam , Inc., pp. 23-34.

11. Elisabeth Hallett, *Soul Trek*, Pp. 175–176.

12. Rebecca Todd. 1998. "More Than I Could Handle, *Guideposts*, (January/February), p. 35.

13. Melvin Morse. 1990. *Closer To The Light*, New York: Villard Books, Pp92-93.

## Chapter 14: Protection From Home

1. Christine Tuttle Monsen.. *Guide Me To Eternity*, p. 171.

2. Susan L. Schoenbeck. 1997. *The Final Entrance*, Madison, Wisconsin: Prairie Oak Press, pp. 44-45.

3. Hartt Wixom & Judene Wixom. 1987. *Trial by Terror*, Bountiful, Utah: Horizon Publishers, Pp. 144, 150-160.

4. Aileen H. Cooke. 1968. *Out of the Mouths of Babies*, Greenwood, South Carolina: The Attic Press Inc., p. 91.

5. Arvin S. Gibson. 1994. *Journeys Beyond Life*, Bountiful, Utah: Horizon Publishers, pp. 199-201.

6. RaNelle Wallace. *The Burning Within*, Carson City, Nevada: Gold Leaf Press, 1994.

7. Hallett, "Purposeful Contact: The Mysterious Power of Our Children To be," Lighthearts.com/articles 5.

8. Dawn Myers. 1994. *Angels, Angels Everywhere*, New York: Avon Books, pp. 79-86.

9. Ann Spangler. 1994. *An Angel A Day*, Grand rapids, Michigan: Zondervan Publishing House, p. 78.

10. Brad Steiger & Sherry Hansen Steiger. 1995. *Angels Over Their Shoulders*, New York: Fawcett Columbine, pp. 31-32.

11. Ibid., p12.

12. Ibid., p. 9.

## Chapter 15: Assurance From Home

1. Carol Jeannie Ehlers & Vicki Jo. Robinson. 1987. *Opening the Windows of Heaven*, Salt Lake City, Utah: Hawkes Publishing Inc., pp. 41-42.

2. Elisabeth Hallett, *Soul Trek*, p. 174.

## Chapter 16: Visits With The Unborn

1. Elisabeth Hallett, 1998. "The Little Girl of My Dreams," Montana.com/lighthearts/letters.
2. Sarah Hinze, 1997. *Coming From the Light*, New York: Pocket Books, P. 15.
3. Bruce Greyson & Nancy Evans Bush. 1992. "Distressing Near-Death Experiences," *Psychiatry*, Vol. 55, (February), pp. 105-106.
4. Albert R. Lyman, *The Great Adventure*.
5. Wheadon, Peter K. 1998. "One More Child?" *The Ensign*, (October), Volume 28, Number 10, p. 63.
6. Theresa M. Danna. www.birthpsychology.com/lifebefore/concept2.

## Chapter 17: Playful Visits From Home

1. Theresa M. Danna, www.birthpsychology.com/lifebefore/concept2.
2. Joan Wester Anderson. 1996. *Where Wonders Prevail*, New York: Ballantine Books, pp. 117-120.

## Chapter 18: Adoption

1. John Denver and Arthur Tobier. *Take Me Home: An autobiography*, New York: Harmony Books.
2. Marie Osmond. 1998. "Marie Osmond Secretly has Baby #6," *Star Magazine*, (August), p. 11.
3. Betty J. Eadie, *Embraced By The Light*, Pp. 135-141
4. Ibid., 143.
5. Ibid., 145-6..
6. Sarah Hinze. 1997. *Coming From the Light*, New York: Pocket Books, pp. 150-151.
7. Ibid., pp. 76-79.
8. Theresa M. Danna. www.birthpsychology.com/lilfebefore/concept2.

## Chapter 19: Abortion

1. Cherie Logan, *Before, Now and Forever*.
2. Exodus 20:12

3. Elisabeth Hallett, Soul Trek, p. 147.

4. Ibid., p. 134.

5. Ned Dougherty. 2001. Fast Lane to Heaven, Charlottesville, Virginia: Hampton Roads Publishing Company.

6. Elisabeth Hallett, Soul Trek, p. 148

### Chapter 20—Returning Home

1. Karlis Osis & Erlendur Haraldsson. 1997. At The Hour of Death, New York: Avon Books, Chapters 6 & 7.

2. Ibid., Chapter 4.

3. Sir William Barrett. 1926. Death-Bed Visions, London: Psychic Book Club.

4. Ibid, p. 13.

5. Ibid. p. 14.

6. James H. Hyslop. 1908. Psychical research and the Resurrection, Boston, Mass: Small, Maynard and Company, p. 89.

7. Sir William Barrett, Death Bed Visions, Pp. 19-20.

8. Ibid., p. 32.

9. Karlis Osis & Erlendur Haraldsson, At The Hour of Death, p. 67.

10. Ian Currie. 1978. You Cannot Die, New York: Methuen Inc., p. 119.

11. Brad Steiger & Sherry Hansen Steiger. Angels Over Their Shoulders, Pp. 172.

12. Ibid., pp. 172-173.

13. Sir William Barrett, Death Bed Visions, p. 75.

14. Brad Steiger & Sherry Hansen Steiger, Angels Over Their Shoulders, Pp. 175-176.

15. Joy Snell. 1959. The Ministry of Angels, New York: The Citadel Press, pp. 46-47.

16, Lance Richardson. 2000. The Message, Idaho Falls, Idaho: American Family Publishing, Pp. 63-64

### Chapter 21: Mission Completed—Our Final Reward

1. George Ritchie 1997, From a taped interview.

2. The Holy Bible, Matthew 22:37-39

3. The Holy Bible, Matthew 25:31-40

4. Lee Nelson, 1990. *Beyond the Veil,* Volume 3, Orem, Utah: Cedar Fort, Inc., p. 99.

5. The *Holy Bible,* James 4:17

6. Lance Richardson, *The Message,* Pp. 88-89

7. Ibid. Pp. 117-118.

8. The *Holy Bible,* John 14: 2.

9. Emanuel Swedenborg. 1990. *Heaven and Hell,* New York: Swedenborg Foundation, Inc. P. 40.

10. Ibid., Pp. 44-45.

11. Ibid., P. 50.

12. Raymond Bayless. 1971. *The Other Side of Death,* New Hyde Park, p. 101.

13. George Ritchie. 1998. *Ordered to Return,* Charlottesville, Virginia: Hampton Roads publishing Company, pp. 39-40

14. Ibid., pp. 40-41.

15. Ibid. p. 44.

16. Ibid., p. 45.

17. John Powell. *Journal of John Powell,* Unpublished manuscript.

18. Christine Tuttle Monsen, *Guide Me To Eternity,* Pp. 85-86.

19. Betty J. Eadie. 1999. *The Ripple Effect,* Seattle, Washington: Onjinjinkta Publishing, pp. 114-115.

20. Ibid., p. 123.

21. Don Brubaker. *Absent from the Body,* Pp. 77-80. 82, 86, 99.

22. International Association of Near-death Studies, Salt Lake City Chapter. 1999. Newsletter.

23. Barbara Rommer, *Blessings In Disguise.*

24. Richardson. *The Message,* Pp. 105-106.

# About the Author

Harold Widdison earned a Bachelors degree in Sociology and a MBA from Brigham Young University. He received his Ph.D. in Medical Sociology in 1979 and taught at Northern Arizona University in Flagstaff, Arizona for thirty-one years before retiring in 2003.

Dr. Widdison became interested in the subject of death, grief, and bereavement two months before his marriage when his father suddenly died in a car a ccident. He later created and taught one of the first courses on these subjects in a university setting. He also had several family members share their experiences with him—one uncle had a NDE (near-death experience) on the operating table and an adopted daughter had a visit from her dead grandfather.

This book is the result of seven years of interviewing, researching and collecting of first person accounts.